The Principled Politician

Governor Ralph Carr and the Fight against Japanese American Internment

The Principled Politician
Governor Ralph Carr and the Fight
against Japanese American Internment

Adam Schrager

FULCRUM
GOLDEN, COLORADO

Library of Congress Cataloging-in-Publication Data
Schrager, Adam.
  The principled politician : the Ralph Carr story / Adam Schrager.
    p. cm.
  Includes bibliographical references and index.
  ISBN 978-1-55591-654-1 (hardcover)
  1. Carr, Ralph L. (Ralph Lawrence), 1887-1950. 2. Governors--Colorado--Biography.
  3. Colorado--Politics and government--1876-1950. 4. Japanese Americans--Evacuation and relocation, 1942-1945. 5. Japanese Americans--Colorado--History. I. Title.
  F781.S34 2008
  978.8'032092--dc22
  [B]
                              2007041157

Printed in the United States of America
0 9 8 7 6 5 4 3 2

Cover and interior design by Jack Lenzo

Fulcrum Publishing
4690 Table Mountain Drive, Suite 100
Golden, Colorado 80403
800-992-2908 • 303-277-1623
www.fulcrumbooks.com

For Cathy.
No detail is too small.

Contents

Acknowledgments

There are few people who know the details of Colorado's state capitol like Carol Keller. For twenty-three years she has conducted tours each Friday at 5,280 feet, and at eighty-two years old, the building's senior volunteer, she shows no signs of slowing down.

She shares the story of Henry Brown dedicating the land, of the installation of the white marble from Marble, Colorado, that would later be used to make the Tomb of the Unknowns and the Lincoln Memorial, as well as why there are three separate measurements designating the building at exactly a mile (5,280 feet) above sea level.

There's a lot of history crammed into the 45-minute tour, but there's one story Keller never fails to share when she brings her groups to the governor's office on the south side of the building's first floor. That's the story behind the plaque that sits out front. A plaque dedicated to a "true American."

She always tells her groups the story of former Colorado governor Ralph L. Carr.

I met Ms. Keller more than five years ago, when former state representative Lauri Clapp and former state senator John Andrews introduced a measure designed to make Dececember 11, Carr's birthday, a voluntary state holiday. I had seen and passed by the plaque many times, as have so many other reporters, lawmakers, and visitors through the decades since Carr served. Understanding why I stopped to listen to Ms. Keller would take a fraction of the time it's taken me since to research and write *The Principled Politician*.

She spoke of a man with principle and resolve. A man who defied public opinion to do what he felt was right. She spoke of a leader.

I was hooked.

In the past I'd read an acknowledgments section of a book

and wonder whether it really takes that many people to write a manuscript. After my journey in this process, which began in early 2002, I'm no longer cynical. Dozens have aided me in this quest, and the following list is likely incomplete.

The research is primarily compiled from three locations: the Colorado State Archives, the Colorado Historical Society, and the Western History Department of the Denver Public Library. They each contain collections on Governor Carr that served an important role in creating this book.

Carr kept every letter, every speech, and every memo he received as governor, and Terry Ketelsen's staff at the Archives, including George Orlowski, Erin McDanal, Elena Cline, Paul Levit, and James Chipman, were beyond patient in helping me retrieve that information. Lance Christiansen spent some of his own time helping to transfer audio recordings of Governor Carr onto formats I could listen to at home, giving me the chance to hear a voice I had only imagined. I can't thank him enough for that gift.

Carr's political career and many of his legal materials are held inside the library at the Colorado Historical Society. Keith Schrum helped get me started, and Ruba Sadi and Karyl Klein were my regular tour guides through those works as well as dozens of Colorado newspapers from the time period. They became friends through the process.

The Western History Department of the Denver Public Libary contains Carr's scrapbooks, and Carr was dedicated to chronicling his every mention in the paper. There are also personal tidbits on his life that were instrumental to creating the fabric of 1940s' Colorado.

As I began, stumbling and fumbling my way through the process of researching and writing a book, numerous people provided information and counsel. Katherine Lynch and Ruth Ann Bauer gave me insight into their grandfather, who unfortunately passed away when both were so young. All along I've hoped to preserve their family's history and treat their grandfather with the respect he deserves.

Lincoln Frager and Hillary Ann Loeffler helped chronicle Carr's legacy in the newspapers of the time. Various representatives from the National Archives and Records Administration, Wichita State University libraries, California State University at Sacramento Library, The Bancroft Library at the University of California at Berkeley, the Franklin D. Roosevelt Presidential Library, the New York Public Library, the Auraria Higher Education Center Campus Library in Denver, and the Lilly Library at the University of Indiana contributed to the research.

Shizue Seigel of the Kansha Project; Marie Matsumoto of the Japanese American National Museum in Los Angeles; John Tateishi, former national director of the Japanese American Citizens League; Virginia Culver; Dave Kopel; Kara Miyagishima; Jan Mackell at the Cripple Creek District Museum; KARE-TV's Brett Akagi; Gil Asakawa; Professor Bob Goldberg at the University of Utah; Merriann Grasmick at the La Junta Chamber of Commerce; Robert Harvey's wonderful book *Amache*; Lowell Thomas's terrific read *Good Evening Everybody*; and John Hopper of the Amache Preservation Society all helped as well.

Edd Perkins took a significant amount of time, through e-mail, over the phone, and by meeting me in person at the First Church of Christ, Scientist, in Denver, to help me understand the basics of Mary Baker Eddy's teachings and how Governor Carr followed some and did not follow others.

KBCO's Studio C channel online provided the soundtrack for my writing process, and seemingly every time I would falter John Hiatt's "Have a Little Faith in Me" would be played, and I'd keep writing.

At the University of Colorado at Boulder (CU), more people should know about the work David Hays is doing in the school's archives chronicling the Navy's Japanese Language School at the institution during World War II. Professor William Wei, Kay Oltmans at the CU Heritage Center, and Karen Gifford also helped. Also, I want to offer a special thank-you to Michele McKinney and President Hank Brown.

Because I was a history major in college, I found the research for this manuscript to be enjoyable, often getting sidetracked by the stories from the summer of 1942 on how my beloved Chicago Cubs still could not seem to win a World Series. The writing, however, was laborious, and I leaned heavily on many people to help bring this story to print.

Thanks to Dr. Tom Noel, history professor at CU–Denver and the preeminent Colorado historian, for asking me in not-so-subtle terms when I was going to stop researching Governor Carr and start sharing the story with the public. His blessing to write, if you will, was the push I needed.

All of the following read either chapters or the entire manuscript to help in its crafting: Michele Ames, Matt Arnold, Jordan Austin, Rebecca Fitzgerald, Dan Hopkins, Helen Thorpe, Alan Salazar, Denver mayor John Hickenlooper, Dan Viens, and my friends from childhood Josh Mitzen, Will Steinberg, and Phil Yau. Reporter-turned-author Mark Obmascik steered me toward his literary agent, Jody Rein, who then steered me toward Sandra Bond. Both were blunt in their feedback and convinced me that I needed a professional editor to help. Having never written a book before, I appreciated their candor.

When I asked my political reporting mentor, Fred Brown, for the name of the best editor he had ever worked with in thirty-plus years in the newspaper business, without hesitation he named Diane Hartman. From our first breakfast meeting, discussing Pat Conroy novels, I have trusted the fate of this manuscript in Hartman's extremely able care. She saved me from me, which may be the best characteristic an editor can possess. Hartman is my hero, and this book would not be published were it not for her efforts.

I appreciate the time numerous public officials spent reading this manuscript once it was completed. Governor Bill Ritter, former governor Bill Owens, Senator Ken Salazar, Senator Wayne

Allard, Mayor Hickenlooper, former U.S. representative Bob Beauprez, U.S. Representative Michael Honda, who spent the first few years of his life at the internment camp in Colorado, and state representatives Paul Weissmann and Rob Witwer. Flossy Aston, Sean Conway, Lindy Eichenbaum Lent, and Cody Wertz helped make that happen.

Thanks to Sandra Dallas, Joyce Meskis, Arnie Grossman, Dick Kreck, Gregg Easterbrook, Max Potter, Patti Thorn, John Fielder, former governor Dick Lamm, and T. R. Reid for their counsel on what to do once the book comes out.

This could not have been accomplished without the help of many of my colleagues at KUSA-TV in Denver. Patti Dennis and Mark Cornetta gave me time off to complete a rough draft of a manuscript, and I will forever be grateful for their trust and faith in me. Further, Lorie Hirose and Adele Arakawa, both with personal histories that made Governor Carr's story intriguing to them, spent time helping me with sources, anecdotes, and feedback.

Governor Lamm and Arnie Grossman provided me the contacts I needed to meet Sam Scinta, the publisher at Fulcrum. When I'm nervous, I tend to talk a lot, so over the first coffee we shared together I rambled to Scinta about everything Governor Carr. Later that day, after reading the first few chapters, Scinta called and said he wanted to publish the book. It's one of the best phone calls I've ever received. Shannon Hassan, Jack Lenzo, Haley Berry, Katie Wensuc, and Erin Palmiter have tolerated my questions about everything and anything publishing and I appreciate their patience with me.

My family is a great help in everything I do. My mother and father, Joyce and Leonard Schrager, plus my sisters, Julie, Sarina, and Abbey, have provided support and feedback throughout the whole process. My aunt June Sochen, as an author and former college history professor, helped guide me every step of the way.

Finally, I offer my deepest thanks to my wife, Cathy, who understood why I needed to go to the library every weekend and why I needed to do research in the mornings and then work in the afternoons. She likely understood from the beginning better than me. Her patience is without peer, and I love her beyond words.

All these people helped, in part, because Governor Carr is the principled politician we all say we want. His is a story unfortunately mostly forgotten by a state and never known by a country.

Hopefully, this manuscript provides Carol Keller with a few more anecdotes to share with the masses on her state capitol tours every Friday.

Introduction
April 7, 1942

The phone was ringing. The phone was always ringing at the home of Colorado's governor and it had little to do with the fact that teenagers had recently lived in the house. The incessant jangling was a constant during the three-plus years Ralph Carr served as the state's chief executive.

From the wood-floored living room to the brick fireplace in the den to the upstairs bedrooms, one could hear its shrill sound throughout the early-twentieth-century home. The leaded glass on the windows, designed to keep out the noise of car horns, held in that godforsaken noise. This was no palatial governor's mansion, but a simple two-story brick structure Governor Carr had purchased years earlier with his small-town lawyer's salary.

Having his home address and number listed in bold type in Denver's city directory invited the attention. It showed the person living at 747 Downing Street was "Carr, Ralph L., Governor, State of Colorado." Phone operators connected Coloradans at all hours of the day.

His teenagers, Robert (Bob) and Cynthia, had begged him to follow the policy of Colorado's previous governors and remove his name from the phone book, but Carr refused.

"The rich, the powerful, the people with status," he told them, "they all have ways of getting their message, their point of view, to you, but the poor man has no way to do this unless he can call you up at home."

Now that they were at college, there was no one else to answer the phone. Carr sat back in his upper-floor study, letting it ring. The antelope, buffalo, elk, and moose heads on the wall, gifts from Teddy Roosevelt Jr.'s most recent Colorado hunt, stared at him. Everyone was looking at him these days, most with disdainful glares. Whispers of his impeachment were growing louder.

It was exactly four months after Japanese forces had attacked Pearl Harbor. Four months since war in the Pacific had led to the deaths of thousands of Americans, including numerous Coloradans. War had been officially declared against Japan, then quickly against Germany and Italy. The draft summoned all able-bodied men to fight. Personal rations of gas, rubber, sugar, and coffee were in effect or imminent. A generation after World War I, the so-called Great War, an even greater conflict was underway. Emotions were raw, specifically toward the "Japs."

Because the West Coast was considered vulnerable to attack, President Franklin Delano Roosevelt had signed Executive Order no. 9066 in February, establishing military zones along the coast and calling for the removal of its 120,000 residents of Japanese descent. Two-thirds of them were American citizens.

Shortly after Pearl Harbor, Carr had been asked by the *Pacific Citizen*, the official newspaper of the Japanese American Citizens League, for his thoughts on how to treat the Japanese living in the United States. Although other political leaders refused the request, Carr did not.

"To the American-born citizen of Japanese parentage we look for example and guidance," he wrote. "To those who have not been so fortunate as to have been born in this country, we offer the hand of friendship, secure in the knowledge that they will be as truly American as the rest of us."

Coming from a governor, the "hand of friendship" became national news.

His black phone jingled again. The hateful tone of the caller was similar to that of recent letters. Inches-thick stacks piled up every day at his office, from all over the state, all with unfamiliar names, but with a common theme.

"This is war," a Mr. Smith scribbled in a postcard, "and I am in favor of getting all Japs out—even if we kill every one of them."

A Mr. Varnum, an attorney in Denver, insisted, "Japs and Whites cannot live side by side in peace and security … Colorado must be kept a white man's country."

Mr. Bradley, a farmer, wrote that he had "heard farmers say they would not tolerate any Japs. … Someone will have to dig a lot of graves for Japs should they be brought to Colorado."

Carr sunk his five-feet-eight-and-a-half-inch frame into an overstuffed chair; the remnants of stale cigar smoke hung in the air from political gatherings of nights past. In his usual blue shirt, the 185-pounder looked seven months pregnant, an ample belly barely covered by the deep red tie. His normally dancing brown eyes were glazed over. The color of his constantly curly hair would soon match the white ten-gallon hat he wore on the campaign trail. Although the eighteen- to twenty-hour days were taking a physical toll, the Japanese "issue" was taking a mental toll.

What Carr lacked in height, he compensated for with a big personality, dominating any room he entered. He loved talking—sometimes in self-taught Spanish—and rarely lacked people willing to listen. There was always another person to meet, another story to share, another problem to solve. Put simply, he "loved people."

"I sense their feelings when I'm around them," he said. "And I sympathize particularly with the poor devil, who, because of circumstances, including often his own misconduct and blindness, gets himself into a place where he needs a pat on the back."

Four months after the Pearl Harbor attack, it was Ralph Carr himself who needed that pat on the back. He needed a night with his books, turning to his personal Abraham Lincoln collection for inspiration. While some of his generation collected stamps, coins, or maladies, the fifty-four-year-old Carr collected everything Lincoln. Friends would send him newspaper articles published on the former president from all over the country. He kept them bundled in an oversized leather scrapbook, pasted along with clippings about his own career.

Carr agreed with what Lincoln said some sixty years before: "I desire to so conduct the affairs of this administration that if, at the end, when I come to lay down the reins of power, I have lost every other friend on earth, I shall at least have one friend left and that friend shall be deep down inside me."

His phone rang again, and it wasn't a friend.

The governor had recently sped across the plains and mountains, from the small towns to the big cities of Colorado, listening to his constituents' concerns. From Grand Junction in the west to Sterling in the east, from Pueblo in the south to Fort Collins in the north, Coloradans were worried about the prospects of even more "yellow devils" coming to the state. That's what the state's largest paper, the *Denver Post*, called them.

Pearl Harbor had brought a fear so palpable to the Rocky Mountains and the country that the parents of Japanese American kids would place sandwich boards around their children's necks, reading "I'm Chinese, not Japanese" just to make sure they wouldn't become targets of racial slurs or worse, victims of violence.

The anger was unlike anything Carr had witnessed before. Even a clergyman wrote the governor, imploring him to "Clean up the JAPAGERMS!"

To Coloradans, the Nisei—second-generation Japanese Americans—were thought to be the same as the Issei, the first-generation Japanese who had never been naturalized. Citizenship did not matter.

Carr made two strong points to anyone who would listen.

First, if President Roosevelt felt that interning the Issei (the noncitizens) in Colorado would help the country's security, Colorado would not object. Carr said Colorado had no greater priority than helping win the war. Those who mailed him letters or called him at home believed he was wrong.

Second, his position concerning the Nisei perplexed even his best friends and created a frenzy of antagonism statewide. The Nisei were American citizens, and Carr believed they must have all the rights afforded any American citizen despite wartime hysteria. If they, or any other American citizen, wanted to come to Colorado, he could not and would not keep them out. He went so far as to tell Coloradans that those American citizens of Japanese descent even had the same right to run for governor as he did, assuming they met the age requirement, of course. Carr *was* a stickler for the rules.

However, the thousands who wrote and called the governor did not differentiate between citizen and noncitizen, between Nisei and Issei, between alien Japanese and American-born Japanese. They were seen as cut from the same "Japanese cloth" and to them, it was a dirty, venomous, savage, and despicable cloth. "We don't want Denver overrun by the yellow race," read one handwritten letter.

A Mrs. Cornell, a homemaker from Boulder, begged the governor, "May God of heaven speak to your soul … no one [wants Japanese here] to see our bodies ravished and raped by the very devil himself."

Mr. Hobbs from Colorado Springs echoed her sentiments. "Don't think for a moment any of these [Japanese] would hesitate to do damage to Colorado … Colorado don't want enemy aliens from anywhere. Let's keep 'em out."

Columnists, neighbors, politicians, and county gossips all wondered. Coloradans threatened open violence to keep them out.

Colorado's senior senator Edwin C. Johnson, a Democrat,

suggested the National Guard be called to keep them out. Leaders in both the Democrat and Republican parties spoke out against housing any Japanese in Colorado. State legislators wanted Carr to call a special session to deal with this "menace."

The state's neighbors were equally venomous.

Wyoming governor Nels Smith said that if anyone with Japanese ancestry were brought to his state, "There would be Japs hanging from every pine tree."

Idaho attorney general Bart Miller said his state wanted to remain pure. "We want to keep this a white man's country."

Carr looked out the window at the half-foot of new snow that had fallen in Denver that April day. A record snowfall that winter was sure to lead to record crops in the fall. He wondered if there would be farmers to harvest the corn and sugar beets since most able-bodied men had volunteered for service or were drafted into it.

These were late-night thoughts and tangents in the broad debate, where Carr never wavered from his main focus. For the sake of those fighting abroad and those supporting them at home, he intended to preserve the Constitution.

He joked he was being cussed in Colorado as often as he was being discussed. The people weren't listening. They certainly weren't understanding.

A Lieutenant Mann from Denver warned the governor about what might happen if the federal government actually sent people of Japanese ancestry to Colorado. "We are sitting upon a seething volcano, Governor," he suggested.

Carr needed some sleep. He blew on his glasses to clean them and thought of what could have been. If he and a friend had struck gold back in 1934 with the five hundred dollars Carr had borrowed on a life insurance policy, he could have been rich.

Instead, his partner ended up selling Fords in California. Striking it rich had also been the goal of his father, Frank, whom he described fondly as a "miner and a tinhorn gambler," never indicating which of the two he admired more.

The governor always considered his father a dreamer and the most compassionate man he knew. He was also his son's hero. Governor Carr enjoyed hearing the story of how his father, shortly before Ralph was born, in 1887, had stopped a mob from lynching an innocent man.

That was courage.

Now Ralph Carr felt as if he were facing his own mob. Every time he spoke to a group about the "Japanese question," he hoped they could see the logic, the reason behind his beliefs. Yet, the hate mail and vitriolic phone calls continued, angry letters to the editor filled the newspapers, and hideous threats against the Japanese living in Colorado continued.

He would not back down. The same reporters who described him as "jovial" and "engaging" and "dynamic" soon began to use adjectives like "stubborn," "determined," and "bull-headed." He had developed a thicker hide as the state's chief executive and compared the bumps of each year in office to "ten years of ordinary living." Carr liked to say that he "didn't take this job to feel the public pulse or to follow the popular demand," but that it was up to governors "to direct public opinion rather than to follow it."

Public opinion, without question, was against him.

Carr was Colorado's first Republican governor since the mid-1920s when Clarence Morley rode the support of the Ku Klux Klan to the state's top job. Morley lost his reelection bid in 1927 and the party had failed to find a leader until Ralph Carr. But now he was desperately tired from being continually attacked by both friend and foe.

As he tried to sleep that cold April night, he remembered the blaring page-one, above-the-fold headline that week in the *Denver Post*: "GOV. CARR STAKES POLITICAL FUTURE

ON HIS JAP STAND."

There was no respite from the clanging phone or assault by mail. He clung to the writings of Lincoln and to his belief in the U.S. Constitution. If he had to answer every explosive call and poisonous letter to combat this war on the home front by himself, then so be it.

His principles were nonnegotiable.

The Denver Post, the state's largest newspaper, took a keen interest in Governor Carr's stand regarding anyone of Japanese descent. All the stories were splashed on the front page with significant detail.

Chapter One
Summer 1938

The imposing black Union Pacific streamliner slowed as it approached Denver before coming to a stop with its familiar hiss, screech, and acrid smell. George Robinson, a tall, straight-backed, and trim man, couldn't wait to step down, stretch his legs, and figure out how to explain himself to his wife, Dolores.

As a white-coated dining-car attendant, he earned ninety-eight dollars a month serving hot cakes and pouring coffee in the seventy-two-foot dining car. He said "yes, sir" and "no, ma'am," dignified and invisible in his serving role.

His boss, Mr. Hansen, let Robinson know he had a future as a "Union Pacific man." But that wasn't appealing to Robinson.

He swung down and strode under the welcoming arch of Union Station, headed toward his home about two miles away in the city's predominantly black Five Points neighborhood.

One of the most prosperous communities of its kind in the West, many of the homes had electrical wiring, plumbing, and garages. Black doctors, lawyers, engineers, and dentists joined cooks, janitors, domestic servants, and railroad workers like George Robinson in a neighborhood a little northwest of the white part of the city. Five Points could boast about the Rossonian Hotel, which had one of the most important jazz clubs between Chicago and Los Angeles. Segregation dictated that while Charlie Parker, Duke Ellington, Louis Armstrong, and Count Basie might play at other Denver hotels, they could only stay at the Rossonian.

Robinson, a lifelong Republican, had been reading in the *Denver Post* about the party's new gubernatorial candidate. Ralph L. Carr was preaching fiscal responsibility and ethical leadership, and Robinson liked that. During his last trip home, he didn't tell Dolores, but he went to see the short, curly-haired, impassioned white man speak in person. Carr was funny and fiery, personable and professional.

"The state is broke," Carr shouted, banging on the lectern and laying out the state's dire financial situation. As he finished his speech, he let the audience know that fixing the problem would take the consent and the cooperation of the public. "This is a job for all the people," he said pointing to the crowd. Robinson felt the finger settle upon him. "When elected, I intend to represent all of the people, all of the sections of the state."

Robinson thought, "Jesus, that's a brilliant man."

That morning, on his train route in the wee hours somewhere west of Nebraska, Robinson scribbled Ralph Carr a note. "After you get elected," he wrote, "I wish you'd give me an opportunity to work in your office. I understand a colored fella can have a job there and I'd appreciate it much if you gave me a chance."

He dropped it in the mail on his trip home, unsure what to expect from Carr, but absolutely sure what he'd hear from his wife. Dolores would ask him if he didn't already have a good job. On the walk home, he settled on his answer.

"I'm just a railroad worker [now], but if I get with the governor of Colorado, who knows what I might do."

Although George Robinson seemed sure Ralph Carr would make a good governor, Carr himself had come kicking and screaming to his candidacy.

He had only begun to build up a law practice and hoped to make enough money to pay off his mortgage and send his two teenagers to his alma mater, the University of Colorado in Boulder (CU). He had recently served as U.S. attorney for Colorado, an exciting job and one that gained him an excellent reputation, but the pay was low.

Carr had negotiated a number of water compacts with neighboring states as an assistant attorney general in the mid-1920s. He successfully argued the legality of compacts before the U.S. Supreme Court in the *Hinderlider v. La Plata River & Cherry Creek*

Ditch Company case. Carr represented the state engineer in his fight with private companies on how to handle diversions from the river. This 1938 ruling dramatically altered water law throughout the West and reinforced the rights of states to decide for themselves how to allocate the waters of interstate streams. Hands down, Carr was considered the preeminent water rights attorney in Colorado.

Colorado was the only state in the country with no water source flowing into its borders, and the people who lived and worked there considered water liquid gold. People died fighting for it, over it, and about it. Water decisions were guaranteed front-page coverage and analysis by nearly all of the state's newspapers.

As a result of Carr winning the Supreme Court case, he was soon being mentioned in political conversations. Two friends and fellow attorneys wrote him, suggesting that he run for governor.

Carr chuckled at the suggestion and responded, "The only time I care to run for governor is in the springtime when the authorities are not aware of it and no one will call it to their attention. I feel that there should be a change at the State House, but I do not think that I am the man for the place. I would alienate 50 percent of the voters the first day and the other 125 percent of them the next day when I expressed my views."

Colorado's Republicans knew the upcoming November election offered an opportunity they hadn't had in more than a decade. The state's budget was in shambles, as was the reputation of the current governor, Teller Ammons, who was known for doling out favors to political friends.

The budget mess was obvious, but Ammons couldn't understand how people were finding out what he was doing. Day after day he got hammered in the *Denver Post* about his deals, despite dire warnings to those inside his office who might be leaking secrets. It was a big mystery, how news got out about one job after another going to a Democratic Party donor. What was going on? Infuriated, Ammons demanded to know who in his inner circle had violated his trust.

The truth proved even more scandalous.

Once the secret was discovered, *Time* magazine dramatized what happened for readers. "Colorado's loud, semibald, profane Governor Teller Ammons shoved himself back from his desk, whisked his office chair aside, stepped to the nearest wall ventilator grill, stared into the dimness of the shaft and emitted an angry oath," according to the September 20, 1937, issue. "There, suspended three feet above the floor, was a crystal microphone."

Further investigation showed two microphones dangling in the ventilator shafts, hooked up to a telephone line that led to the apartment of a private detective five blocks away. They had been installed months before and were the conduits spilling the governor's private conversations to the newspaper.

The private eye, a *Denver Post* reporter, and an attorney were indicted by a grand jury and eventually convicted on eavesdropping charges. Ammons was not charged with anything. Later he commented that the worst thing to come out of the mess was that his mother heard about it and said, "I didn't know Teller used that kind of language." Republicans said the tapes revealed the way Ammons rewarded his friends at any cost. The average Coloradan tended to agree.

Even Ammons's fellow Democrats were beginning to take him on in public.

State senator A. Elmer Headlee complained to reporters that the entire state was being run "by the Denver city hall and the [Democrat political machine]." Critics argued that during Ammons's two years in office, because of his strong ties to the teachers' union, he had bankrupted the state by refusing to divert money raised by a newly formed state income tax designed to help schools. Money for what the state needed was not being distributed fairly and was not sent where it was most needed. State employees were not being paid and wards of the state were not being fed. Ammons pushed another tax increase through the legislature, and instead of paying the bills, he created sixteen new boards, bureaus, and commissions.

Carr called the current state of affairs a "political monster." He voiced the sentiment of the public when he said, "Rich and poor today find the hands of the state officeholders dipping deeper into their pockets than ever before." Even Democrats like Senator Headlee wondered aloud about the effectiveness of the current administration's fiscal policies.

"Colorado can have everything she needs, meet every just and legal obligation without additional taxes, if only we will apply good business principles in the handling of our state's affairs," Headlee told the *Denver Post*.

Carr had been involved in party politics for years. He enjoyed talking at Republican dinners throughout Colorado, and had campaigned vigorously for mayors, state representatives, state senators, county commissioners—anyone who believed as he did in the principles of fiscal responsibility and less government regulation.

In 1938, the state Republican convention was held in Colorado Springs at the fancy Antlers Hotel. On Friday, August 5, Carr took his law partners and Bob, his fifteen-year-old son, to the Springs. They hoped to stay overnight to see one of the prominent Republicans, Charles M. Armstrong or Benjamin W. Snodgrass, nominated as candidate for governor, setting the stage to defeat Governor Ammons in November. As soon as he arrived, Carr went to work persuading party members to include a provision in the platform stating that Colorado knew how to control its water better than the federal government.

Late in the afternoon, state GOP chairman John Coen, a wide man—hard to miss in a white suit and black tie—approached the Carrs and pulled Ralph aside. His massive girth expanded as he spoke.

Three very animated minutes later, Carr returned to Bob and said, "Well, we've got to get out of here. We've got to go back to Denver."

"Why?" asked Bob.

"That's the third man who's come up to me and said, 'Nobody likes the candidates for governor, so stick around, lightning might strike for you.'

"I don't want any part of that lightning," he told his son. "I'm not interested in running for governor. I'm sorry you're going to miss the fun part of the convention, the nominating of candidates, but we need to go."

Carr told his young legal associates—Jack Shippey, John Reid, and Jean Breitenstein—that he and Bob were going home. He didn't want to set aside his life for a two-year term as the state's chief executive. After going out to dinner and visiting some relatives, he returned home to Denver just after 10:00 P.M.

As he walked in, he could hear the phone ringing.

"It's a number from Colorado Springs," said his housekeeper, after speaking with the operator. "It's the same number that's been calling all night long."

Carr ignored her and the phone.

"Aren't you going to [answer]?" she asked.

"I know what they're calling about and I want no part of it."

Five minutes later, the phone rang again. Finally, Carr answered.

"I'm not interested," he said and, then hung up.

The phone continued to ring.

Around midnight, after more phone calls from more groups, Carr relented, believing he was destined to have a sleepless night.

"Okay, I'll come down to speak with you, but I'm not happy," he told the last caller.

He sent his legal assistants Breitenstein and Reid to the convention to tell party members that the reason he didn't want to run was because his law firm's finances were fairly precarious, and that he was the one who brought in business—he felt that leaving the firm wouldn't be fair to his young partners. He grabbed his son, Bob, and they returned to the hotel, where they checked back into the room they had hastily abandoned only eight hours earlier.

It was 3:30 A.M., so both put on pajamas to get ready for bed.

The phone rang. Breitenstein and Reid were calling from the lobby and to report that they had failed in their duties.

"You're going to have to go talk to them yourself, Ralph," they said. "[The members] know it's a sacrifice for you. It's a financial sacrifice. It's a family sacrifice. They know you haven't thought about it. … [But] we can't talk 'em out of it."

Reluctantly, Ralph Carr pulled on a pair of suit pants over his pajamas, left his top on, stepped into a pair of slippers, and put on his hat before heading out the door. The dawn was coming and with it a stunning view of Pikes Peak, the mountain that had inspired English professor Katharine Lee Bates to write "America the Beautiful" in her Antlers Hotel room back in 1893.

Room 50 was packed with cigar- and pipe-smoking Republicans. Chairman John Coen was there, his bulk covering up the identities of two delegates he was lobbying on Carr's behalf. Colorado Supreme Court justice Haslett P. Burke, who often quoted Shakespeare, sat by himself in the back of the room. The most formidable guest among them was former U.S. senator Lawrence C. Phipps, who controlled the Denver Republicans. He had nominated Carr for the U.S. attorney position in 1929. Now he was openly supporting Benjamin Snodgrass for governor. Phipps had been the de facto head of the state party for years, anointing various candidates to office, but his status was being challenged.

Colorado Republicans realized that the weakest candidate on the 1938 Democratic ticket was the current governor. Despite the wishes of Phipps, prevailing wisdom was that neither Armstrong nor Snodgrass was strong enough to beat Ammons. Coen believed Carr could get both Republican and Democratic votes, as well as the support of people who ordinarily would not vote on election day. The state party chair was not prepared to see his master plan ruined by an unwilling candidate.

Coen convinced Armstrong to step aside and run for state treasurer, promising he wouldn't have to go through a primary and he would have the full support of the party. Despite Coen's pleas, Snodgrass was not willing to concede. Phipps was fuming.

The crowd in the room wasted no time asking Carr to run for governor. He wasted no time rejecting the offer.

"What about George?" asked Carr.

George Birdsall was mayor of Colorado Springs, the second-largest city in Colorado.

"I've got health issues, Ralph," said Birdsall. "Can't run."

Carr spun to another face in the room. "What about you, Nate?" Carr pleaded.

Fort Collins banker and cattleman Nate Warren had run unsuccessfully for both U.S. senator and governor, so voters knew his name. Surely his connection to Colorado State College, the state's second-largest college, would help.

"Same thing as George," answered Warren. "Health problems."

"Harry, how about you?" begged Carr. "Why not run Harry?" he said to the group.

Harry Mendenhall was president of the Rocky Ford National Bank and a widely known Arkansas Valley rancher and stockman. He paused, looked his friend in the eyes, and said, "Ralph, you're known everyplace."

It kept coming back to Carr. He finally tried talking about conditions they'd have to meet before he would agree. Terms he thought they would consider unreasonable.

"I don't have the finances and I don't want to have to do anything to raise money," he said. That was first. Then he added that he was sure to do things they wouldn't like, "Because if I'm governor, I'll call the shots as I see 'em. I won't be beholden to anybody."

"That's fine, that's fine," the group chorused. Phipps shook his head, the lone dissenter, seeing his plan to get Snodgrass elected evaporate before his eyes.

Carr left Room 50 without making a decision. The convention was set to start in a few hours, which would give him enough time to get a little sleep, clean up, and make the kind of choice that would impact all their lives.

The next morning, Chairman Coen and others approached Carr outside the main hall, looking for an answer. The convention had started an hour and a half earlier and tensions were high.

"Still wait and see," Carr told him. "Bob and I have been here a long time and we need a piss break." So father and son, plus Jean, Jack, and John, the legal associates, excused themselves to head toward the marble urinals of the Antlers Hotel men's room.

"I know they realize it's a sacrifice and that they said no strings attached," Carr said to the group safely ensconced in the bathroom. "This is not what I want to do. It'll be hard on you guys because the law practice is doing well."

"We don't want you to run, either," said Jack, "but it doesn't look like you've got any choice."

"Aw, hell." Carr washed his hands.

Shortly before noon, he allowed his name to be submitted to the Republican state convention as a candidate for governor.

Pandemonium ensued. "It was something that caught everybody's imagination," his son, Bob, said later. "It was just one of those things that caught on like wildfire."

Phipps encouraged Snodgrass to run and discouraged him from pulling out, but Carr's momentum was too great. When the delegates from Colorado's sixty-three counties had voted, the unwilling candidate had won a decisive victory, 733 to 442. Aside from the 238 delegates Phipps delivered from the Denver delegation for Snodgrass, Carr dominated the rest of the state. The *Denver Post* called it a "political resurrection."

"Throwing off the defeatist attitude, which has paralyzed them politically since the 1936 landslide, delegates to the Republican state assembly suddenly decided they have a chance in this 1938 campaign," read the next day's lead story.

Republican optimism grew Saturday night when Snodgrass announced that "in the interests of party unity," he would withdraw from a forthcoming primary battle with Carr. He pledged his allegiance and encouraged his supporters, even Senator Phipps, to do the same. At last they had a promising candidate.

Sunday morning, the party faithful left the balloons and confetti behind and headed out on the campaign trail. The first stop was the San Luis Valley in southern Colorado, Carr's home for years before moving to Denver. The visit was not arranged to pay homage to the candidate's roots, but because Carr had a client he was representing in court there that Monday morning. It would be his last official legal business until the election.

As the Republican caravan pulled into the valley, Carr was reminded of his last election experience in the area. It was the only time in his adult life he had run for office. In 1918, Twelfth District judge Charles M. Corlett had died, leaving a vacancy to be filled in that November's election.

Carr submitted his candidacy, running on a platform that included promises of "legal efficiency on the bench" and "justice to all." He took out a few advertisements in the paper, but a bout with the flu kept him from doing much campaigning.

The Twelfth District did not respond. Carr lost to Democrat Jesse C. Wiley.

When Carr and the other candidates arrived in the valley fresh from the convention, many residents wanted to talk about that twenty-year-old race. The Democratic Party chair from the area made it a point to find the gubernatorial candidate.

"Ralph, do you remember when you lost for judge?" he asked. "You lost for judge because I stuffed the ballot box against you."

Carr fired back, "You're not going to do that this time, are you?"

"This time," the Democratic chief said with a smile, "I'll stuff the ballot box *for* you."

The *Denver Post* was the largest paper in the state and decidedly Republican leaning. It joined the Carr bandwagon a week later in its page two column called "That's That."

"The vital issue of the campaign as Ralph Carr sees it, is giving the citizens of Colorado an 'efficient, economical, and American form of government.' Certainly there has been neither efficiency nor economy in the Ammons administration …

"Even if Governor Ammons had the ability to be a good executive, he still would be under an unbearable handicap. For he is a puppet of the Denver city hall machine. … He is under the machine's thumb all the time. NOBODY HAS ANY STRINGS ON RALPH CARR. He is independent of the influence of political machines and political factions. He is free to run the governor's office in the way which will best serve the state as a whole."

One incident that was indicative of how Carr ran his life and his campaign involved another Republican who was usually on the campaign stump with him. Archibald Lee was set to take on Senator Alva Adams in November. The Seventeenth Street Denver lawyer failed to adhere to Carr's most definitive political rule: never speak beyond the bladder capacity of your audience.

Senator Adams was well known, respected, and liked by many Republicans, including Carr. He was seen as an independent, which made him popular throughout the state and made Lee's job particularly challenging. One night, the caravan arrived in the ranching community of Springfield, Colorado, for a chamber of commerce event.

Lee went first because he was the first Republican on the ballot. The more restive the audience got, the longer he spoke, trying to convince them of his positive qualities. He went well past when the group was set to leave. Carr waited patiently for close to an hour. When he finally got his chance to address the crowd, he said, "We're behind our schedule. We were supposed to be on the road an hour ago and we just don't have any time now. I'm very happy to have been here and met you all, but there's no time for any speeches, we have to go."

The place was in an uproar, with crowd members shouting, "No! We came here to see you."

Carr headed back on the road. Archibald Lee never made any more trips with the Republican caravan; he became a political lone wolf and was trounced in November.

For the five months of the campaign, Carr zeroed in on the current bureaucratic excess. Not a speech went by without him mentioning the sixteen new boards, bureaus, and commissions created during Ammons's two years in office. Carr reminded the crowds of the "political henchmen who are now ringing your doorbell asking you to perpetuate them in their jobs." An increased service tax, use tax, income tax, "taxes upon this and taxes upon that," served as easy marks for an able litigator now turning his courtroom skills to the political stump.

Phrases like "financial chaos," "political incompetency," and "financial and moral bankruptcy" were staples of the average Carr speech. "Let's be specific," he said to a statewide radio audience. "What does this mean to you as an average citizen? If you eat food, if you wear clothes, if you need medical attention, if you are born or if you die—you are a taxpayer in Colorado."

He spoke to a state still mired in the Depression, where many residents were living on three dollars per month. Instead of providing relief for those families, taxpayer resources were being diverted to what Carr called "fat salaries for useless political employees." His message was compelling.

"I intend to give this state a business administration," he said. "I intend to eliminate waste and inefficiency in state government and I intend to conduct the people's business with the same care, with the same determination, that I would if it were my money which is at stake."

Carr articulated the problem; his friends showed how he could be the solution. They were quick to point out that when the last Democrat-controlled legislature created a State Water Conservation Board to protect the state's most valuable resource, they turned to a Republican—Ralph Carr—for legal advice.

Even the Democrat who succeeded him as U.S. attorney for

Colorado was gracious. Thomas Morrissey had crossed swords politically with Carr numerous times. But when he was being sworn in to his new position, he told a reporter, "I hope I prove as competent as the man I am succeeding, Mr. Carr. If I do, I shall consider my administration an entire success."

Governor Ammons responded to Carr's claims in the only way possible—he told voters he would bring change and push for more government efficiency. Carr responded that the creators of "this political monster" were now saying they would destroy it if voters gave them another chance. In fact, throughout October, the Democrats would discuss his issues and adopt his solutions. But Carr knew he had the momentum.

On November 8, when the votes were counted manually throughout the majority of Colorado, the results were clear. Well before midnight, Governor Ammons called Carr to concede. The man who made the decision to run for the state's highest office near the urinals at the Antlers Hotel was now Governor-elect Ralph Carr.

George Robinson read the results in the next day's paper and felt vindicated. He had picked a winner and was thankful Colorado had agreed. He wondered if his letter had been read or considered. After two more trips to Omaha aboard the streamliner, Robinson had his answer. His anxious wife told him he had been summoned by a Mr. Hill in the Symes Building.

William Hill was a Fort Collins businessman hired by the governor-elect to hire staff and run his transition team. "I had no more idea I was going to get that job than I thought I'm going to get a million dollars, and I know I ain't getting that," Robinson thought to himself as he waited to see Hill.

There were sixty-seven applicants for the one "colored" position the governor was allowed to hire in the 1930s. The position was classified as a messenger or valet.

Hill said to Robinson, "You wrote a letter to [Carr] that you wanted a job with him if he got it, so you're an applicant ... "

George Robinson (second from the right, next to Governor Carr) said he had more respect for his boss than any man aside from his father. After hearing Carr speak for the first time, he said, "Jesus, that's a brilliant man." Robinson applied to be Carr's valet, but the new governor would instead assign him to the front of his office, so the first face you saw entering the Colorado governor's office in 1939 was an African American man. Robinson would become one of Carr's most trusted companions. Courtesy of the Colorado Historical Society

"I'd love to have it, but don't take me seriously," Robinson told him. "I don't know the governor. I just know he's a good man."

"We'll let you know. We don't promise you anything, but we'll take up your application and compare it with the others and you'll find out who gets the job."

When George Robinson got home, he finally told Dolores he had written Carr asking for a job. As expected, she pointed out sharply that he already had a job.

"Yes, yes, but I was just thinking about I'd like to have that job. If I had that job, I could be something."

"You should stay where you are," she said.

Two weeks passed and Hill called Robinson, telling him he had made the cut of eight. Dolores's unhappiness cranked up a notch.

"You're the dumbest man I ever saw. What do you know about the job? How much does it pay?"

"Don't worry," he told her, amazed he was still in consideration.

After one more trip to Omaha, Robinson came home to a message telling him to come to the state capitol, where the governor-elect had moved into the office he would occupy for the next two-plus years. Only two candidates remained, Robinson and a man who worked at the Denver Country Club, from a leading black family in Denver.

Robinson was ushered into a little wood-paneled room in the back of the governor's offices. Fairly soon, the door flew open and the man who was described by his hometown newspaper as a "boundless, never-tiring human dynamo," came face to face with the man whose letter he had saved for months.

"Your letter said, 'After you get elected, I'd like a chance to work with you,'" Carr said. "How'd you know I was going to get elected?"

"I didn't, Governor, but I thought you should've been … and it'd be a shame if you didn't get elected."

Carr looked him up and down for a couple minutes, the silence unnerving Robinson.

"You were the first one before I was elected to ever ask for a job and on account of you being the first one, I think I oughta hire you.

"Something tells me you'd probably be pretty good because you can look ahead of times. If I hire people like you around me and they can look ahead for me, maybe I can [do] this job pretty [well] ... because maybe you'll see something else one day. Let's shake hands now."

Robinson was floored, stunned. He was being hired.

"I'm going to put you out there in that front office," Carr told him, "on your honor."

Nobody had ever used the word *honor* with Robinson before. It was "like [having a winning] lottery ticket."

Robinson expected to be a valet, but instead he would be an information clerk, answering phones, escorting luminaries into the governor's office. This was much more than being a messenger.

Ralph Carr made sure that the first face visitors saw as they entered the Colorado governor's office in late 1938 was that of a black man. And Dolores could be happy that her enterprising husband was now making a hundred and twenty-five dollars a month, a nice raise from the railroad.

Chapter Two
January 10, 1939

Soon it would be time to get into the car waiting outside and ride a short distance to the state capitol, where Ralph Carr would put his hand on the Bible and take the oath of office as governor of Colorado.

His family began to gather. Son Robert, daughter Cynthia, Carr's mother, Mattie, and brother Merle would be seated in the front row in the state house chambers. All morning his home had been filling with friends and supporters, with well-wishers calling constantly.

Upstairs, Cynthia was dawdling a bit. She had two outfits; one sedate for today's formal ceremony. Then, much more exciting, the sixteen-year-old had laid out a blue gown with taffeta bodice and net skirt that she'd dance in at tonight's celebratory ball.

That morning's banner headline in the *Rocky Mountain News* read: "Carr climbs long trail from Cabin to Capitol." Indeed, the road had been a steep one, but what he was about to do could have been predicted by those who knew him well.

Carr had three heroes: One was his father. Another was William Gilpin, the first territorial governor in Colorado. And, as a guiding light, he studied and revered Abraham Lincoln.

Governor Gilpin had, in fact, been appointed by Lincoln. Carr thoroughly enjoyed Colorado history and he knew that Gilpin had arrived by stagecoach in 1861 to take office in Denver, wearing riding boots and a swallowtail coat. A large crowd had welcomed him to town. Gilpin noticed a secession flag waving as he rode through the town. Soon enough, Gilpin stood against those who opposed Lincoln's policies of preserving the Union. He prepared a code of laws that ensured that Colorado would remain a slave-free state. He also equipped the First Colorado Volunteer Army to support that cause.

Carr remembered a story told about Gilpin in the closing years of his life. He had been called to the witness stand in a criminal trial in the old district courthouse of neighboring Arapahoe County. When asked his occupation, the long-bearded Gilpin replied that he fancied himself a "pioneer." Carr liked that.

Lincoln was his hero of heroes, who had of course faced down half a country in his stand for what he believed was right.

Before the election, Carr had told friends—only half-jokingly—that if elected, he would become the "most hated man in Colorado," because he would follow his principles. He promised Coloradans that things would be dramatically different with him in state government.

"Regardless of what it does to me," he said, "you may rest assured I will be governor in fact as well as in name."

It had been a long climb. He was born December 11, 1887, in Rosita, Colorado, at a time when miners reached Colorado's mountains by stagecoach or wagon. The "Centennial State" had come into being in the heat of gold fever, when train tracks were laid across the stunning and treacherous Rocky Mountains. His family followed the gold-mining fortunes from Rosita to the silver mines in Aspen. From there, they moved to Cripple Creek, called the "richest cow pasture" on earth—cows could graze there, but the ore underneath made some men wealthy and others giddy with anticipation. It was the place to be in 1894 if you wanted to pan for gold and strike it rich.

Somehow, Carr's father didn't have any kind of luck at all, so times were hard for the Carr family. Starting at age six, Ralph held a number of jobs to help put food on the table. He carried ore samples from the mines and also sold newspapers in the saloons. Before he was ten, he saw a man shot in a barroom brawl; it remained a vivid memory.

His mother insisted he go to school and study. He became well versed in writing, literature, and Latin, and even taught Latin verbs to other kids when he was only six.

Although he won a partial scholarship to the University of Colorado, he worked as a package wrapper at a coffee company in Colorado Springs for a year to earn the rest of the money he needed.

At CU, Carr became well known. Nicknamed "Trolley Carr" by his friends, he was described in the yearbook as, "A good friend and a good worker; what more could a man be?"

He joined Delta Tau Delta, where the brothers would sit around and sing favorites like "Shine on Harvest Moon" and "Moonlight Bay" and "I Wonder Who's Kissing Her Now" at the end of evening meals.

Carr served as the athletics editor for the *Silver and Gold*, the student newspaper. Later he became an assistant editor. He helped run the junior prom and served on the governing board of the *Colorado Monthly*, the school's literary magazine. He was awarded the Heart and Dagger, the symbol of the Senior Honor Society. He so excelled academically that he was appointed an assistant to Professor M. F. Libby in the philosophy department his senior year.

Everyone assumed Carr would work at a newspaper when he graduated because he loved to write. Sports were a passion for him, and when writing about it, he could get a little carried away. Describing a CU–Colorado College baseball game for the school paper, "It was a slaughter of the innocents. The bloodthirsty [Colorado College] Tigers who have played such havoc in the ranks of collegiate baseball are no longer to be feared. Their nails have been clipped and their molars removed, so that the nine striped animals with dragging tails … looked more like shorn lambs than the much vaunted bullies of the forest which had come in with flying colors the day before."

While working for Professor Libby, Carr noticed and got to know one of his students, Gretchen Fowler. Soon they became a couple, never leaving each other for long.

Their walks were filled with conversation, sometimes about topics brought up by Professor Libby, who delivered lectures designed to inspire and stir. Ralph couldn't stop talking, questioning, wondering, and Gretchen was content to listen and to tease him about not being able to get a word in edgewise. She was his sounding board, as patient as he was impatient. He felt he could tell her anything. Sometimes she felt he would try to tell her everything. They laughed a lot together and shared a desire to make the world a better place.

Their walks through Boulder would inevitably lead to the enormous sandstone boulders surrounding the school, which every Colorado student, including Ralph, had tried to scale. Many, like Ralph, were unsuccessful. Their romance bloomed against the backdrop of the pine-scented forests that surrounded the school and, during fall, the shimmering heart-shaped leaves of aspen. The strong autumn sun made those leaves look like pennies.

Gretchen had grown up in Colorado Springs, where her grandfather was one of its first settlers. She was academically ambitious and had insisted on leaving home to attend college in Boulder. She pledged Chi Omega sorority, but left her friends two years later to marry Ralph.

About the only failure of Carr's college career was when he lost his race for student body president by a landslide to fellow student Todd Storer in 1911.

Defying expectations, he went on to CU Law School.

After graduation and a small wedding ceremony, he and Gretchen moved to the mountains, where they lived in a few different towns before moving to Antonito, in the heart of the San Luis Valley in southern Colorado.

Many consider this area magic. It is the world's largest alpine valley, at an average altitude well above seventy-five hundred feet.

There are sweeping vistas with varied vegetation and different geologic formations at every turn, and often the dusk glows with lavender and pink overhead. Sometimes double rainbows score the sky after a rare rain.

The Carrs enjoyed their life in Antonito. It was a place of no pretense. Unlike people in the cities, folks stopped them on the street to see how they were doing and waited patiently for an answer.

Carr hung a black and gold shingle outside his Main Street office that read, "Ralph L. Carr/Lawyer," and waited for clients. The town was so small that when the chamber of commerce secretary had a few drinks and boasted there were eight hundred people living there, everyone humored him by agreeing.

He and Gretchen adopted two children, Bob and Cynthia, and enjoyed the quality of life small towns afford. He taught himself Spanish to be able to serve a larger population of clients. He served as the Conejos County attorney, and still found time to take the kids out for the best trout fishing in Colorado.

"If you're in a little town like Antonito," Carr said, "you learn to do everything. Country lawyers are the best because they have to learn everything. [We] have more time to sit around and read more law books than lawyers in the city."

His practice flourished and he quickly attracted the attention of lawyers around the state. After eleven years in Antonito, he was tapped by attorney general William Boatright to serve as Colorado's assistant attorney general, focusing on water issues. Despite loving the valley, he and Gretchen felt the education for their two children would be better in a bigger city. Then, following just two years of hard work in the attorney general's office, President Herbert Hoover selected him in 1929 to be the U.S. attorney for Colorado, the state's top federal law enforcement officer.

In taking the federal job, he would trade his concentration on streams and water compacts for the very different work of dealing with and capturing bootleggers and gangsters.

Fishing was Ralph Carr's favorite form of stress relief. For a man whom a coworker once said "had no hobbies," Carr loved trout fishing on rivers like the Conejos outside of Antonito, Colorado, where he started practicing law. He enjoyed going with political types like former President Herbert Hoover, as well as taking his kids, Robert and Cynthia. Courtesy of the Colorado Historical Society

Enforcing the country's Prohibition laws was the top priority for that office. At the time, Denver authorities didn't know what to do about the notorious Joe Roma gang. In southern Colorado, brothers Sam and Pete Carlino held the liquor monopoly and were causing trouble there. Like Americans most everywhere, Coloradans wanted alcohol, and laws were broken to buy or sell it. Many of the federal enforcement agents and Denver police officers were corrupt, leaving Carr's job among the loneliest in the city. During an era when people in his position sold out to the highest bidder, no one questioned Carr's character. He wouldn't take a dime or a drink.

He prosecuted the organized crime families with vigor, achieving numerous victories and subsequent headlines. However, before Roma and the Carlinos could be sent to prison, they were shot dead in the streets. Carr wondered if he would suffer the same fate, but his integrity may have saved him.

Carr's memory of people was legendary. Nearly a decade after Prohibition had been repealed, Carr ran into one of the bootleggers he had prosecuted at a campaign stop outside a Denver church. The man was stopping everyone entering the chapel, saying, "If you [promise to] vote for Ralph Carr for governor, there's free beer," at the tavern he owned down the street.

Carr pulled the man aside and whispered, "Didn't I send you to prison?"

"Oh, yeah," the man said, smiling.

"Well, why are you campaigning for me?" Carr asked.

"That's simple," said the bar owner. "When I was bootlegging, sure you prosecuted me and I served some time [in prison], but you were the only public official we weren't able to buy. Now I'm an honest businessman and I want another [honest man] in office."

The only thing missing as he waited to be escorted into the state house on that cold January morning in 1939 was his wife, Gretchen. She had died three years earlier, leaving her soul mate a widower with teenagers to raise on his own. A complication from diabetes, untreated for religious beliefs, had caused her death suddenly and unexpectedly. His mother helped, but he trusted no one's instincts the way he trusted Gretchen's. To ease the pain, he threw himself into work, getting the law firm on solid financial ground before being "sidetracked" into politics.

Carr's full attention on that January day was focused on a budget problem greater than he had envisioned. The state deficit was $1.8 million and there was a rumor that he would be forced to shut down many state institutions and lay off hundreds of workers to balance the budget. The superintendent of the state mental health facility had come into his office recently and tossed $115,000 worth of unpaid grocery bills onto his desk. The merchants of southern Colorado had been "patriotically feeding forty-five hundred charges of the state simply because they still had confidence in their state government." But as the superintendent told Carr, they were now weary of that sacrifice.

State finances were a mess, but newspapers of the day were excited about Carr's chances of succeeding. The *Boulder County Miner and Farmer* said, "[Carr] goes into office the freest and most independent man ever seated in office in this state. He will never lose prestige by any acts of commission and can only fail by acts of omission."

The *Denver Post* editorialized, "Governor Carr will start his administration with the all-important backing of public sentiment. The vote last November showed that the great majority of the people, Democrats and Republicans alike, believe in his ability, trust his judgment, and want him to succeed."

At 11:40 A.M., the committee of lawmakers appointed to escort the new governor headed for his chambers. Across the street in Denver's two-square-block haven known as Civic Center Park, Battery B of the 168th Field Artillery of the Colorado National Guard was standing at attention, waiting to fire a salute. The guns had been moved off the capitol grounds because the concussion from the rapidly firing guns rattled the building's old glass windows.

Ralph Carr, his mother, Mattie, his son, Robert, his daughter, Cynthia, and the family dog celebrate his inauguration day in 1939. Carr was a widower; his wife, Gretchen, died three years earlier due to complications from diabetes. The two were soul mates, and he trusted no one the way he trusted her. Courtesy of the Colorado Historical Society

About three thousand people packed inside the state house chambers and hundreds of others gathered in the hallway outside to listen over loudspeakers. The crowd rose to applaud as the state's Supreme Court justices and then the governor walked down the center aisle. Carr kissed Cynthia and patted Bob on the head before climbing the steps to the dais.

He wore a three-piece dark suit with a carnation in his lapel. Smiling, he took the oath of office administered by his friend, Chief Justice Burke, who had won reelection in November. They had come a long way from Room 50 in the Antlers Hotel only five months earlier.

"Do you swear to uphold the Constitution of the United States and the State of Colorado and perform the duties of your office to the best of your ability?"

"I do."

Guns across the street immediately fired nineteen times in an official salute to the chief. Friends and family came up to congratulate Colorado's new governor as he stood on a platform filled with flowers and palms. Governor Ammons "remained glumly in his seat" until Carr turned to shake hands with him before the cameras.

"The house will come back to order," said the new lieutenant governor, John Vivian. "Ladies and gentlemen, Governor Ralph Carr."

This political pioneer knew there was no turning back. His speech elaborated on the themes he had taken to Colorado voters: fiscal responsibility and ethics in government. The address was carried live on radio stations across the state.

"By the vote at the last election, the people of Colorado pronounced certain mandates directed to the legislative and executive departments with respect to the conduct and operation of their state government which no public official, either elective or appointive, may ignore.

"Our basic trouble is not financial. Our temporary fiscal

problems are but symptoms of poor organization and bad management."

As Governor Ammons grew more uncomfortable, Colorado's new governor announced plans to abolish many of the state bureaus and boards established during the last administration. He told state workers to expect a drastic reduction in the expenses of nearly all state departments.

He proposed shifting the net income tax benefiting schools into the state's general fund to pay the bills. Trained attendants at the state's hospitals and prisons had been paid on credit for months. He suggested paying them in cash the following month.

"The people were advised of this in the campaign and they know that the filler must be paid. Either a new tax must be voted [on] or we must find the solution in some such fund as this."

He was not only asking Colorado's schools to sacrifice, but said state workers needed to sacrifice as well. He told the crowd that anyone who joined the civil service to have an easy job financed by the taxpayers, and not to work for the betterment of the state, could expect to be fired.

Forty minutes later, many lawmakers sat in stunned silence. No one could remember an inauguration speech so controversial and so blunt in its message. Special interest groups were on alert and politicians were on guard. A tepid round of applause followed Governor Carr as he left the chambers.

Carr knew he'd have trouble reforming Colorado's state government. The bureaucracy had not been built in a day and would not be deconstructed quickly either. The Republicans controlled the state house, and the Democrats ruled the state senate. Enacting dramatic change, he admitted in a letter to Edward Leach, a former CU classmate and then publisher of the *Pittsburgh Press*, would be a challenge.

"My administration cannot be Republican because we didn't take enough men into the [State] Senate," he wrote. "Up to now, both papers [*Rocky Mountain News* and the *Denver Post*] have been behind me in everything I have suggested and if I can keep them in line, I may be able to whip recalcitrant Democrats into the picture strong enough to put over my campaign pledges."

Controversy erupted immediately, with some people supporting Carr's strong moves and others denouncing what they thought was high-handed "reorganization."

Some suspected Carr had higher ambitions. "Carr is trying to get himself elected to the United States Senate or the vice presidency by balancing the state budget," said Senator Rudolph Johnson (D-Boulder).

Colorado teachers had visions of schools closing, districts going bankrupt, and children being endangered. One school superintendent told the governor that the district was saving money by cutting resources that went directly to the students. He also told Carr, however, that the administrators' and teachers' salaries had been maintained. Carr exploded and told the superintendent that if he ever heard the district was skimping on its students again to give benefit to the adults, he would "throw [him] out of this window."

In years past, the usual political back and forth would have led to gridlock; this time they had a different governor and no one could anticipate his next move. He asked the state's radio stations for airtime to deliver a Republican version of a fireside chat. The fifteen-minute speech just nine days after he became the state's chief executive took the case straight to Colorado citizens.

"People of Colorado, you are facing a crisis tonight," he said. "I do not care to be listed as an alarmist, and I do not enjoy going on the air to discuss matters as serious as I have to present to you. Because you have refused to face the facts and because some of your representatives in the 32nd General Assembly seem inclined to dodge the issue, I am forced to present a true picture to you and then, to ask you and your legislators what you and they are going to do about it."

Carr laid out the state's financial straits.

Salaries of state employees—those operating the State Home for Dependent Children, nurses and doctors at Colorado General Hospital, and those working for other state institutions—were not being paid. There was no food for those being treated at the Colorado Hospital for the Insane. There was no fuel to transport convicts from the state prisons to court hearings. The state's infrastructure was crumbling, bit by bit—and quickly.

To address the state's $1.6-million deficit, Carr had suggested shifting income tax revenue from the schools to cover the many gaps. To those furious about this idea, he pointed out that the income tax amendment allowed for it, and besides, payment had already been made to Colorado's schools for the next nine months, so they would be fine.

Carr sternly told the teacher's union, "There is no reason for the closing of a single school."

He invited solutions from citizens of both political parties, saying he was "ready and anxious to work for any practical solution." But he lamented, "Tonight when our state cannot pay her obligations, when the cries of unfortunate women and children can almost be heard, no solution is offered other than a protest."

Carr called on citizens to send letters, telegrams, and make phone calls to legislators urging them to act, even those who questioned his "sincerity and honesty" in describing the problem.

"People of Colorado—this is your problem. As your governor, I have given you the facts. The result is in your hands."

Four days later, he went back to the airwaves to convince those who might be "wobbling" about a solution, and he spoke strongly to those who continued to fight change. He told the radio audience that his correspondence since his first speech was ten to one in favor of his solution.

To the Denver teachers' union specifically, Carr said he remained a devout believer in those who chose education as a profession. To the recalcitrant lawmakers battling a new governor's ideas, he demanded results.

"Repeatedly, they have been challenged to present some practical, workable solution of the problem if they did not agree with that of the governor," he said. "And tonight what do we have? Not a single constructive idea has emanated from that body."

Carr realized no solution would appease all Coloradans. Yet, to avoid the problem altogether was not an option.

"The situation cannot be sidestepped," he said. "The crisis will permit no delay. It takes courage in the face of criticism and attack to go forward. God grant that the lawmakers of Colorado will see their duty and by their votes will convince the people of Colorado that they are as big as the emergency which confronts them."

The public campaign worked, but not without compromise on both sides. Carr would soon sign a measure into law, diverting 65 percent of the school money to cover the state's bills. It had the support of a large majority of state lawmakers.

At the same time, he and his allies opposed "every bill intended to levy a new tax against the already-burdened property owners of Colorado." One bill that added a direct levy on property passed the legislature. Carr vetoed it, calling it a "back-door tax." The governor promised that if more needs arose, they'd be met through tax cuts, not tax increases.

In the midst of his challenging first months, Carr's mother died from a heart attack. Mattie Carr was seventy-five. In her obituary, the *Denver Post* wrote, "One in search of those qualities which made the western pioneer the symbol of courage, tenacity, and faith need not look beyond the life and character of Mrs. Carr."

Before the funeral, Carr read once more the letter his mother had written him when he was named U.S. attorney. "My dear Ralph," she wrote, "I have been trying to find a short time all by my self [*sic*] when I could sit down and think of the blessing that came to me when you was [*sic*] given to me the sweetest most lovable baby in all the world and all through the years that followed how proud I was of you …

"I always want you to remember your father's words the night before he passed on. 'There isn't a man that walks the streets of the United States today who is a better man than Ralph Carr.' It was his last message to you, Dear. And you are surely fulfilling his faith in you."

He put the letter down and took a deep breath. He was now alone in raising his kids. But work took his mind off his losses.

Dealing with the gigantic financial morass was the biggest challenge of his first two-year administration, and certainly the most important. But he was faced with a couple of other crises that would have tested any leader.

On the first of July, two days after the *Post* had complimented Carr for his plan to balance the state budget, he was surprised to see this headline: "Carr swings open prison doors." Readers were told, "Governor Carr has been paroling and pardoning convicts SECRETLY and without asking the advice of the warden of the penitentiary."

Of the seventeen criminals whose sentences had been commuted or pardoned over the last four months, seven were rapists, according to the paper. "The governor says he is 'not going to embark upon a pardon and parole orgy.' He isn't going to do that? HE ALREADY HAS DONE IT."

Nobody should have been surprised by Carr's policy. During the campaign when the topic came up, he was quoted widely by numerous papers saying, "I think the matter of paroles, pardons, and commutations is one of the most important things that comes before a chief executive … after investigation, if I think a man should be given clemency, I will extend it to him and I will not care what critics may say."

Faced with blistering public criticism, Carr remained true to his word and refused to back down. He said he would continue to issue commutations or grant parole in cases he considered deserving.

"I looked into their backgrounds, the nature and circumstances of their crimes," Carr said of the seventeen men he helped.

"I also talked with their relatives to find out just what the chance of rehabilitation was."

As to why he didn't publicize his decisions, he said he felt "any publicity would work to the hardship of the convicts, whose principal aim is to get a fresh start in life." Further, he told judge John Palmer, a friend for decades, "May I say to you that I am going to use the pardon power even more than some newspapers think I have any right to."

Carr traveled to the bleak state prison in Cañon City, along the Arkansas River in southern Colorado, once a month. He met prisoners individually to discuss their requests. His background as both a prosecutor and defense attorney gave him insight into a judicial system that he felt needed to treat some convicts with more of a "pat on the back" than a punitive sentence.

"Ralph Carr was a great judge of character," said Myrtle Graham, who worked in the governor's office. "He could tell about a person by spending some time with them." She said none of the men Carr pardoned ever ended up back in prison.

A third situation that challenged Carr's leadership skills happened on a hot August 2 morning, when he was fishing along the Colorado River with former president Herbert Hoover. An aide called him to a nearby telephone where he heard a garbled message, "Strike at the Green Mountain Dam out of control. Gun shots right by the tunnel at Heeney. Two to five people killed, others wounded. Lines of communication are broken. Public highways barricaded by armed men and more are reportedly on their way."

Union workers building the Green Mountain Dam along the Continental Divide had walked out because they wanted the project to remain a closed shop (with union membership required). Nonunion workers and the local farmers, who for years had wanted the dam to help water their crops, confronted them. Armed with deer rifles and shotguns, the nonunion workers and the farmers broke through the union picket line to take over the dam workings. Dozens of shots were fired. In response, the union workers blew up nearby bridges and erected barricades to prevent reinforcements from coming to help their opponents. The union men were vastly outgunned and feared for their safety.

Carr sent his personal driver, Colorado courtesy patrol officer Myron Donald, to investigate and report back. When Donald pulled up to the dam at dusk, he was stopped by bullets "whizzing over his head." He got out of the car, walked in front of the car lights, and let the combatants see his sky blue uniform. He calmly faced the guns and told both sides to stop shooting.

He saw four hundred armed strikers with their sympathizers facing off against three hundred fifty more heavily armed non-striking workers, farmers, and what he called "vigilantes" who had come from Denver looking for a fight. Donald called Carr and told him that he needed to act immediately.

After hanging up, the governor ordered up the Colorado National Guard to "save the lives and property of American citizens." It was the first time in Colorado history that the guard was used to keep the peace in a strike to protect both sides, including the strikers.

By nine the next morning, three hundred guardsmen in full battle regalia rushed toward Green Mountain in scenic Summit County; they faced a grim scene. But by that afternoon the intervention had worked. The violence stopped and both sides disarmed. The early reports of fatalities had been misleading.

"It appears this morning that the reports as to the persons killed were not true, for which I am very happy," the governor said in a statewide radio address that evening. "I am still happier in the knowledge that action was taken before such tragic results actually developed.

"I have notified all groups that I am not taking sides one way or the other. I have nothing to suggest as to the type of agreement that should be entered into as I have no chips in the game."

The newspapers raved about the governor's actions. The

Denver Post wrote, "Governor Carr acted with commendable decisiveness and dispatch." The *Pueblo Chieftain* reported that the "strikers rose practically as ONE man and said, 'Thank God and Governor Carr for sending the troops in.'"

Before leaving for Denver to confer directly with the adjutant general of the National Guard, Carr went to say good-bye to Hoover, his fishing pal and political patron. They'd have to grill some trout another time. The Republican icon, still with significant clout nationwide, had appointed Carr the U.S. attorney from Colorado during his presidency, and Carr always sought his counsel and favor.

"Good! I knew you could do it," Hoover said.

So far, despite his unorthodox ways and his cut-to-the-chase manner, Carr was passing test after political test. Politicians on a national level were taking notice and his name was being mentioned for higher office. His first term as governor had set a high standard and it looked like he could do just about anything he wanted to. However, it was a pivotal time in history, and pretty soon everything would blow to pieces.

Chapter Three
November 1939 to 1940

In 1939, Lowell Thomas was likely the second-most recognized man in the United States, behind President Franklin Delano Roosevelt. He was the most popular radio commentator in the world, and by the happiest of coincidences, he was good friends with Ralph Carr.

What began when both were young newspapermen seeking their way in life, living and working in the same mining town in Colorado, would lead both to successes they'd never imagined.

Thomas was called the "golden voice of radio," and his career spanned fifty years, taking him around the world to cover war and peace. Listeners knew the familiar way he began each broadcast, "Good evening, everybody," and the way he ended, "So long, until tomorrow." They trusted him and hung on his every word.

Lowell Thomas wanted Ralph Carr to be vice president—at least. He teased Carr about going even higher. And America took notice.

Although Thomas was born in Ohio, his father, who was a doctor, took his family West in 1900. He had heard that the streets in Victor, Colorado, were paved with gold. He planned to indulge in his favorite pastime of geology. Young Lowell climbed Pikes Peak before he was fourteen, and he lived in the camp when it was producing millions of dollars of gold every year.

Carr was five years his senior and lived in the tiny town of Cripple Creek, around Battle Mountain from Victor, Colorado. Both young men went off to school, Carr to CU for his undergraduate degree and then to law school, and Thomas to Valparaiso University in Indiana. Thomas returned to Cripple Creek prepared to do what "young scholars in mining camps have always done." But before he ever swung a pick or shovel, he was offered a position running the *Victor Daily Record* for ninety-five dollars a month.

It was a great place to be a reporter.

"In any given ten-day period, you could count on a shooting spree in a gambling hall or one of the red-light districts, a holdup, a fire, a mine accident, and an indignant reader proposing to horsewhip the editor," Thomas wrote. "There were also rodeos, prizefighters, evangelists heralding imminent doom for sinners. … It was an opportunity to intrigue any young man with a taste for the great human drama."

Six months into the job, Thomas was stolen away by a group from Denver starting a second newspaper in town, the *Victor Daily News*. Lowell Thomas would describe his replacement at the *Record* as "the ablest young man they could get." That man was Ralph Carr.

At home, while waiting on the results of his bar examination, Carr joked that he would put Lowell out of business in thirty days. Although they "hated each other in print," they became the best of friends, sharing stories and talking politics over coffee nearly every night after the newspapers had been printed. Both soon left to go out into the world, but their friendship continued for the rest of their lives; they kept in touch, corresponded, and gave each other advice.

Thomas furthered his career as a print journalist, then broke into the career he became famous for—radio news broadcaster.

Two and a half decades later, Thomas's support for his old friend, now the governor of his beloved Colorado, would lead to accusations from other national media outlets that Thomas was actively promoting Carr for higher office. Carr acknowledged using Thomas's name for publicity purposes "in a shameful manner" during his gubernatorial campaign and hoped his friend would "someday feel that the action was justified." In return, Carr sent Colorado-grown celery that Thomas could not find in the New York markets.

The two joked back and forth.

"Whatever you do, don't overwork," Thomas wrote on January 9, the day before Carr would be inaugurated. "There may be a

Ralph Carr and Lowell Thomas were friends and newspaper rivals in Victor, Colorado, before either one of them achieved any national prominence. Thomas would write the book *With Lawrence in Arabia* and become arguably the second most well-known person in the country, behind President Franklin Delano Roosevelt. Thomas used his radio program, newspaper articles, and his connections with high-powered Republicans to help thrust his old friend into the national spotlight. Carr was being mentioned as a vice presidential candidate, and even as a possible presidential candidate, due, in part, to the fact that he was being so actively promoted by a power broker like Thomas. Courtesy of the Colorado Historical Society lot of fun ahead and you'll have to conserve your physical power in order to get the most out of it. Have you ever tried an hour in a gym? I haven't. But they tell me it is a great idea."

The five-eight, 187-pound Carr wrote back a week later. "I am too lazy to work out in a gym. … If you try it first, then maybe I will too."

Thomas watched what Carr did as governor. He was impressed Carr had met and conquered a state budget deficit without raising taxes. He also agreed with Carr that the New Deal had run its course and it was time for private industry to take the government's place in stimulating the economy. Thomas began to drop not-so-subtle hints about his old Victor newspaper buddy joining Thomas Dewey, his neighbor and the Republican district attorney in New York, in an East-West ticket for president and vice president. He felt the combination would be sure to beat the Democrats in 1940.

"I have a hunch that almost nothing now can stop [Dewey] from getting the nomination," Thomas wrote Carr in March 1939, fifteen months before the 1940 Republican Convention, "and, I'd like to put your name before the convention, for vice-president . How about it? By then, you may want to enjoy a brief vacation in Washington, get away from the Colorado financial puzzle …

"I am positive that you can handle the vice-presidential assignment just as ably as 99 percent of the gentlemen who have held that post in the past. It would be great fun to help put you over."

Carr believed Dewey needed "a few more gray hairs" before running for president, and as far as his friend's suggestion that he could make it to the national political stage, he brushed it aside. "I am not yet ready to think that I am in the national picture. I have a big job in Colorado to complete first."

Thomas was not the only one promoting Colorado's governor, who had only been in office for a few months. One of Carr's high school classmates, Harry Denny, made news in the Denver papers in late March when he echoed Thomas's sentiments about a Dewey-Carr ticket at a luncheon.

George Emick, owner of the Cascade, a café named after the mountain resort town where it stood, put up a sign in the restaurant window that read "Carr for President in 1940."

On his home turf, the *Denver Post* editorialized on May 22 that Carr was a "strong potential candidate for the Presidency." In Denver on a campaign stop, Donald W. Hornbeck, the chairman of the National Young Republican Foundation, said Carr is "decidedly among the possibilities for the Presidential nomination."

One day in June, Thomas sent a box of "Carr for President" buttons to the governor's office at the state capitol. Carr's secretary brought the box into the waiting room and "before he got through, he had them plastered on the coat lapels of as many persons as he had buttons." Carr said, "Naturally it reached the newspapers and now they are figuring all kinds of things about my future candidacy. Those things are in the laps of the gods. I am just trying to do a little job day by day and so far have had all the breaks."

Reporters were noticing the extra attention being paid to Carr. United Press International reported on June 28, "The consensus ... was Thomas and Dewey, probably acting on the advice of national Republican leaders, were seeking to drum up a boom for a western man on the national ticket in 1940."

The "little job" Carr described for his friend entailed trying to remake Colorado state government and continuing to be frustrated in his efforts to do so. The Democratic senate, outnumbering Republicans two to one, blocked his reform plans.

Carr admitted to Thomas that he was "bull-headed and refusing to compromise." He went on to say, "Like all crusaders, I think I am right. As you well know, that is the most pernicious form of self-righteousness and I should be ashamed of myself, but again, like crusaders, I justify my conduct."

In July, he asked all state bureaus and departments to cut costs by 10 percent. He decided he would trim their payrolls until "foolish expenditures" were halted and state workers stopped spending their time "drinking coffee and Coke in the basement cafeteria of the capitol."

One month later, the request became an edict as Carr, who had promised to run the state as a business, refused to take no for an answer. To those who forecast economic ruin, he reminded everyone that his earlier plan to pay the state's bills had resulted in no schools being closed. "No children [were] deprived of an education," he said. "No teachers [were] thrown out of jobs."

Carr's national prominence grew. In August, he hosted the 1936 Republican presidential candidate Alf Landon. The former Kansas governor came to Bear Creek for a little fishing and politicking. The visit was duly noted in the press.

Political speculation got hot when Carr went to the East Coast to convince Wall Street bondsmen that Colorado was a great place to invest. While there, he hobnobbed with the Republican elite. First, Carr attended an October football game at Yale University with former president Herbert Hoover, where he sat on the fifty-yard line and hummed the Yale fight song.

Next, he had a conversation about the 1940 campaign at Lowell Thomas's country house in Pawling, New York, with both Hoover and Dewey.

At the same time, his lieutenant governor back in Denver, John Vivian, was steering the political conversation about his boss in a different direction. Vivian wanted to see Carr run for the U.S. Senate in 1942 against Democratic incumbent and former Colorado governor, Edwin C. Johnson. "That's what I'm trying to get Carr to do," said Vivian. "The vice presidency would be nice, but I'd rather see him get the senatorship."

Although the interest was genuinely flattering to Carr, it seemed premature. He had no problem believing his budget-balancing politics were needed at the national level, but he did not believe he would be the one to bring them to Washington. He returned from the trip and told reporters that any stories of him becoming a vice-presidential candidate were "just bunk." That did

Ralph Carr and former President Herbert Hoover watch a Yale University football game. Hoover appointed Carr to be U.S. attorney in Colorado, and Carr always turned to the Republican leader for political advice. Despite being governor of a small state, his budgeting success and skill in marketing his ideas endeared him to national political leaders like Hoover who were looking for Republicans to voice opposition to President Roosevelt's New Deal. Courtesy of the Colorado Historical Society not stop the state's newspapers from offering their varying opinions on the topic anyway.

Despite his denials, Thomas turned the national spotlight on Carr once again by writing a flattering profile of him in the *New York Herald Tribune*. "North, South, East and West, you can hear the G.O.P.'s prayer. 'Please Heaven, send us a candidate!'" Thomas wrote in the January 28 *Sunday Magazine*. "A candidate who is a whirlwind campaigner, a candidate who can capture the ears of radio-listening millions. A candidate who will know how to handle Congress, how to balance the budget, how to keep us out of war, how to settle the difference between capitalists and labor!

"Why not begin the search with the highest state in the Union? [Look] to Ralph Carr ... a wizard in the [Colorado] governor's chair."

The *New York Times* called him a vice-presidential candidate and editorialized, "When Governor Ralph Carr of Colorado announces to the nation that 'the way to save money is to stop spending it,' he is quoting common knowledge in the simplest and plainest possible English, and, in so far as he is trying to add to the electorate's store of political wisdom, he might as well have proclaimed that if a man falls into the sea, he will get wet. Yet, it happens that Governor Carr is not just a fountain of old copybook maxims, but is one of the nation's most successful money-savers in an executive office."

Carr was invited to preach his message of fiscal responsibility all over the nation. He spoke about the party's founder at a Lincoln Day audience of seven hundred Republicans outside Detroit. "Lincoln would have known that spending and lending is unsound and that thrift and the full payment of debts ... is simple and common honesty," he told an applauding crowd. The next month, he barnstormed in New Mexico, Oklahoma, and Texas, talking to Republican voters.

The attention would have flattered any politician, and Carr was no exception. He had received an entrée into a world that few men knew. Yet, he remained unconvinced he was ready to live in that world full time. He told his college friend Ferdinand Lockhart that he didn't believe any conversation that included him as a vice-presidential candidate was either "geographically or politically wise."

Of the candidates set to vie for the presidency, the one who had not paid Colorado's governor a visit or an open compliment in the press was the one who captured Carr's attention. In the late part of 1939, Wendell Willkie had formed a group of acquaintances around the country to help him prepare for a run, according to the *New Republic*.

The group was filled with businessmen, not politicians. It included a bank president rather than a union president, and a corporation representative rather than a state representative.

Carr was impressed with Willkie's "unusual intellectual capacity." He saw a "natural, open-minded, straight-thinking American." The general public and the media called it the "Willkie phenomenon." Both men were from modest homes, and had done manual labor before becoming lawyers. As politicians, they shared a common belief in saying what they thought.

Willkie opposed FDR's Tennessee Valley Authority, which sought to provide low-cost power and flood control to hundreds of thousands of Americans. He believed that government did not have the constitutional basis to enter the utility business. Carr had personally argued against an overreaching federal bureaucracy numerous times. What impressed Carr even more was Willkie's determination to take his campaign directly to the people by writing articles for major media outlets like *Forbes*, the *Saturday Evening Post*, *Life*, and the *New York Times*.

But as Republicans descended upon Philadelphia for their June convention, few gave Willkie a chance. The exception was Ralph Carr. The *Rocky Mountain News* said, "The governor isn't picking out a bad horse to ride. Maybe our Mr. Carr figures that, if Willkie is nominated, he would like to have Colorado's governor for a vice presidential running mate."

The Philadelphia crowds were enthusiastic wherever Willkie appeared. He arrived with petitions supporting his candidacy signed by four and a half million voters. Carr received three hundred telegrams and a petition with ten thousand signatures on it from home, all supporting Willkie.

Colorado's leading business leaders told Republicans they could not expect financial support in the upcoming November elections if they did not support Willkie.

Yet, when the Willkie campaign formally announced that Carr was supporting their candidate, there was a near rebellion by Colorado's eleven other delegates. It was generally assumed that the chairman of a delegation represented the wishes of its delegates. Carr's decision to support Willkie without formally polling his delegation earned him the rebuke of Colorado's other delegates. A red-faced Carr threatened to resign his chairmanship. He was insulted that the delegates were questioning his "honesty and integrity."

Colorado's delegates were not the only Republicans questioning Willkie; others felt he wasn't Republican enough. He had attended the 1932 Democratic National Convention and even donated a hundred and fifty dollars to FDR's first campaign. He hadn't switched party affiliations to Republican until November of 1939, just seven months before he asked the party to nominate him as its candidate for president. In fact, his fellow Hoosier, former Indiana senator James Watson, refused to endorse him, saying, "I may welcome a repentant sinner into my church, but I wouldn't want him to lead the church choir."

Willkie's opponents were Ohio senator Robert A. Taft, the son of the late president William Howard Taft, Thomas Dewey, and Michigan senator Arthur Vandenberg. All three had courted Carr's support before they ever arrived in Philadelphia. Yet, the day the main convention business got underway, after Indiana congressman Charles Halleck nominated his fraternity brother Wendell Willkie,

Ralph Carr took the microphone to second the motion.

With both of his children in attendance and on the Philadelphia Convention Center floor, Carr told the convention that the ills Colorado faced were the same ones the entire country faced. He said, "We must march back up the hard hill we came down so fast, to return to industrial, to agricultural, and to social America as we used to know it."

He told Willkie's story, from his humble home to the Wall Street boardroom, successes all along the way, before concluding it was Willkie's devotion to financial responsibility that made him the perfect candidate. "If we are ever to save this country, we must first save business. Every one of you is in business—big business and little business, farmers, stockmen, laboring men, industrialists—you are looking for a man with the ability and the character to mold every faction of our people into a unit.

"The people are demanding him. We are here offering to the American people the one man who knows, the one man with the soul, the one man with the ability to do it. It is an honor to second the nomination of Wendell Willkie!"

Two days later, it took six rounds of voting before Willkie won a majority of the delegates, shortly after midnight. He told reporters he was happy, humble, and proud. Now Willkie needed to find a running mate. He turned first to those who had supported him from the beginning.

He turned to Ralph Carr.

Inside his suite in the Benjamin Franklin Hotel, Willkie and Carr discussed the vice presidency. Ralph Carr told his son, his secretary, and his staff that he had been invited to be one heartbeat from the presidency.

The invitation made political sense. Willkie, now based in the East, could benefit from a western politician like Carr. They could be the two outsiders taking on FDR, the ultimate insider seeking an unprecedented third term in the White House. Willkie and Carr shared the philosophy that government should be run as a business.

Ralph Carr and 1940 Republican presidential candidate Wendell
Willkie joke around during the month Willkie spent in Colorado
following the nominating convention that summer in Philadelphia.
Carr seconded the nomination of Willkie at the convention and was
offered a spot on the national ticket by the businessman. However,
Carr turned down a chance to be vice president to finish the job of
reforming Colorado state government that he had promised voters
he would accomplish. Courtesy of the Colorado Historical Society

Agencies, bureaus, and commissions would be forced to become more efficient or be downsized in their administration. Belts would be tightened. It was a match sure to energize the party, and more important, could possibly shift the philosophy of government.

Lowell Thomas's efforts to promote his friend had succeeded. There was just one hitch: Carr didn't accept the invitation. It would not be the last time Colorado's governor passed up a major opportunity in Washington.

Carr's secretary Myrtle Graham explained it simply, "He didn't want to leave Colorado." Carr felt he wasn't done reforming at home, so leaving would be a betrayal of his word. He'd run for reelection as governor instead, his two-year term coming due in November. So when Willkie came to Colorado shortly after the convention to regain his energy and plan the campaign for the next four months, he came as the guest of Governor Carr, not as his running mate.

Carr was photographed with Willkie everywhere, from eating deep-fried Colorado mountain trout rolled in cracker crumbs to Frontier Days in neighboring Cheyenne, Wyoming. At each stop, Carr introduced the man he hoped would become president.

The current administration didn't care about the individual, he'd say. What they wanted was an ever-expanding central government, operated by politicians for politicians. Those bureaucrats claimed they knew how Americans should conduct their private affairs, Carr continued, and were telling Americans how many acres of ground to plow, what price they might receive for crops, how many livestock they might keep, and what doctrines their children should be taught.

Although the campaign in Colorado looked grand to outsiders, Carr silently bristled when Willkie forgot the names of his staff members and couldn't make appointments on time. "It just used to make [him] furious," said Graham. "He'd have things planned to the minute and [Willkie] was never on time. Ralph Carr had absolutely no patience for that. I think for that reason, if nothing else, he wouldn't have run with him."

After Willkie left Colorado in August, Carr turned to his own reelection campaign. He told voters the promises he made as an outsider in 1938 were only partially accomplished. Trying to pass reform measures with the Democratic obstructionists in the state senate was like running to school uphill, barefoot, and in the snow both ways, he said. He encouraged Coloradans to stay the course.

He told a group of Young Republicans, "If I hear any Republican voicing any alibi or apology for anything I've done in office, I am not going to be a candidate on the Republican ticket. … We are on the right side."

In Republican strongholds, he was considered a hero, a political breath of fresh air bringing life to a previously moribund party. For example, a visit to Burlington, on Colorado's eastern plains, received this glowing front-page review: "The very humanness of the man, his sincerity, his untiring efforts for the good of his fellow citizens of the entire state, his utter disregard for self in his efforts to do his very best for Colorado, his keen perspective and his brilliant mind," the *Burlington Call* reported, "all these attributes mark him as a truly great man. Party lines were forgotten and Burlington folks knew only that here was a friend."

Critics from all sides were quick to attack. The Democrats circulated a campaign poster of a little girl waiting outside the governor's office with cobwebs covering the door, implying he was never around. The image of an absent governor, more interested in national politics than Colorado politics, became a theme.

Carr figured his critics had already had the chance to fix things when they were in charge and they didn't do it. They were the machine, the establishment that sought to benefit at the expense of Colorado taxpayers. The fact that his administration had balanced the budget without raising taxes was highlighted in every campaign speech he made. He promised to keep it balanced and not impose new taxes if reelected.

"What have we done to justify your returning us to office?" he asked in a speech on October 15. "We have taken the income of the state of Colorado. We have lived within it. We added not a dime of new taxes. We cut the [tax] levy for state purposes last October and we balanced your blooming budget."

Three days later, he told a raucous crowd, "Some wise man has said the most sensitive part of the human makeup is the pocketbook nerve."

Carr had his own clever supporters, including Robert Furlong of Denver, who wrote a song called "Carr for Governor" to the tune of a famous ballad written after World War I. It started:

> There's a son of Colorado who has won his spurs,
> Our citizens are therefore pleased when this occurs.
> They admire this man who has clearly shown,
> That he wears no man's collar but his own …
> Well, Governor Carr is such a man, as we'll know,
> He has put the State upon its feet, statistics show.
> He has the courage, brains, and tact,
> His administration proved that fact.

Making a bigger impact was a statewide radio address by Carr's campaign manager, Max Goldberg, a former sports commentator and announcer. For fifteen minutes, Goldberg articulated why "his friend" should be honored with another two-year term.

"Let's forget, for this next fifteen minutes, about political parties and all the babble and confusion of a political campaign. Let's forget about charges and countercharges. I want to talk to you about a man," began Goldberg. "I want to slash right through that web and talk about Ralph Carr, the man. I want to talk about him simply because I, as a citizen of Colorado, believe he is the best governor this state ever had. … I am proud to know him because he is a great man, and he would still be a great man if he had no title and no public office."

Goldberg reminded listeners of the dismal state of affairs when Carr took office. He faced a budget in peril, a political system gorging on its taxpayers, people going hungry, a state in disrepair. Perhaps Coloradans had forgotten that dangerous time, which he said, in itself, is "the most eloquent tribute that can be paid to Ralph Carr."

Goldberg went on to say, "He not only hung his hat in the corner; he took off his coat and rolled up his sleeves. Day after day he worked sixteen and twenty hours a day. Week after week, he worked seven days a week. At every step and every turn, he ran into new obstacles, new opposition of selfish groups, new pessimism of men who said the job couldn't be done."

Colorado had been sick and dying, Goldberg said, now it was well. The state that had been bankrupt was now robust and strong. It was a stirring tribute. Despite accusations hurled by his Democratic opponents, Carr had facts on his side. The state's budget had been balanced with no new taxes. No school had been closed as a result of his plan to shift money from education to pay the bills. He did not need nor did he want to engage in any negative campaigning.

His Democratic opponent George Saunders passed out a flyer accusing the governor of converting himself into a tourist at the expense of the taxpayers "with the sole purpose of organizing a political machine with destructive tendencies, instead of progress."

Part of the flyer read: "It is true that both candidates are natives of Colorado. This does not prove anything. A mother can bear two sons, one a thief and one with a human heart; so this is the case."

Newspapers rallied to Carr's defense even if their editorial policies leaned toward the Democrats. They admired that he would not personally attack his opponent. "Governor Carr's record of clean campaigning, of refusing to stoop into the mudslinging so common in some Colorado campaigns, may well be imitated by future candidates," editorialized the *Boulder Daily*

Camera.

Carr left nothing to chance. He visited every fair possible, riding so many horses that he said he "[pulled] leather [saddles] every time [he] got into an automobile." He traveled seven thousand miles on the campaign trail, seeing the aspens, sumac, cottonwoods, and oak trees turn shades of yellow, gold, crimson, and bronze "known only to the mile-high altitude" of his favorite state.

During his final speech that was broadcast on four statewide radio stations on November 4, he thanked the people of Colorado, saying, "My only motive in entering the campaign two years ago was the hope that I might repay something of the great debt which I owe to the people and to this state."

The strategy that had served him well throughout the previous two years continued. It was the economy that people cared about. The taxes they paid. The jobs they held.

"No man alone may claim credit for what has been done. It is your accomplishment as well as mine. It is, in essence, the accomplishment of an alert and determined people who saw their state tottering to ruin and simply would not permit it.

"I stand here tonight, then, only as the symbol of an achievement in which I was privileged to share, and for which you chose me as a leader. …

"I stand here tonight representing your achievement in saving Colorado from the ignominy of bankruptcy and restoring her to a proud and secure place among the States."

Twenty-four hours later, when the polls closed on November 5, Willkie would win Colorado and gain more votes nationwide than any other Republican candidate against FDR, yet still be walloped overall. His political career had peaked.

The man he'd continue to correspond with for years to come had a much better outcome. Colorado voters overwhelmingly endorsed his vision, 60 percent of the vote to 40 percent. Ralph Carr won reelection by fifty-five thousand votes.

A campaign card given to voters before the November 1940 election highlights Ralph Carr's budget-balancing abilities. The man who first decided to run for governor around a urinal in a Colorado Springs hotel would decisively win another two-year term, sending this political star even higher. Carr was being asked to speak around the country as a voice of spending restraint and balanced budgets in contrast with the New Deal policies operating in Washington.

Chapter Four
January 1941 to December 1941

Like a lot of crusty Colorado men, Farrington R. Carpenter swaggered a little as he walked. He was known as a maverick and tried his best to live up to that reputation. Right after taking the job as Colorado's first director of revenue, he went after Governor Ralph Carr.

It was brought to his attention that the governor owed twenty dollars in taxes. Carr had received a thousand dollars from the state and had not paid taxes on it.

"Nobody had dared try to collect it," Carpenter said, "so they dumped the problem on me."

Without hesitation, Carpenter, who was not so affectionately referred to around the capitol as the "son of a bitch who is raising hell with the state government," strode into the governor's office. Carpenter had a stubborn streak and knew the message that would be sent if the governor, "Mr. Accountability in Government" himself, was allowed to skate on a past-due tax bill.

He walked in, greeted his friend of decades, threw the bill on his desk, and said, "Why don't you pay your taxes, Ralph?"

"Oh, I paid that tax long ago," Carr replied.

"No, you didn't," Carpenter insisted.

Carr called for his assistants to check his records and find the receipt. They couldn't find it right off the bat. Carr asked them to search some more. When they returned a few minutes later, they still had no receipt.

"Why don't you pay up now and have it over with?" Carpenter said. And as the governor was begrudgingly taking out his personal checkbook, Carpenter remembered one more thing.

"Wait a minute," he said. "Please add penalty and interest. They come to $6.48 more."

"I thought the interest and penalty on the first offense was discretionary with the director," Carr pleaded. "You don't mean to say that you're going to make me pay it?"

"I sure am," Carpenter said. "People have been dodging these taxes for seven years. If I knock off the penalty and interest for you, everybody will say I give personal favors."

That check for $26.48 sat on Carpenter's desk for only a few days before it was put to use. A Denver auctioneer and his high-powered attorney came to complain about an unpaid service-tax bill sent by Carpenter's office. The man said he'd pay the bill, but he wanted the interest and penalty waived because it was his first offense.

Without hesitation, Carpenter picked up the governor's check and said, "Governor Carr signed this for tax, penalty, and interest ... that's the way he was treated by this department when he failed to pay his tax."

The auctioneer and his lawyer headed for the cashier.

Carpenter's reputation was solid—he earned his reputation as "the meanest man in Colorado." He loved his job; a *Rocky Mountain News* reporter saw him burst into Carr's office a few weeks into the job, and overheard him say, "I'm certainly having fun as a fella sez when the sow ate up his little sister."

When Ralph Carr began his second two-year term in January 1941, reorganizing state government was at the top of his agenda. He intended to start with the Department of Revenue. He knew he could work at a slower pace than he did in his first term when budgets had to be balanced or people wouldn't eat and state employees wouldn't be paid. Yet, he felt the importance of this mission was equally important.

Roosevelt's New Deal policies—like the enormous Social Security program—took money, and involved getting matching funds from the states. Colorado's tax collection had to keep up. In 1941, tax collectors in the state worked for three entities—the state treasurer, the state auditor, and the state attorney general, with no coordination or supervision. Carr wanted to use a business model that would streamline the process.

It would be a significant task to merge government departments to prevent redundancy and improve efficiency. "It can not be done in one legislative session," he explained to *Capitol* columnist Alva Swain. "However, a good start can be made."

That start was known as the Administrative Code Act, or Senate Bill 383. It put all tax collecting under a newly created Department of Revenue. The streamlining paid for the program. Carr would call it "one of the most progressive steps in the history of our state government."

The measure passed through the legislature with only two dissenting votes. Still, its success was "only as good as the people implementing it," Carr reminded both citizens and lawmakers. The goal was economy in government, but without efficiency that was impossible.

Carr needed an unbending force to help him get started on his goal. He called Carpenter, who led the life of the small-town lawyer that the governor once enjoyed.

"Hello, Ferry, this is Ralph Carr."

"Hello, Governor. How are things under the capitol dome?"

"Fine. Just fine," Carr said. "But they'll be better when you take the appointment I'm about to offer you. Ferry, will you accept the position of director of Revenue? I need you in Denver to head the department. We need somebody with your reputation of integrity. I want you to start right away, as soon as you can. I want you to take the job."

A day later, at a salary of sixty-five hundred dollars, which was fifteen hundred more than the governor himself was earning, Carpenter moved to Denver to work for another political maverick. In his first year in office, tax collections increased exponentially, often forcing the governor to defend the "meanest man in Colorado."

"It has been the custom since the time of [the] Nazarene to criticize the tax collector," Carr said. "He has never been a popular member of organized society."

Carr started out his second inaugural address on January 9, 1941, with the clear message that Colorado state government must be streamlined so that every cent of taxpayer money would be spent wisely. Then he talked about the most serious issue everyone faced—the possibility of a second world war.

"We can almost see the outline of structures rising against the western skyline, designed for the production of death-dealing war equipment on a war basis; the eastern air is alive with the planes of fighting birdmen whose wings may carry them we know not where.

"We are not Republicans, we are not Democrats. We cannot be in this crisis. We are Coloradans. We are Americans."

Still, after the inauguration, Carr felt it his duty to criticize FDR's policies when he disagreed with them. He especially felt that the president stepped hard on the Constitution when he opposed letting each state determine its own water future. Carr called the president's decision "as foreign to the principles of Americanism as darkness is to daylight."

Carr despised the New Deal. He often let people know that he was for less government, whereas FDR wanted more. Carr wanted individuals to make decisions for themselves. He believed FDR wanted the government to make decisions for those individuals. The governor said, "The New Deal has usurped the powers of the state [and] undermined personal liberty." To a Republican who loved Abraham Lincoln, there was no political ideology more onerous.

He equated the New Deal with "totalitarianism, if we don't stop it." The totalitarianism he warned about was already evident in Germany, Italy, and Japan as tanks began to roll across Europe, Africa, and Asia, and warplanes menaced. Even with the dark, forbidding climate all around, Carr believed it essential to continue his fight for the principles of the Constitution. He called it a "holy crusade" against the programs of the New Deal, which he believed could threaten Colorado's way of life.

One federal proposal in particular that worried Carr was the 1941 Arkansas Valley Authority Act (AVA) or, as the governor called it, a "menace and a threat." The act sought to capitalize on public support for the Tennessee Valley Authority (TVA). Designed to provide electricity and flood control to one of the poorest areas of the country, the TVA had revitalized the region it covered. But that was in a different part of the country, a part with different resources and different needs.

Water was the lifeblood of every farmer in Colorado. The governor liked to quote western author Harvey Ferguson, who said that in the West, "thunder is sacred and rain is a god." In this parched area of the country, Carr said, "men guard their water rights as they do their homes and their lives." Without irrigation—manipulation of the water supply—there would have been no development, no growth, no life in the West.

Only a week after his inaugural address, Carr called for a special joint session of the legislature to talk solely about the AVA, which he felt would be devastating to the state. "It provides for the organization of a federal corporation with such extensive powers over the basins of the [Arkansas River] that, if even only partially exercised, it would destroy Colorado's control over the waters of the Arkansas River and jeopardize every decreed water right belonging to Colorado's farmers.

"While I do not care to be classed as an alarmist," he told lawmakers, "my warning goes further to every person in the country who clings to the belief that under our Constitution there remains something of sanctity in the doctrine of states' rights."

To Carr, who had spent his career fighting for the legitimacy of various water compacts negotiated by states throughout the West, and who had even won a case on the subject before the U.S. Supreme Court, the AVA was an insult. Water deals in the West took years to work out, and sometimes it took years more arguing about them in court, but it was always the state's representatives at the table, not some distant federal agency purporting to know best. Under the AVA, current irrigation rights held by farmers, by cities, and by ranchers, would be made subservient to the Authority's whims. It was feared that a lower river state like California, with a larger population, would benefit at the expense of mountain states like Colorado.

The AVA sought powers of eminent domain. It could require states to construct dams, tunnels, or canals. Further, no state could do anything on the river without the consent of the Authority. Compacts between states without permission would be banned.

"In short," Carr told lawmakers, "the whole system of life within these river basins is to be altered and changed to conform with a theory of government which nullifies constitutional rights and leaves individual states stripped of everything but their names."

He pointed out that every drop of water from the Arkansas River in the state of Kansas running from Dodge City west into Colorado had been spoken for by farmers in the two states. There was no more wiggle room for an authority to change the equation unless citizens were to lose what they had used for years. The entire southeast quarter of Colorado would be impacted— twenty-four thousand square miles covering crops worth around $11 million to $13 million a year.

Land without irrigation, the governor said, would sell for $.50 to $2.50 an acre. With irrigation, ranchers and farmers could get $25 to $250 an acre for their land.

"There looms the greater question of federal encroachment on the powers of the state," he said to the house and senate members. "Your very right to sit here, as legislators representing a separate state is questioned by the provisions of this Act. Either we are to continue to retain some semblance of state rights and state individuality, or else we are to surrender every power of self-determination.

"You men of the West are brought to the verge of a bloodless civil war testing your rights under the constitution."

Carr was truly galled that the authors of the AVA, the men who had penned this bill, had not visited the area, or even spoken to the water boards or the irrigation experts in the areas that were impacted. They had simply assumed that because public sentiment in the states covered by the TVA was positive, it would be in the Arkansas River area as well.

He took his opposition on the road, speaking to the U.S. chamber of commerce that was meeting in Washington state.

He told the business leaders that before it was irrigated, Colorado was "capable of sustaining only the prairie dogs, the rattlesnake, the bison, the sagebrush, the rabbit brush, and the cactus plant."

Carr even received backing from Colorado's senior Democrat in Congress, Senator Alva B. Adams. Adams was on the Senate Committee on Irrigation, and any AVA legislation would need to cross his desk before it could ever get to the floor of the full Senate for a vote. Carr and Adams were equally hostile to the project.

For years, the White House had advocated a national plan to prevent floods throughout the country. President Roosevelt told reporters in January 1934 that the issue could best be handled by Congress and the resources of the federal government.

Adams clearly opposed that policy, but his Democratic colleague Senator Edwin C. Johnson did not. Johnson was known throughout Colorado as "Big Ed," as much for his large stature as his personality. He told reporters it was his plan to "debunk the propaganda of Governor Carr against the proposed Arkansas Valley Authority." He explained Carr's opposition as an example of a politician protecting the corporate big shots. He accused Carr of siding with the power companies who stood to lose money if the government created the AVA.

When Johnson was Colorado governor in the mid-1930s, the two had stood together to protect the state's water rights. Yet, now he believed Carr was aiming to challenge him in the

November 1942 election and Johnson had no desire to do him any political favors.

In his pocket, Johnson carried around a note from President Roosevelt on the topic, which read as follows:

Dear Ed:

You are absolutely right about AVA and Carr is wrong.

More power to you.

FDR

Johnson had been a consistent foe of the president's for years, even though they shared the same party affiliation. In fact, Johnson had once called him "the high priest of intervention." Yet, he showed Roosevelt's AVA letter to everyone he could.

The letter got so worn from constant use that syndicated columnist Drew Pearson said it resembled a "museum piece." Johnson would eventually make photocopies to ensure its longevity.

The rhetoric between the governor and the senator peaked with dueling columns, published by the *Denver Post*. Johnson labeled the governor "impetuous, impatient, AMBITIOUS" and the "right bower of the power octopus." Carr, no stranger to heated rhetoric, did not attack Johnson personally. He focused his words on the AVA, which he called the "most menacing threat ever made to the general welfare of the western states."

Support for Carr's position skyrocketed. An editorial cartoon printed by the *Post* summarized the public sentiment. A woman dressed as "Miss AVA" was pictured sitting at a dinner table speaking to Governor Carr. "Ralph, I'll have some nice water rights consommé, and some of your land salad, and some dam site chops, and some electric power soufflé."

Carr's character responds, "Why you hussy, you!"

Galvanizing the governors of the other seventeen western states with telegrams, phone calls, and letters, Carr locked in sixteen to protest the policy to the White House.

With Carr leading the charge, the AVA never came up for a vote in Congress. The votes to pass it were not there.

His national standing grew. He was summoned all over the country to speak on topics of national importance. In Los Angeles, Carr told a group of reporters that balancing the national budget would be easy—he had already done it in Colorado. "When your money's gone, stop," he said simply. "That's the way to balance the budget."

Carr also repeated another theme—why he felt it was his patriotic duty to criticize the president—even as war clouds loomed. He used the Constitution and what it symbolized as both a sword and a shield. "It is not disloyalty to oppose and to question the policy of one who has not yet proved himself omnipotent and to require that he too be limited and circumscribed by those same ideals and standards governing others. We insist that the president recognize and follow the Constitution which created him."

The trip to California fueled rumors about his personal life. From the time his wife died, gossips paired him romantically with many women, especially those shown in newspaper photos with him. One 1939 photo shows a nervous smile on his face as Miss Atlantic City slipped her arm through his—he knew the talk that would follow.

Rumors got back to Mrs. Sam Rankin, a woman you could set your clock by every morning at 6:30 when she would be out sweeping her walkway in tiny Florence, Colorado. Carr, Lowell Thomas, and other Cripple Creek citizens revered her. She served as a surrogate mother, reminding them to eat three meals a day and to get enough sleep. Carr wrote to her three or four times each month.

"Don't get worried about my being married," Carr assured her after the California trip and when another photo with other politicians and an attractive brunette made its way to the local paper. "I have plenty to take care of now without taking on the added responsibility of a wife. There's gossip every time the governor is seen with a woman, but that doesn't mean a thing."

Ralph Carr is sitting next to Miss Atlantic City, who has put her arm through his. Numerous women flirted with the widower in the governor's office through letters and conversations. He welcomed the attention and flirted back, but nothing more. He would tell friends that he had "plenty to take care of now without taking on the added responsibility of a wife." Courtesy of the Colorado Historical Society

It's obvious, though, in his correspondence that he enjoyed flirting with both married and unmarried women—he was the ultimate pen pal, complimentary and humorous.

He wrote to Mrs. Alda Hyndman, when they saw each other after a hiatus of forty years, "You should not have been flattered that I remembered the color of your hair and the little hat which you wore. My child, you would stick in the memory of any person who ever knew you, and as a child you were not only bright and interesting, but you were beautiful."

Meanwhile, many of the women who sent him letters were flat-out suggestive.

"My dear Ralph," wrote Edith Clark in April 1941, "I see by the paper—and hear over the radio—you are in the midst of a wild blizzard-y snow storm again. You see, THAT is the reason (ahem) I never could or would (2-ahems) marry you. (A DOZEN AHEMS!!) It is such a cold climate, and I'd look like H--- in an outing flannel night-gown."

She followed up a few weeks later. "Listen Ralph: I know! I'm in the doghouse—even with a muzzle on, after that 'outing flannel' episode. I did lead with my chin on that, didn't I? But couldn't get the dern letter out of the mailbox after I had mailed it—just too bad. Someway, I was so sure you would know I was neither 'propositioning you' nor was I 'proposing to you' but it was sorta 'fresh' at that. SORRY!!!!!"

Carr enjoyed every single moment of attention. Life was going well for Colorado's governor, fresh with personal and professional accolades. But the governor's secretary, perhaps the woman closest to him and the best observer, knew that he was married to his work. "He worked all the time," Myrtle Graham said, pointing out that he didn't golf, didn't play bridge or poker or tennis. She couldn't remember him having any hobbies, although he enjoyed singing and sometimes sang tenor in a quartet. He even played the guitar on occasion.

He was demanding but fair, and always willing to laugh.

One time, another secretary, Marian Powell, sat at one of the chairs in front of Carr's big desk, taking dictation on a note the governor was sending to his friend, Mr. Gurley, at the Rio Grande Railroad. When he ended it, he said, "Say hello to all the little Gurleys." However, when Powell typed up the last sentence, she spelled it "Girlies."

"While many [bosses] would have fired her over a mistake like that," Graham said, "Ralph thought it was the funniest thing."

Office humor was some solace in a world increasingly in conflict. From the beginning of his term in 1939, Carr had been sounding an alarm about the state of the world and what he believed was the inevitable involvement of America in a war.

"A man who sits calmly on his back stoop," he said, "while a prairie fire consumes the homes of his neighbors, secure in the belief that the wind will change its direction and save his dwelling just because he wills it so, is a poor philosopher."

On June 7, 1941, coincidentally at the same time the Japanese were planning a bombing raid on a strategic suspension bridge the United States and others needed along the Burma Road to provide aid to China, Carr established the Colorado Council of Defense.

"Our country has called," he said, as he appointed the two-hundred-member citizen group. "Colorado is responding as the Centennial State has always answered a summons from the national government. ... Every man, woman, and child in Colorado is an active member of this Council of Defense. We face a grave moment in our lives. Citizens must not wait to be called. They must volunteer their services and generously aid in the consummation of this plan. It is a service which all will cherish in the years to come."

Two days later, the governor sat at an unofficial preview opening of the Red Rocks Theater. It was the world's greatest open-air theater, right outside Denver, created out of sandstone by nature and nurtured by federal government workers. As the Denver Junior Symphony Orchestra played that June night, the music could be heard clearly at every seat. It was one of the last civic projects Colorado would see for a long time. From then on, the machinations of war took over.

Hundreds of workers had been hired in the last two months at the Remington Arms Company facility located in Lakewood, just west of Colorado's capital city. Thousands more would follow in the next few months. The complex was named the Denver Ordnance Plant, and by fall, its four manufacturing buildings would produce a million .30-caliber shells every day. It was one of the nation's largest and most efficient small-arms ammunition facilities. An order to expand the facility by two hundred thousand square feet to produce larger shells came shortly after the first of two hundred buildings opened that summer. It cost taxpayers $3 million and would double in size by the middle of 1942.

Lowry Field, located on the east side of Denver, had begun training air force pilots and crew in 1938. During the buildup to the war, it increased facilities to deal with bigger demand. Fitzsimons Army Hospital, also east of town, graduated two hundred and fifty medical technicians each month who were prepared to travel the world for their country.

"Know that while the names of heroes may adorn the headlines of the newspapers," Carr told the 1941 Fitzsimons graduating class, "in the record of tomorrow, a greater, a finer, a more brilliant record will be written of those unselfish ones who went forth to defeat suffering rather than to promote it."

Carr believed that if freedom were to succeed abroad, America's democracy needed to be reinforced at home. His theme throughout the latter half of 1941 focused on the rights of the individual.

"I maintain that so long as there persists in this world a nation made up of 130 million thinking human beings, where men have the right to gather in public assembly, to voice their individual opinions without fear ... and where he is protected from attacks by any man or group of men so long as he does not use his rights to injure others—then there is hope," he said at a dedication of a junior college.

As America was pulled closer to war, Carr did not challenge the president's and Congress's decisions about intervening in the conflict, but instead how they chose to treat their own citizens during the crisis. When Carr was invited to speak to Colorado's Fourth Congressional District convention, he emphasized the principles he believed were clear in the U.S. Constitution.

"The individual is supreme and government is established only to protect and to foster his rights," he told the Republicans gathered.

A few days later, Carr stressed to a group of teachers, "As government is strengthened, so is the individual necessarily weakened. Every time the individual submits to a central government for a solution of another problem of business or life, there is a consequent surrender of individuality, of privilege, of right."

Carr believed that everyone who came to his office was of equal importance. He turned no one away. In addition to scheduled appointments with foreign and domestic leaders, he always welcomed his friends from the San Luis Valley, including the Spanish-speaking ones. They would be escorted into the governor's office without a hint of hesitance to meet with their old friend "Rafaelito." If they needed help, their amigo was there, no matter how busy his job became.

For example, when Epiminio Garcia wrote Carr a note saying he was at the Colorado General Hospital and needed to see him, Carr didn't hesitate. "Would he please come?" the note read. For an old friend from Antonito, the answer from Carr was, "Which room is he in?"

"He left a group of politicians in his office [to go see him]," his secretary said. "It didn't bother him in the slightest to have [some politician] sit and wait for him while he was talking to someone who didn't make a darn bit of difference as far as his politics were concerned because [Carr] took care of a lot of people. He never did turn his back on anybody."

One of Carr's longtime friends, William Grant, told a similar story. "I was never in Ralph's office," he said, "when he wasn't talking to a poor Spanish American, keeping someone in a three-piece suit waiting."

He was a politician that *Rocky Mountain News* columnist Lee Casey claimed came from the "liberal wing of the Republican Party." It's one reason he got along so well with Senator Adams, whom Casey would describe as "representing the conservative wing of the Democratic Party." Both giants of Colorado politics were typical western lawmakers: individualistic, fiscally responsible, and fair.

When Carr heard in late November that Adams wasn't doing well, he was troubled. Although similar politically, they were opposite in personality, with Carr extroverted and warm and Adams introverted and "a bit cool," according to Casey. Yet, to those who knew him the way Carr did, Adams was beloved and universally respected.

Adams's father (also named Alva) had served as Colorado's governor on two separate occasions; his uncle William (Billy) had also been governor for three terms. The latter's picture hung on the wall of Carr's office as a sign of respect. Adams's family guessed they were relatives of the Massachusetts Adams clan (former presidents John and John Quincy), but as Senator Adams told Casey, no one had ever "taken the trouble to look the connection up."

On December 1, 1941, Colorado's senior senator suffered his fourth heart attack and died at his Washington apartment. Adams had told no one but his secretary of the first two attacks and carried on as usual, saying he hadn't been sick since he was thirteen years old. A third attack in late November had kept him home for a day before he went back into the office, to "dispose of a few pressing matters." After hearing the news, his doctor ordered him to bed.

Five days later, with his wife, a son, and a daughter by his side, he would suffer the final, fatal attack. "Colorado's finest citizen," according to Governor Carr, had died at age sixty-six. Adams's doctor said the cause was coronary thrombosis, a blocking of the arteries surrounding the heart. The *Denver Post* reported it had been induced by "overwork on major legislation." One colleague said Adams had been working with him on an amendment to a bill the night before he died.

Just below the headlines announcing the senator's death in the December 1 and 2 newspapers, both major Denver dailies had articles about who would be appointed to fill Adams's spot, and more important, whether Governor Carr would tap himself to fill that spot. Carr found that talk insulting to the memory of the man he said "symbolized everything that was fine and big."

"It would be indelicate in the extreme," he told reporters, "for me to make any statement regarding Senator Adams's successor at this time."

Adams was the third high-profile figure to pass away in Colorado within the last couple months. Carr had a vacancy to fill on the Colorado Supreme Court with the death of Justice Francis Bouck just a week earlier and a special election was set for December 9, 1941, to fill the spot of the late Fourth District congressman Edward Taylor. Some Republicans told the *Rocky Mountain News* that no decision was likely on Adams's successor until after that special election.

The governor was tempted by the prospect of moving to D.C.

"He told us there were some things he'd like to say on the floor of the United States Senate," said his assistant George Robinson, "that didn't fit in the governor's office."

Whoever was appointed to fill Adams's spot would have to run the following November to serve the remaining two years of his term. Colorado's other senator, Edwin Johnson, was also up for reelection in November 1942. The two major Denver dailies differed in their interpretations of what the governor would do. The *Post* reported, "Governor Carr might seek the short term [Adams's spot], instead of running against Johnson. GOP strategists might figure that this would assure them of one seat in the Senate."

The *News* speculated to the contrary, "[Governor Carr] could [although his closest friends say he will not] resign, let Lieutenant Governor John Vivian take over and have Mr. Vivian appoint him to the Senate. ... In the final analysis, Governor Carr probably would do himself and the party unity more good if the appointment goes to another man."

As Governor Carr stood outside Adams's old brownstone home at the corner of Orman and Colorado Avenues in Pueblo for a final good-bye to the senator, he was surrounded by congressmen and senators from Washington. There were men in the crowd that day who hoped to fill Adams's seat. They included one-time senate candidate Nate Warren; Lawrence Phipps, whose father had served as a Colorado senator for years; and Archibald Lee, who had run for the seat back when Carr was first elected governor in 1938.

Hundreds of people braved the cold, fifty-five-mile-per-hour winds to pay their respects and to honor a "Colorado statesman," as the newspapers called him. Would Carr command that respect if he went to Washington?

He would tell the public his intentions after the congressional special election in five days. The *Rocky Mountain News* reported Carr would take "speedy action" to fill the empty spot. He told the paper he was "swamped with recommendations" on behalf of numerous aspirants for the job.

And among those being recommended by Colorado citizens was Carr himself.

Chapter Five
December 1941

Mary Lathrop was only five feet tall and one hundred pounds, but she had no problem commanding attention. Denverites knew her as one of the city's top real estate and probate lawyers and the first woman to be admitted to the American Bar Association.

She and Ralph Carr had an annual date to celebrate their birthdays together—December 10 would be her seventy-sixth birthday and Carr would be fifty-four on December 11. This year's dinner party was planned for Saturday night at the swank Cosmopolitan Hotel.

The governor's staff referred to Lathrop as a "little toughie" and it was clear their boss enjoyed her stories. If there was anyone who could spin a tale like the governor, it was Lathrop. She was a brilliant lawyer, and the first woman allowed to practice before both the Colorado Supreme Court and the U.S. Supreme Court. In spite of that, Carr knew there were men who refused to participate in cases she was involved in.

Lathrop loved the verbal repartee she could share with her much younger friend. Like the governor, she had been a journalist before becoming an attorney, and in the early 1900s she worked for *McClure* magazine covering the Cripple Creek labor strike, the very strike where Lowell Thomas's dad had shoved him under the table to keep him safe from the shooting that ensued.

On December 7, one week before the birthday party, Lathrop read in the morning paper that President Roosevelt had sent a "personal message to Emperor Hirohito," the Japanese leader. Its specific contents were undisclosed, but the United Press wire service reported that it asked for a "maintenance of peace in the Pacific." In recent days, the Japanese diplomatic corps had called the Americans' conditions for that peace "utterly impossible," and a government spokesman said that "Japan's 'patience' may be tried only a little longer."

The two sides were still talking. They were still negotiating. But that would end before many Americans finished their morning coffee.

The horrible, shocking news spread rapid-fire, with frantic radio broadcasts and "extra" editions of newspapers with huge screaming headlines being hawked on the streets. America had been attacked by Japanese warplanes at Pearl Harbor in Hawaii. Three thousand U.S. servicemen and servicewomen had been killed or wounded. The Japanese had attacked the Philippines. They had attacked Guam. They had attacked Hong Kong. Americans throughout the Pacific were in danger.

Governor Carr was on Colorado's Western Slope that day, finishing up a barnstorming tour for Republican Robert Rockwell, who was hoping to be elected Colorado's Fourth District congressman. The campaign had taken on a decidedly "lackluster" feel, according to the December 7 *Rocky Mountain News*; a snowstorm had covered the area, discouraging heavy voter turnout. Both political parties anticipated that only a third of the voters who turned out in the November 1940 election would cast ballots a little more than a year later on December 9.

After hearing about the attack on Pearl Harbor, Carr called Denver immediately and set up an emergency meeting of the Colorado Council of Defense for the next morning at ten. He and his driver jumped in his 1940 Buick and headed across the Continental Divide late at night, although snow was in the forecast. As dawn broke, at about 7:10, the governor came across "a shivering group of working men standing close to a great wood fire almost twelve thousand feet above sea level with the thermometer several points below zero."

The men were working on an exploratory tunnel bore to be driven 5,483 feet under Loveland Pass to serve as part of a strategic defense roadway network. They had chosen that Monday morning to picket the project to ensure they'd receive fair wages.

Two-plus miles above sea level, Carr witnessed a celebration of the American way of life that allowed for such freedom of expression. He believed it was not just the country itself that had been attacked by the Japanese at Pearl Harbor, but also its belief system.

When he got back to Denver, Carr told reporters, "When I drove in from the Western Slope this morning, the same old sun was coming up. It's the same sunshine, but we don't see things in the same light we ever have in the past. ... Things have been set in motion which have taken American lives and property and which threaten the complete destruction of all Americans, of everything which we have established and called American ...

"Every American this morning is engaged in this warfare. We are engaged in the fight for our very existence and for the perpetuation of those blessings of life which we have won only by centuries of effort, suffering, and intelligent planning under the guidance of our Maker. Coloradans are ready."

The governor met with the Council of Defense in his executive chambers. One of his first acts was to mobilize the new Colorado Home Guard, which had roughly two hundred men, to immediately secure the state's utilities, bridges, tunnels, and reservoirs against sabotage. Volunteers would be needed to help, he said.

"We are all a little hysterical and jittery this morning," the governor acknowledged. "But let us not permit our emotions to cause us to do anything we may regret."

Moments later, Carr stopped the meeting and turned up his radio. There was silence among the seventy-five men and women who would plan the defense of Colorado.

"Mr. Vice President, Mr. Speaker, Members of the Senate, and of the House of Representatives," President Roosevelt said to an emergency joint session of Congress at 12:12 EST. "Yesterday, December 7, 1941—a date which will live in infamy—the United States of America was suddenly and deliberately attacked by naval and air forces of the Empire of Japan."

The *Denver Post* reported "an air of grimness and purpose about the gathering in the governor's office. Federal and state officials, captains of industry, leaders of labor sat tense and grave-faced."

The president concluded his speech with the words all Americans had dreaded for the better part of the last two years. "Hostilities exist. There is no blinking at the fact that our people, our territory, and our interests are in grave danger.

"With confidence in our armed forces, with the unbounding determination of our people, we will gain the inevitable triumph—so help us God.

"I ask that the Congress declare that since the unprovoked and dastardly attack by Japan on Sunday, December 7, 1941, a state of war has existed between the United States and the Japanese empire."

When the president finished speaking, the men in the Colorado meeting rose, heads bowed, to listen to the National Anthem on the radio.

"Until today, a lot of people just wouldn't believe a war was possible," Colonel Paul Newlon, the executive vice president of the Defense Council said. "Now, all forms of organizing for defense will receive an immediate impetus."

It might have been 3,337 miles from Pearl Harbor to the Colorado state capitol, but the reverberations felt from the Japanese attack were evident in that meeting. The governor commandeered the private squadron of planes from Colorado Springs who were serving as part of the Home Guard. He conferred with the group about asking for federal help in protecting Colorado's industrial and military installations.

Major Oscar Yorker informed the group that Lowry Field had already strengthened its military guard to "sufficiently" deal with the emergency. Colonel John Temple echoed those sentiments for Fort Logan in Denver, which was serving as a sub-post for Camp Lowry, where more guards had been posted, even though the facility remained open to the public. At Fitzsimons

Army Hospital, Colonel Frederick Wright had increased the military police force on duty, and visitors were being subjected to a more "careful check."

The council approved a telegram to be sent to police chiefs and sheriffs statewide imploring them to be "especially alert to prevent and handle sabotage" and encouraging them to advise the council of any protective needs within their areas that could not be handled by the local authorities.

And then, roughly twenty-four hours after America had been attacked by the Japanese, Governor Carr switched from state defense to moral defense. He read a telegram from the editor of a Japanese-language newspaper in San Francisco, condemning the Pearl Harbor attack in the most vigorous of terms.

"This should remind us," the governor said, "that we have among us many of a new generation of Japanese people born in the United States—sincere, earnest, and loyal people.

"I want to caution the defense council against taking the attitude that because a man may be brown skinned, he is our enemy. We must be sensible about these things."

As the governor was preaching restraint, however, society was speaking a different language. The enemies were no longer the Japanese, but the "Japs," in headlines, in stories, and in conversation.

Even those who were American citizens were considered suspicious. "Most of the Japanese in the [Arkansas] Valley have already registered or become naturalized, but the potential threat is not diminished," reported the *La Junta Daily Democrat*.

Calls began flooding into the local offices of the Federal Bureau of Investigation, the Immigration and Naturalization Service, the U.S. District Attorney, and the Denver Police Department to report concerns about espionage, sabotage, even a neighbor acting strangely. Some were phony, some were genuine concerns; all would be checked out.

George Gillespie, who ran a mining company in Idaho Springs, was worried about his property. He remembered there had been Japanese students from the Colorado School of Mines who visited his properties and "took pictures and many notes." That was enough to warrant a note to the governor about a possible incident of espionage.

George Lilley, who ran a wholesale potato company in Monte Vista, Colorado, knew of at least a hundred Japanese families in his area of the state. He wrote, "Friend Carr: Am wondering if you consider it advisable to use any precautionary measures relative to Japanese subjects in and around Ft. Garland, San Acacia, Mesita and Jarosa, Colo. ... Personally and especially at the present time, I cannot regard any Japenese [*sic*] subject as a trusted citizen."

Twenty vulnerable spots around Denver were given immediate twenty-four hour protection by order of the police chief, August Hanebush. Specifics were not given, but Captain Harry L. Wood told a meeting of all police captains and sergeants, "The best way to protect such places as waterways, dams, pipelines, railroads, power lines and transformers, and telephone communications is to be thoroughly cautious from the start." Special anti-sabotage units worked eight-hour shifts, stopping and questioning all suspicious people.

Weld County sheriff Gus Anderson arrested two Japanese in northern Colorado at a hotel "after being told they had been contacting Japanese families in the area." He seized several maps, a large quantity of literature printed in Japanese, and photographs of Rocky Mountain highway passes.

The Denver FBI office was placed on twenty-four-hour emergency duty, ready to take action immediately, according to its agent in charge. Gordon Nicholson told the *Rocky Mountain News* that despite press dispatches saying FBI offices in other cities were rounding up all Japanese aliens, he had not received orders to that effect. U.S. Attorney Thomas Morrissey asked Colorado's local police officers to report any action against "Japanese aliens who may be dangerous to the public peace or safety" to the FBI and not to make any arrests.

That was fine with Adams County sheriff Herman A. Farney, who told the Associated Press, "We expect no trouble," referring to the northern Colorado agricultural area where roughly three hundred Japanese Americans lived. "The greater part of the foreign-born Japanese who operated truck farms in this area have returned to their native country in the last few years."

In reality, numbers from the 1940 census in Colorado show a somewhat different story. Of the state's population of 1,123,216, there were 2,734 people of Japanese descent.

Almost 70 percent were born in the United States and were called "Nisei." The rest were designated "aliens" by the census, meaning they were "Issei," not American citizens. In many cases, they had no choice in the matter. Naturalization for many Japanese aliens had been barred by presidential proclamation in 1913. An immigration act passed by Congress a decade later reinforced that philosophy. A "gentleman's agreement" between leaders of the United States and Asian nations agreed to prevent the further importation of members of "yellow races" into America. Only Japanese ex-servicemen who fought for the United States in World War I were exempted from the citizenship ban. Yet, even if they wanted to become citizens—to become Americans—they were not allowed to by law.

Regardless of their legal status, from December 7 forward many people lumped them all together.

As president of the Japanese Young People's Christian Conference, Violet Otsuki tried to calm the nerves of Denver residents by stating a desire to be considered "like all other Americans." She told the *News*, "The majority of the Japanese in the Denver area are native-born Americans. While our parents may have come to this country from Japan, they came because this was the country of their choice. We are Americans by birth and our parents by choice."

Still, the rush to retaliation was demonstrated at the Denver recruiting offices for the armed services. "I was spit on by some of those Japs when I was in Japan several years ago," said one man in line. Another cried when officers told him that at age sixty, he was too old to enlist. Colonel T. N. Gimperling said the army recruiting stations would remain open until the last man was accommodated. The navy was planning to do the same thing. The marines, who were expecting recruits to be ready for hand-to-hand combat in the Pacific, committed their recruiters to three shifts and being open twenty-four hours a day.

The *News* reported, "Men who pleaded with tears in their eyes that their advanced years be waived and their services accepted, men with false teeth and men who swore they were 'about 30' though their hair was gray." An extra full-time phone operator was brought in to handle the overload of calls from men looking to enlist.

"So, they really want to fight. Well, we'll just give 'em a real one whenever the head man says the word," said one soldier.

The governor's office was flooded with requests for executive clemency from men with records that prevented them from serving. Staffers at state draft headquarters switched from civilian clothes to military garb.

Banks across Colorado froze the accounts of Japanese "enemy aliens," according to the *Denver Post* and the *La Junta Daily Democrat*, and businesses were warned against doing business with noncitizens. The order applied to accounts and credits of American branches and businesses in Japan as well as the personal assets of noncitizen Japanese residents.

"For example," the *Post* reported, "a man born in Japan may have lived in this country for forty years. He may have a reputation above reproach, own his home, be loyal to the United States, and honestly indignant over the attack made upon us by his native land. He may have grown children and grandchildren who are native American citizens. Yet, financially speaking, he is an enemy alien. He cannot draw checks against his account in a bank. He cannot open his safety deposit box."

Public sentiment, according to the *News* reporter at the Navy Recruiting Station, was that "most [recruits] ... would like to get into the middle of a fight in the Pacific today, if possible."

Forty-year-old Alfred Kears, an interior decorator, returned to Lowry after going AWOL twelve years earlier. "Here I am," he told the provost marshal. The *News* reported Kears had enlisted in February 1929 and served only twenty-six days, ten of which were in the hospital, before simply walking away because "that food up there was something awful."

He came back because "the United States needs all of the support it can get ... I figure the army can use me now."

Within days of the Pearl Harbor attack, photos of Denver residents in Hawaii, the Philippine Islands, and all throughout the Pacific region who hadn't been heard from since December 8 lined the pages of the two major dailies in the city. People like Ralph Keeler, a former *Rocky Mountain News* reporter who was now a first lieutenant with the intelligence department in the Philippines, were deemed missing. His wife waited for information.

People like the parents of William E. Loveless yearned for news at their Denver home. Their son had been aboard the USS *Tennessee* at Pearl Harbor.

As did the parents of Ralph and Russell Gabbert, brothers who were both at Pearl Harbor. "We are waiting anxiously to hear from our sons, of course, but I don't suppose a private cablegram could get through now," said their father. "We aren't going to worry about the whole situation because we're sure the Japanese will soon be beaten."

That night, following an all-day meeting of the Council of Defense, Governor Carr took to the radio for a short, seven-minute speech to assuage his citizens. "I am confident about what Colorado can do," he said. "I am confident about what my people will do."

He described plans to guard public structures like the capitol, tunnels, railroad and highway bridges, and water treatment plants, and how volunteers would be needed to accomplish those goals. "Will not the people of Colorado immediately get in touch with their several sheriffs and mayors to the end that local organizations may be established to carry on this work? This is the first time that a call has been made to the public generally to participate in this great work. I know we shall have a ready response from every corner of the state."

Privately, he feared paranoia and pandemonium from a collective public afraid of its shadow. He had told the council its single most important job right off the bat would be to keep "our feet on the ground and our heads clear." The next day brought word of more Coloradans unaccounted for in the Pacific and fear to their family and friends.

The navy also reported that more than a hundred Colorado men were working on base construction throughout the war zone. They were in places like Honolulu, Wake Island, Guam, and the Philippines, all of which had been attacked by the Japanese. Their names were not released. Many were recent college graduates, engineering majors at the Colorado School of Mines.

Among the correspondence the governor received was a pledge of loyalty sent by George Nakagawa, state chairman of the Japanese American Citizens League, on behalf of those "Japanese Aliens, many of whom are our parents, who are residents of the State of Colorado and most of them continuously so for the past thirty to forty years, we are directed to say: they immigrated to these United States in search of a land where they would have the right to live, the right to express themselves, and the right to be free and equal people."

That message was seconded to an overflow audience at the University of Colorado by its president, Robert Stearns. Three thousand students and faculty crowded into Macky Auditorium on the center of campus while another thousand listened on a loud speaker outside to a speech that the World War I veteran entitled "Steady."

"We have in our community a number of American citizens of Japanese origin," Stearns said. "We have no reason to doubt their loyalty. I bespeak the consideration of every member of the community for the feelings of these people."

The Colorado Council of Defense met again, and Carr accepted the recommendations of many committee chairmen to establish local defense councils to serve as a first line of defense. Telegrams were sent to the mayors of all Colorado communities in an effort to spread the national war effort to the entire state.

Local councils were asked to follow the lead of the state council, to set up committees on firefighting, police activities, medical problems, public works, utilities, public relations, and education, and to maintain vital public services. The goal was to train local officials who could react quickly in case of emergency. Smaller communities around the state that did not have mayors were encouraged to join a county defense council.

On December 10, one day after he sent out the telegrams, Carr followed up with letters to all mayors, emphasizing what he had said before. He also received a telegram from Minnesota governor Harold Stassen on the topic of "enemy aliens." The head of the National Governors' Conference was recommending that states turn over that issue to the FBI, which Carr told the *News* was his policy in the first place and that "there would be no duplication or interference in this effort from the state."

Requests to help were overwhelming his office.

By wire, mail, phone, and in person, Carr received offers of support from the Colorado's seventy-five hundred Boy Scouts, and from retired servicemen with the American Legion, the Veterans of Foreign Wars, and the Disabled American Veterans. The state medical society made available its doctors, nurses, and technicians; the bar association offered the services of its lawyers; the service engineers volunteered their expertise. The Motion Picture Operators Union of Denver volunteered search lights. Local gun clubs offered weapons training, the radio stations their commercial time.

As Carr deliberated before speaking statewide again that evening, he realized he was governing a powder keg. Antagonism toward the Japanese was running high. He had already received reports from the highway patrol office in Alamosa, Colorado, that a guard had to be placed in the area to "prevent any outbreak between white residents and about thirty Japanese families." Captain Joseph Monnig told the Associated Press that a plot to burn a Buddhist chapel had been uncovered and other threats of violence by "young hoodlums" had been reported.

"People of Colorado, fellow Americans," Carr began in his speech that night. "As governor of Colorado, I want to express my pride in the people of this state for the manner in which they have received the news of the happenings in the Pacific. Not by hysterical expressions nor by panic-stricken public demonstrations ... but quietly, calmly, and as intelligent citizens."

He said the "avalanche" of offers to help—too numerous to count—filled him "up with this confidence in this dark hour. ... All Colorado stands ready and willing to do its part." He noted that although he was grateful for everyone who volunteered to guard against sabotage, bought war bonds, and cut down on precious supplies like gas and rubber, Carr made it clear there was one thing he did not want Coloradans to do.

"The federal government has sent a suggestion that the apprehension of aliens is not a new problem and is being taken care of by the Department of Justice. Accordingly, every state agency, every individual is asked to keep hands off."

Then he made a stronger plea than the president or any other national leader had since Pearl Harbor. "And it is my urgent request that no person may say or do anything which might cause embarrassment to some individual who is as truly American by reason either of birth or adoption of this country and his unselfish patriotism as you and I ...

"Let us remember that America is the great melting pot of the modern civilized world. From every nation of the globe people have come to the United States who sought to live as free men here under our plan of government. We cannot test the degree of a man's affection for his fellows or his devotion to his country by the birthplace of his grandfathers. All Americans had their origin beyond the borders of the United States. If there are among us those who are wrong or who are unfriendly to our country and its people, we have men who know it and who will ferret them out.

"Let us, as products of this philosophy of government and life, be Americans first of all in the crisis which confronts us tonight."

Reaction from the public was mixed, ranging from the unemployed minister who wrote the governor to "Clean up the JAPAGERMS" to the retired lieutenant living in Denver who believed Colorado's "racial prejudice has so become integrated into our American social order as to make one shudder."

On Carr's fifty-fourth birthday, Germany and Italy declared war on the United States, and the governor received a note from the Kobayashi family, who lived a mile and a half north of him.

"Your statement of our case, that of American citizens of Japanese ancestry, and that of other minority groups most seriously affected by this war, was one of the most decent, democratic, and AMERICAN utterances we have heard come over the radio since the fateful and horrible events of last Sunday."

Carr sent the legislature's Interim Committee home after telling members there was "nothing for it to do now, in view of the war emergency." Then he ordered the expansion of the Home Guard tenfold, from two hundred men to two thousand, to be located throughout the state. He knew that bad news would inevitably arrive. He likely heard it from Adjutant General Harold Richardson, who ran the state's National Guard, or from one of the military officials attending a Council of Defense committee meeting.

The parents of twenty-year-old Russell E. Gallagher were notified at two in the morning. A War Department telegram arrived at their Aurora home, notifying them that their son had been seriously wounded at Hickam Army Airfield in the Pearl

Harbor attack. No specifics were given, only that his injuries were "serious."

The *Denver Post* reported that he was "the first soldier from the Denver area to be reported among the casualties of the Japanese attack on Pearl Harbor." Carr knew Gallagher would not be the last. He had heard the radio reports of the Japanese government claiming to have sunk the aircraft carrier USS *Lexington* off the shores of Hawaii. The 36,000-ton *Lexington* carried more than two thousand men.

Gallagher's mother told the *Post* of the time a few years back when her son had used CPR to save two members of a swimming party at Bluff Lake, just east of Denver. He was just a couple years older than Carr's son, Robert, who was already making noises about joining the Naval ROTC at Boulder.

Within a week, more Colorado victims' names were released by the Navy Department in Washington. The *News* reported that Ensign Thomas McClelland, former radio technician, left behind a wife and two small daughters. The death of twenty-three-year-old Henry Weber left six sisters and his parents in Denver crying for him. Seaman William Blackwood, widely known as a skilled amateur baseball pitcher, could not be found. That's what the telegram to his parents said.

Bad news reached all layers of Colorado society. State representative Roy Chrysler lost his grandson at Pearl Harbor and wrote the governor, "God knows I want to do anything I can to avenge that dastardly murder."

The recruiting stations continued to be filled with stories of people willing to "get in this ruckus." Wesley Ford Frazier, all of seventeen years old and 104 pounds soaking wet, showed up with his thirty-six-year-old father, Luther, to enlist in the navy. A recruiting officer had sent Wesley home a week earlier when he only weighed ninety-nine pounds, telling him the navy only took men who weighed more than their duffel bags. Three steaks and some vitamins later, he reenlisted, bringing his dad with him.

"It will take a lot of us to get the trouble settled in smart fashion," his father told the *News*.

Colorado's Japanese-American community continued to try to prove its allegiance. Nearly a hundred residents in Pueblo County signed a loyalty pledge "without evasion or secret reservation of mind," and Carr continued to try to reassure them. To the national president of the Japanese American Citizens League (JACL), he sent a note that would be published in an emergency edition of the *Pacific Citizen* newspaper, the organ for the fifteen thousand members of the JACL in the United States.

"We have come to a time that tries men's souls. On the part of many there comes the necessity for patience, fortitude and great courage. On the part of others, for understanding, tolerance and kindness.

"To the American-born citizens of Japanese parentage, we look for example and guidance. To those who have not been so fortunate as to have been born in this country, we offer the hand of friendship, secure in the knowledge that they will be as truly American as the rest of us.

"This is a difficult time for all Japanese-speaking people. We must work together for the preservation of our American system, for the continuation of our theory of universal brotherhood."

Carr put out this statement about the same time as one issued by Congressman Martin Dies, who ran the U.S. House Committee on Un-American Activities. Dies said there were Japanese spy elements in the country. The general and admiral supervising Pearl Harbor told superiors that their biggest concern was sabotage from the significant Japanese population in Hawaii. No one believed that more than three thousand Americans could have been killed by surprise without the help of someone on the inside.

Intense fear and hatred toward the Japanese blossomed in Colorado. The *Rocky Mountain News* published an article entitled, "Here's How to Distinguish Chinese from Japanese." Unfortunately, Dr. Alex Hrdlicka of the Smithsonian Institute said, people had only a 30 percent chance of doing that successfully. But, he said, the "Japanese have a clever, smarter expression, the reflection of their materialistic and commercial interests."

Although the governor had no trouble allowing the FBI to handle surveillance and law enforcement related to enemy aliens, he continued to have trouble with the top-down approach that was a hallmark of FDR's government. For example, New York mayor Fiorello LaGuardia, who doubled as the director of U.S. Civilian Defense in Washington, sent a telegram on December 13, about "rules for the guidance of individuals in case of air raids." LaGuardia sent many flyers directly to Colorado schoolteachers from the Washington office, and Carr was frustrated with being told how to handle his state during a time of emergency. He wanted all pamphlets sent to his Council of Defense, whose members could then decide the best way to distribute information from Washington.

"Because of the peculiar conditions existing in this part of the Rocky Mountains, because of our comparative isolation, and mostly because of the fact that I see no reason in stirring up a people already aroused about a menace which can reach us only some time in the distant future, if at all, I would prefer that handbills or pamphlets giving instruction of what to do during air raids be not distributed through Colorado at this time.

"Please do not misunderstand me in this connection. There is no desire to hold back on any activity which is necessary. But we must keep our people in a calm state of mind."

The federal government was also recommending experimental blackouts for all communities, to see how they would handle an attack that would take away their electricity. The governor told a hundred and fifty county defense officials that, despite their desire, he did not feel there was a need. His goal was to keep the hysteria associated with a possible blackout mitigated. Less than an hour later, the meeting was stopped when a fuse blew on the master control board at the state capitol, sending everyone into the dark for a good fifteen minutes. Needless to say, everyone was on edge.

A telegram from President Roosevelt brought the states' rights issue into better context. The president had requested that, due to national defense, all duties performed by Colorado's State Employment Service and its unemployment compensation be federalized. Carr okayed the move as long as supervision returned to the state after the war, treating it as a leasing of its resources during a time of need. If it were to remain federalized, he suggested that an act of Congress would be required.

"Every day there is some new evidence of a determination in high places to centralize power in the federal government," Carr wrote in a letter to Montana governor Sam Ford. "We must fight it while we give every support to the Nation's problems. At the end of this we want forty-eight states still independent and active agents in a great federal union. We want no separate entities, but we don't want to exchange our present form of government for one of absolutism."

He knew these were the types of issues he could address more directly from the U.S. Senate. Already the papers were clamoring for him to appoint a successor to fill Senator Adams's seat, with the *Rocky Mountain News* editorializing, "Name Him, Mr. Carr! The appointment of a nine-month senator is not of major consequence ordinarily. It is of major concern in wartime."

The *Gunnison News-Champion*, located in Colorado's southwest, encouraged the state's chief executive to head to Washington. But Colorado's governor felt he had given a pledge to the state's voters in 1940, committed to a style of government they had not seen in years, and now, with war at hand, he could not break his word.

For the second time in two years, he would pass on a significant political opportunity.

"I think it would be a mistake for me to leave Colorado now," he wrote Henry Lake, editor of the Gunnison paper. "If I have anything in my soul which is calming and quieting, now is the time to use it on our people. If I served my own selfish wants, I should go down there. But I must stay at home and do the job until the term is completed. What I do thereafter is in the lap of the gods."

George Robinson remembers Carr telling his staff, "The people didn't elect me to be United States senator and if they want me, I'll let them elect me. I'm going to give it to a man I think's entitled to it and who'll be a good senator."

That December, he appointed Republican Eugene Millikin to fill as much of Senator Adams's shoes as possible. He described the fifty-year-old Denver attorney as a "Republican of today" which the *News* interpreted as meaning "a Republican of liberal sympathies who is in full accord with the administration's determination to win the war." Millikin was a classmate of Carr's at the University of Colorado and served as the head of the Civil Protection Committee within the Council of Defense.

The World War I veteran described himself to the *News* as "a man without a hobby, unless you'd call work a hobby."

As the forty thousand Christmas lights were placed by John Malpiede, electrician for the city of Denver, on the city's tree, Carr knew this Christmas would be unlike any other he'd experienced. This year, because of the war, a number of families would spend the holiday grieving.

Without question, the Japanese were winning the battles in the Pacific. General Douglas MacArthur was struggling to hold the Philippine Islands. Japanese bombers swarmed over the capital of Manila and cut off communications to numerous islands. The fighting was fierce, and everyone knew the casualties would be high.

Carr had been told that his voice could sway a bird off a tree. It radiated warmth and had a grandfatherly tone that was soothing to the ear. Myrtle Graham said that even when she knew what he was about to say, she would still find herself stopping to listen. As Christmas 1941 arrived and he heard word from some around the state that people were depressed, the man described by the *Pueblo Chieftain* as having a "rotund Santa Claus stature" sought to quell the feelings of some that "there will be no more Christmas." He offered solace through a statewide radio address.

"Above the confusion and grief and apprehension of war, let us remember this: this is not so much a war between nations and peoples—it is a war between the true and the false. It is a war in which the Christmas spirit must survive. It must survive the spirit of barbarism—of animalism—in which honor, integrity, the brotherhood of man and the dignity of the individual have no place whatsoever."

As Coloradans huddled by their radios that December 23 night, it was snowing in much of the state. Blankets and tea were the condiments of choice with a main course of storytelling by their governor. Carr told of a call to help a young girl just across the border in Scottsbluff, Nebraska, who had been poisoned and was suffering from an attack of botulism. While thousands of Americans were dying abroad, Carr highlighted a survival story closer to home.

"To try to relay the necessary serum by automobile," the governor said, "would be slow and hazardous under existing traveling conditions."

It was hard to find help. A year earlier, Maj. Harry Wellman of the 120th Observation Squadron, had made a similar "mission of mercy" to southwestern Colorado. But now, like so many other Colorado fathers and brothers and sons, Maj. Wellman and his squadron had been called to duty and weren't available.

With the 120th Squadron gone, a group of local flyers with private planes had joined together and volunteered to help. In this emergency, they went into action and delivered the necessary medicine. What might seem a small action took on bigger proportions at Christmastime.

"They reached Scottsbluff, started for home a short time ago, and as we are on the air, they are up there actually," the governor said in his calming baritone-bordering-on-tenor voice. "[The] wing commander and his fellows have proved that our defense efforts are effective and worthwhile. They have justified the pride which we have expressed in our people's response.

"Tonight as we gaze out across the Pacific and pray for those men under General MacArthur who are trying to stem an overwhelming tide of Japanese, we are trying to retain something in our souls of the teachings of the Nazarene to soften the picture.

"And in the years to come after peace has been reestablished, they will tell the story around the fireplaces in the homes of westerners of the flight of Colorado's volunteers in the interest of love and peace and friendship.

"This action of our flyers tonight," he concluded, "exemplifies the attitude of all Coloradans—of all Americans—at this Christmas season."

Chapter Six

January 1942

What would Lincoln do?

It was a question Ralph Carr applied to even everyday problems. Lincoln was his hero; Carr studied his life and tried to emulate him. No date on the calendar was more sacred to Colorado's governor than Lincoln's birthday. The consommé and chops aside, talking at the Lincoln Day dinners let him engage in an exploration of his political hero's principles and practices, which offered guidance to be applied nearly eighty years later.

Since he became governor in 1939, Carr traveled the country over to spread Lincoln's legacy. He spoke on a dais in New York City with former president Herbert Hoover, extolling Lincoln's "patience, frankness, and honesty." He went to Nashville, Tennessee, where he joked about how foreign a concept it must be to have a Northerner singing the praises of another Northerner in the South.

He was a Lincoln aficionado in every sense.

He collected newspaper articles on the former president, always buying the February 12 big-city papers from Chicago and New York, looking to glean something he could practically apply to modern-day life. He viewed Lincoln's second inaugural address with nearly as much reverence and fervor as the Lord's Prayer. "Malice toward none" seemed the moral equivalent of "forgive us our wrongs as we forgive those who have done wrong to us."

They shared similar roots; both were from humble beginnings. Lincoln, the "rail-splitter's son," grew up to become a "country lawyer" before entering politics. Carr, the miner's son, grew up to become a "country lawyer" before entering politics. The governor was known to joke while he was in office, "I've always wanted to be a lawyer, but I've had so many interruptions. Maybe someday I'll get started."

Lincoln's principles and policies certainly had an impact on Carr's. For example, on the issue of criminal justice, Carr regularly fought the legislature for reform, saying, "Prevention is the answer to a large portion of our criminal problems."

Carr saw Lincoln's mental strength when it came to an issue like preserving the Union. Despite attacks both real and threatened from all over the country, Lincoln believed and persevered to accomplish that goal. Similarly, Carr, when faced with a less important decision about reforming state government, refused to back down from critics even when it would have been the easier road to take.

"[Carr] surveys a situation, decides what course is best, and then drives right through like a fullback with a football," said his friend Max Goldberg. "Ordinary men would have trembled at problems. … They would have winced, weakened, and wilted. Not Carr! … He swept opposition aside like chaff before the wind."

Carr and Lincoln were both "people people," enjoying company and stories. Both believed those who shunned the advice and counsel of others could not be true leaders. Lincoln fired General John Fremont from his position leading the army's Department of the West in 1861, saying, "His cardinal mistake is that he isolates himself and allows nobody to see him and by which, he does not know what is going on in the very matter he is dealing with." Carr solicited advice from everyone he contacted.

"Everybody he'd meet, he'd find out what they were interested in," his son, Bob, said. "It's not like polling, but more like if you take a picture, you're going to have different perspectives based on where you're standing. He wanted all sorts of views. Most people tend to look at life as pictures with not much variation, but Dad looked at life as a sculpture from all the different points of view, very diverse points of view."

Carr said Lincoln applied "the same simple reasoning of the country lawyer addressing a jury of farmers to the questions of government." Without apology, he used the word *liberal* numerous times when discussing Lincoln, saying the word had been co-opted by the New Dealers of the day who were, in reality, practicing "pseudo-liberalism."

"Lincoln was a liberal, a true liberal," Carr said during a 1940 speech. "There are people who masquerade under the term "liberal" who are so open minded that like mountain goats they jump from crag to crag, leaving one as soon as another appears in view.

"But the true liberals are those who consistently follow the proposition that liberty means freedom to exercise individual rights unaffected by external restraint or compulsion.

"While not expressed in this exact language, the underlying theory of the Constitution is found in the proposition that every man may use the talents which God has given him, may reach any goal toward which he sets his eyes, and may enjoy the fruits of his ambition, his study and his toil, provided only that he does not use his powers to injure his fellows."

Carr adopted the Lincoln belief that "by viewing a man's actions through that man's eyes, a more sympathetic understanding is afforded."

At the dawn of 1942, with his country at war and his state struggling to find its place in the conflict, Ralph Carr wondered what Lincoln would do in his position. Since his last speech to Colorado on December 23, the war had grown more grim.

Wake Island had been officially captured on Christmas Eve. Hong Kong was occupied on Christmas Day. They were locations many Americans hadn't known existed, but now they represented yet another example of Japanese success in the Pacific. Wake, the tiny atoll in the Central Pacific defended by marines and civilian forces, was to be home to an American air and submarine base, but it was taken after twelve straight days of bombing.

Hong Kong, controlled by the British for so many years, capitulated after three weeks of intense attacks. English, Canadian, and local Hong Kong soldiers died trying to hold the island, but without question the most emotionally devastating news of the new year came with the fall of the Philippine capital of Manila.

There were more than thirty-one thousand American soldiers under the command of General Douglas MacArthur stationed at the Philippine garrison. Faced with an unwinnable battle against an overwhelming enemy, MacArthur abandoned Manila on Christmas Eve and it was occupied by Japanese forces on January 2.

Carr sincerely believed "conditions create leadership necessary to meet crises," and as he deliberated on his Lincoln Day speech for the following month, he wondered what Lincoln chord to hit, what Lincoln story to tell, what Lincoln point to make.

The new year brought new restrictions from the federal government and new complaints from Colorado's governor. With 90 percent of the country's rubber supply coming from the Far East, and only a year's supply on hand during peacetime, the government implemented a freeze on the sale of new passenger car tires.

In the West, where public transportation was not nearly as common as in the metropolitan cities of the East, cars—and, thus, rubber—were needed to get products to market, to get tourists to the ski areas, and to get many people from point A to point B.

"I am working eighteen to twenty hours a day trying to keep Colorado right up at the head of the procession in support of the war, but I am going to retain the right to suggest that they are taking too many powers unto themselves in the name of war," wrote a cynical Carr to Lowell Thomas on January 14. "We've got to keep this theory of government intact and when we lose the plan of separate states, and the central government of delegated powers, then—goodbye Democracy."

After he posed on a tandem bicycle with patrolman Floyd Christiansen, clad in his overcoat, wingtips, top hat, and briefcase with the initials *RLC* in hand, he received a note from Wendell Willkie crediting him for setting an example that "will do a great deal of good in the present national emergency." Willkie said he

Ralph Carr rides a tandem bicycle with patrolman Floyd Christensen after rubber restrictions were imposed by the federal government during the war. Carr chafed under the numerous regulations implemented by East Coast bureaucrats who he believed did not understand life outside of the nation's capital. He preferred to encourage his neighbors to be patriotic by voluntarily giving up certain material goods rather than being required to do so. The photo was shown in numerous papers nationwide, and Wendell Willkie wrote Carr that he looked "handsome, business-like and athletic" on the bicycle built for two. Courtesy of the Colorado Historical Society was "handsome, business-like, and athletic on that bicycle built for two."

Carr chose to answer the note seriously.

"There is one thing that continues to worry me," he wrote. "The determination to take over state rights and activities in the name of war offers much concern. ... The determination to merge all employment agencies in the federal government, with no agreement to return these functions at the end of the emergency is a cause for great concern.

"Should there not be some sort of an understanding that these powers which are definitely those of the state will be returned at the end of the emergency? I think it with all my soul, and I hope somebody will either speak up and allay our fears or else come out frankly and say that it is their determination to accomplish this thing and there is no idea of returning those powers to the state at any time."

His feelings were not shared by large numbers of Americans. In fact, only "a scant five percent of Americans believe the present democratic system is breaking down." That came from pollster Elmo Roper, as quoted by the *Rocky Ford Daily Gazette-Topic*.

Practically, Colorado was being flooded by families from the West Coast "war zones." Trains, buses, and automobiles were daily bringing a sharp increase in the number of residents, and Carr told the Associated Press, "There is evidence that the influx will increase."

"There should be sufficient housing suitable for the accommodation of families now in exodus from the Pacific Coast," Carr wrote in a letter to the chambers of commerce in Colorado. He urged the business and city leaders to discourage landlords who may want to set unreasonable rentals for Japanese and other families moving into the state.

Carr spent much time dealing with the war and often with its unexpected ramifications. A note from Ed Christensen, a former neighbor in Antonito, exemplified his frustration over things he couldn't control. Christensen had two hundred forty acres to farm, and three sons to make it work, producing food for the family and for the market, until the war. With one son already in the army, Christensen's two other boys were examined, checked out, and told to prepare to head out.

"I cannot work this land without them," he wrote to the governor. "[It] is impossible to hire help as have tryed [*sic*] last fall and we could not get help to gather our crop. Some of it we did not get out of the ground because we did not have help.

"I'm willing to do all I can to help our country but I believe the boys can do more good on the farm then they can in the Army as there has got to be food raised for the Army to eat."

Carr's frustration with what he knew would be both a labor issue and a moral dilemma oozed out in his response.

"My dear Ed," he began, "I know your problem in connection with your boys being drawn in the service. I heard an officer in charge of the conscription law talking yesterday and he gave farmers no comfort or hope. He made it plain that farm boys generally are within the age limits which the Army needs. Unfortunately, I have no control over the conscription ... I don't know a thing I can do."

One thing he felt he could control was what people learned about one of their enemies: Japan. With Dean Clifford Houston at the University of Colorado, Carr helped plan a statewide radio campaign to educate people about "the Japanese and their ideals." Houston described it as an "aid in developing an intellectual morale at this time, not just the emotional type of morale."

After the drumroll faded, the radio announcer said, "Our enemies and allies—we know them, yes—in a way we know them. And yet, how much do we know, know in detail about the nations we are fighting with and fighting against?

"It is to answer hundreds of questions like these—questions of fact—that the University of Colorado and this station bring you this new broadcast series."

CU professor Earl Swisher, an authority on the Far East, delivered the first broadcast on the topic of Japan. For the next half hour, Dr. Swisher detailed the history of Japanese society, most recently the evolution from the feudalism and samurai rule, which broke up in the late 1870s, to the emperor-ruled country of 1942. A country where the state religion, Shinto, "stresses the Japanese emperor's being a god and the divine origin of the Japanese race" and children are "indoctrinated with the state religion."

He described how the Japanese military holds "a superior constitutional status" and how the code of the Japanese Army called for committing suicide rather than being taken prisoner "simply because … capture is an unbearable disgrace. … It is the guiding creed of the army we are now fighting against."

If the information was frightening to a state ignorant about its enemy, it was understandable. Japan was a warring nation with more than 70 million people, almost as large as Hitler's Germany, and had nearly 250 million other Asians under its rule. The Japanese could not make the Koreans or Chinese fight for them, but they could use them, Dr. Swisher stated, to produce the materials Japan needed to fight. "Even allowing for resistance," he said, "[Japan] has more than twice as many effective workers as we have."

Maybe most depressing, Coloradans heard that America had sold raw materials like steel, iron, and copper to Japan in "even greater quantities since 1936," now likely being used against U.S. troops. "Her people—her own Japanese people—are fanatically united; and obviously they are all the more so recently, since their army and navy have been able to feed them victory after victory."

Swisher concluded his sobering address by helping Coloradans understand why the Japanese held such anger toward Americans.

At the end of World War I, the Japanese wanted a clause in the peace treaty recognizing racial equality, and it was refused by the American negotiators "largely because no one took it seriously." Then, in 1924, the Federal Immigration Act branded the Japanese as ineligible for citizenship and it was "so great an affront

Japan was on the verge of declaring war on us then and there." Many Japanese who had lived in the United States for decades simply could not become naturalized.

"The Japanese remember" these insults, Swisher concluded, "and now, having struck us at what is perhaps the last possible moment, they are after revenge up to the hilt."

In that arena, with those facts, Governor Carr tried to tamp down the public's hysteria and its attitudes toward the residents of Japanese descent. It was an increasingly hostile situation in many areas of the state. Navy recruiter E. H. Riley announced that men who signed up in La Junta in southeast Colorado would be given "hunting licenses for Japanese."

Carr's incoming correspondence was filled with prognostications about doom on the Pacific Coast, to be aided and abetted by Japanese spies in America. "Believe me Governor," one letter read, "last eve while praying for our boys in the islands; the LORD spoke to me saying 'Tell Governor Carr to notify the people on the West Coast to 'dig in' for they must be ready in ten days.'"

The governor tried to diffuse the anger by sharing examples of positive contributions on the part of Colorado's Japanese Americans with reporters. Stories like that of twenty-two-year-old Henry Harada, an American-born Japanese (or Nisei), who left his farm behind to join the army at Fort Logan. Stories like the loyalty petition signed by Frank Muramoto, to whom Carr wrote, "Yours is a difficult position at best. Men whose hearts are truly loyal, however, will eventually be recognized and rewarded for their attitude."

The governor forwarded and publicized an effort by the Japanese American Citizen's League in rural Blanca, Colorado, which had earlier required an armed detail to protect its Japanese American residents, to raise money for the war effort. The JACL collected several tons of scrap iron, raising $38.75 for the cause. "It shows their patriotism, their good citizenship and their good judgment," Carr wrote to Blanca mayor George Opincar.

Yet, there was also tangible evidence blaming spies or "fifth columnists" for Pearl Harbor. The term came from the Spanish Civil War in the mid-1930s; loosely defined, it meant a clandestine group bent on undermining its own country's security. The federal government did nothing to stop the fifth-column rumors and innuendo of what happened at Pearl Harbor, even though privately it was receiving contradictory evidence.

Secretary of War Frank Knox told reporters, "I think the most effective fifth-column work of the war was done in Hawaii." The president appointed Supreme Court justice Owen J. Roberts to "investigate and report the facts" surrounding the Pearl Harbor attack. What he received lacked documentation but increased fears among military personnel and civilians alike about the true threat of those of Japanese descent in America.

The Roberts Commission concluded that more than two hundred spies were acting under Japanese authority in Hawaii before Pearl Harbor, many of whom had not registered with the FBI as required by federal law.

"It was believed that the center of Japanese espionage in Hawaii was the Japanese consulate at Honolulu. It has been discovered that the Japanese consul sent to and received from Tokyo in his own and other names many messages on commercial radio circuits. This activity greatly increased toward December 7, 1941," the commission report stated. "It is now apparent that through their intelligence service the Japanese had complete information. … They knew, from maps which they had obtained, the exact location of vital air fields, hangars, and other structures. They also knew accurately where certain important naval vessels would be berthed."

Alien Enemy Hearing Boards were established by U.S. attorney general Francis Biddle to expedite charges against those who would commit espionage and sabotage against the country. One was set up in every federal court district, including one in Colorado. From the get-go, they were criticized for being too soft on those accused. The FBI rounded up hundreds of Japanese aliens in Hawaii alone.

The "Washington Merry-Go-Round" syndicated column reported on "congressional probers" who were putting the "microscope" to the three-member boards around the country. The columnists wrote that members of Congress had received numerous complaints about the board members "having business and social connections with enemy aliens, and to have displayed suspicious reluctance to deal forcefully with influential questionable enemy aliens."

The questioning was seen as a "mounting undercover feeling on Capitol Hill that the spy and fifth-column problem in the country is not being met with the rigorous realism needed. Privately, members of Congress are saying that certain [members of the administration] seem more concerned about what they term 'civil liberties' than the security of the nation."

For Ralph Carr, civil liberties meant the Bill of Rights, and that meant fighting for those principles at any cost. That's what Lincoln did. "Principles are as true as truth and will live as long as God's creation," Carr once said. But Carr was not ignorant of another Lincoln saying, uttered during his first debate with Stephen Douglas in 1858: "With public sentiment, nothing can fail; without it, nothing can succeed. ... Consequently, he who molds public sentiment goes deeper than he who enacts statutes or pronounces decisions."

Ralph Carr was losing the battle for public sentiment. He was getting daily briefings on aliens who lived near infrastructures that were strategically significant. Front-page articles about Japanese turning in scores of cameras, guns, and shortwave radio sets to police stations across the state led to speculation about why they had these materials in the first place. Law enforcement officers like La Junta Police Chief D. H. Houghton said that no deadline had been set for the "alien surrender" of these possessions, but told the *La Junta Daily Democrat*, "Unless they are turned in immediately, warrants for the arrest of those aliens in possession of the articles will be issued and federal authorities informed."

Sure, there were some supporters for benevolence toward those of Japanese descent. From the First Methodist Church in Boulder, Rufus Baker complimented the governor on his "reasoned sanity and good sense," which he felt "should appeal to every lover of America."

Carr treated the Constitution and its principles as sacrosanct, claiming it "is the cornerstone of the greatest work of human hands" primarily because "the people were sovereign and the government and its administrators were the servants, and not their masters."

The sentiment along the West Coast was decidedly more antagonistic and fearful. Army records show that nearly six hundred Japanese aliens were initially picked up in the week immediately following the Pearl Harbor attack. The FBI, making regular spot raids, was turning up guns, radios, cameras—all materials the government feared could be used in another attack on U.S. citizens. Shinto priests, judo instructors, labor leaders—all were swept up in the wave.

Meetings had taken place in the early part of the month between Lieutenant General John L. DeWitt, who ran the Western theater of operations, and representatives with the Department of Justice. The result, according to United Press on January 29, was that "the Justice Department in a move to prevent espionage and fifth column activity similar to that preceding Pearl Harbor today set in motion a plan to remove the 186,000 enemy aliens residing in defense areas in eight far western states."

However, that was not enough for many West Coast residents. Allowing "a Jap" to simply move inland from the harbor areas of San Francisco, Los Angeles, or Seattle, but still live within the city limits, brought vehement objections from residents all up and down the coast. They wanted the group physically removed from the area, citizenship notwithstanding. Security took precedence.

"Civil liberties" were being stressed too much.

The concept of physically detaining any Japanese was first brought to the public by Mississippi congressman John Rankin who, from the floor of the U.S. House of Representatives just eight days after Pearl Harbor, said, "I'm for catching every Japanese in America, Alaska, and Hawaii now and putting them in concentration camps and shipping them back to Asia as soon as possible. ... This is a race war, as far as the Pacific side of the conflict is concerned." Rankin shouted from the well of the House floor, "The white man's civilization has come into conflict with Japanese barbarism. ... One of them must be destroyed. ... Damn them! Let's get rid of them now!"

That belief was echoed by prominent Mutual Broadcasting commentator John B. Hughes in early January. Five months before Pearl Harbor, in his *News and Views by John B. Hughes* segment, he had predicted that something ominous was going on in Japan. He likened it to the "tense crouch of a great cat in that moment before springing to attack." Now, after Pearl Harbor, he too sounded the call to imprison anyone with Japanese ties, saying the threat of espionage was too great.

Hearst syndicated columnist Henry McLemore waited until the end of the month before saying, "Speaking strictly as an American, I think Americans are nuts. Twenty-four hours in Los Angeles have convinced me of this. We are at war. California is our key state, not only because of its airplane industry but because its shores offer the most logical invasion point. So what does the government do about the tens of thousands of Japanese in California? Nothing. ...

"You walk up and down the streets and you bump into Japanese in every block," McLemore wrote. "They take the parking stations. They get ahead of you in the stamp line at the post office. They have their share of seats on the bus and streetcar lines. This doesn't make sense. ...

"Everywhere that the Japanese have attacked to date, the

Japanese population has risen to aid the attackers. Pearl Harbor. Manila. What is there to make the government believe that the same wouldn't be true in California?

"I am for the immediate removal of every Japanese on the West Coast to a point deep in the interior. I don't mean a nice part of the interior, either. Herd 'em up, pack 'em off and give 'em the inside room in the badlands. Let 'em be pinched, hurt, hungry, and dead up against it."

The situation was so inflammatory that everyone wanted a shot at the Japs—even kids like ten-year-old Minor Mullins. The Limon, Colorado, lad made the front page of the *Rocky Mountain News* when he wrote the Navy Recruiting Station in Denver, "Dear Sir: May I enlist in the Navy? I am ten years old. Mother said I may. I believe I can kill Japs just like jackrabbits. Thanks, Minor Mullins."

Ralph Carr did not have personal history upon which to base his benevolence toward those of Japanese descent. As governor, he had met with Japanese American leaders in Colorado as early as 1940, when tensions between the Far Eastern nation and the United States were growing, but he didn't have good friends of Japanese descent. Carr's most publicized story as it related to the Japanese came out during his first political campaign and went all the way back to his college years.

He was an enterprising newspaperman, working his way through college and law school by writing for the *Rocky Mountain News* and *Cripple Creek Times*. One day he was covering Boulder County sheriff M. B. Capp's search for a Japanese fugitive who was wanted in a murder. They followed his trail seventeen miles northwest to the tiny town of Lyons, where a number of Japanese laborers were working on a pipeline. Denver detectives joined in the search that lasted all night, ending at dawn outside a tall barn perched on a hillside.

"The tracks apparently ended at the barn door, which was locked from the inside," Carr told the *Rocky Mountain News* in

1939. "Sheriff Capp told me I was the smallest in the group and asked me to climb up to a window in the rear of the barn and go through and open the door.

"I managed the window all right, but it was pitch black inside. Not wanting to appear afraid, I let myself down off the sill and let go. I dropped fifteen feet, landing in the hay. Just as I struck, a horse coughed and almost scared me to death." The Japanese fugitive was not inside, but the police officers had a good laugh at Carr's expense.

But the tension in 1942, though, was no laughing matter. Despite Pearl Harbor, Carr was convinced any talk of internment, confinement, imprisonment—whatever word was used to describe what was being suggested for American citizens—was simply wrong. "We are talking of the rights of American citizens," he said. "We are talking of those things which have [built] this country. We are still entitled to live under the most [benevolent] form of government that has ever been devised by man."

As he began to write his Lincoln Day address, he thought of Lincoln's famous statement that he had "faith that right makes might and in that faith let us to the end dare to do our duty as we understand it."

Governor Carr believed he knew his duty. And he had an answer as to what Lincoln would do.

"While we as citizens render to the nation everything of loyalty and encouragement and support, may our government do nothing which will weaken us or render it difficult for us to work efficiently to that end.

"We know Lincoln today as a man of strength as well as of tenderness and we know that in his efforts to be sympathetic, to be fair and to be just with his fellow men, he often violated the human rules set up by those who called themselves strong," Carr wrote.

"Let us follow in the footsteps of Lincoln. Let us so conduct ourselves that we can assure the men who have gone into service and those who will follow them before this issue is settled that the form of government which they are leaving, the Bill of Rights which offers them security, freedom, and opportunity, will continue to function and that they will find upon their return, the same kind of government in the United States of America as existed when they went away."

That would not be easy, especially when it affected his own family. His son, Bob, wanted him to fill out a consent form so he could join the Naval ROTC on the CU–Boulder campus. The nineteen-year-old was adamant in wanting to contribute to the war effort. The rules said he had to be twenty-one.

Carr signed the consent, and on January 23, Governor Carr's only son became an apprentice seaman. The conflict in the Pacific was calling.

Chapter Seven
Early February 1942

Robert Warren's job was to lure tourists to Colorado during the middle of a world war.

Not surprisingly, he was having trouble coming up with a good catchphrase. How do you communicate the blue "spacious skies," the "amber waves of grain," and the "purple mountain majesties" in an advertising campaign to a world that seemed to have gone crazy?

And yet the state's economy depended on Warren's success in bringing in tourists, even in a time of war.

Colorado had plenty to boast about. "America the Beautiful" had been prompted by a spectacular view of 14,110-foot Pikes Peak. The Maroon Bells mountain range outside Aspen, later captured photographically by Ansel Adams with a crystalline lake in its foreground, was an idyllic location. The Great Sand Dunes provided enormous mounds of finely grained sand and a natural desertlike atmosphere, with mountains and sagebrush not far away. The mesas and canyons of southwestern Colorado were home to the ancient Anasazi cliff dwellers, one of the few man-made wonders in his gorgeous state. The Berthoud Pass ski area and its 425-plus inches of snow each year beckoned to those wanting to vacation on the slopes.

Still, according to the state's hotel association, "During the past several years, the tourist business in Colorado has decreased while that of other Western states has increased." With a freeze on the sale of rubber, looming fuel restrictions, and a country still emerging from a depression, Warren knew his ad campaign had little room for error.

Tourism was an $80-million-a-year business for Colorado, placing it behind agriculture in terms of importance, but still a vital cog in the state's economic engine. Warren had been hoping for a seventy-five-thousand-dollar ad campaign funded by his boss and political mentor, but Governor Carr wasn't willing to loosen the purse strings when state government had only recently been in significant debt.

Warren was kicking around the slogans "Cool Colorado … year-round playground" and "The state that tops the nation." He wasn't sold on either and was asking for input from people all over the state. It had to be perfect. Americans couldn't be expected to spend too much money or time on their vacations at a time when the country's affairs seemed to suck the collective breath from their guts with the daily headlines.

One group of people Warren was sure he did not want coming to Colorado were people of Japanese descent, no matter what economic benefit they might bring. He did not want them tending to Colorado's fields. He did not want them working in its cities. He did not want them living on its property.

He knew how Colorado's farms were being affected by the military draft. Governor Carr had told him about Leo Kiefer, who had taken over the family farm that his father could no longer tend, only to be drafted into the service. Fred Lowenhagen was farming a hundred to a hundred and twenty acres on his Fruita farm, also taking care of his widowed mother, and he had gotten drafted. Same story for Bud Musselmann and Billy Byers. The point of view of Farmer's Union Local No. 149 echoed that of every other local in Colorado: we want to win the war, but we need to leave the boys on the farm to grow and harvest the crops to do so. Yet, putting Japanese workers in the sugar beet fields, the onion fields, the potato fields, and the bean fields was not the answer for Warren.

He had heard the cries from West Coast politicians to send "the Japs" inland, away from their military establishments. Those cries had been deafening and unanimous from Washington State to Arizona. There were one hundred twenty thousand potential spies living in those areas, and until they were removed, it was argued that the country would not be safe from sabotage and espionage.

Warren felt it was his job to let the country know where Colorado stood on the issue. The state's economy depended upon it.

He began contacting chambers of commerce, parent-teacher organizations, and Spanish American groups in all four corners of the state for support. He chose Valentine's Day to launch what the *Rocky Mountain News* called a "one-man drive" against the "settlement of 45,000 to 85,000 Japs in this state."

"It would ruin Colorado as a tourist attraction," Warren said. "The only reason any group favors importing the Jap aliens is because of a possible labor shortage and that can be cared for by our ally to the south, Mexico.

"If the Japs were used in our fields, no one would eat the vegetables and products they raised anyhow. ... Before the government brings them here, it should consult the people of Colorado."

Rocky Mountain News editor Jack Foster sent a telegram to Carr, who was out of state. "Bob Warren's announced opposition to war board plan to move Jap aliens here and his campaign to arouse Spanish-Americans, farmers, PTA, Chambers of Commerce and other groups, makes statement from you vital. Please wire us your position soonest."

The governor never responded.

On a day where "the far-flung Japanese offensive stretched" toward the Pacific island of Sumatra, Warren's campaign got front-page headlines statewide. His campaign was met with immediate support. Four prominent farmers in Weld County, north of Denver, issued their own statement designed to "keep California Japs out of Colorado."

"We have found no farmer who wishes to use [imported Japanese] labor," their statement read. "Northern Colorado will have hundreds of boys in battle against the Japanese. Casualty lists will come in ... it is not well to scatter among us strangers, already suspect, who might be a provocation for people losing their heads and doing things that might result in reprisals against prisoners in Japan. We cannot see the wisdom of drafting our own boys, skilled farm workers and replacing them with enemy aliens."

Despite assurances from all levels of the government that Japanese suspected of being unfriendly to the United States were being investigated by the FBI, the idea of bringing a potential problem closer to home only led to more worries. One Colorado State College instructor worried about the water supply in Fort Collins and throughout the Poudre Valley that surrounds it. "One subversive alien in the bunch might wreck the entire Poudre Valley irrigation supply system," Economics instructor E. F. Resek told the *Fort Collins Express-Courier*.

The *Denver Post* chose to forsake the holiday of affection with an opinion column filled with vitriol. "Colorado's answer to suggestions that this state import thousands of Jap aliens and give them jobs in the sugar beet fields should be: 'TO HELL WITH THE JAPS! KEEP COLORADO AMERICAN!'

"The United States and Japan are at war. THE JAPS ARE ENEMIES OF THE AMERICAN PEOPLE. JAPS SLAUGHTERED 3,000 AMERICANS OVER AT PEARL HARBOR. And now it is proposed that Colorado help 'avenge' this monstrous crime by providing paying jobs for the brothers and cousins of these gory-handed murderers! That's enough to throw any American into a fit!

"The most asinine thing Colorado could do, even if there were no war, would be to take over a part of California's Jap problem. If the Japs are allowed to get a foothold in Colorado's farming areas, the same thing will happen that already has happened along the Pacific coast. They will starve out American farmers and workmen. Because of their lower living standards, the Japs will undersell and run out of business our own Colorado farmers. COLORADO IS AMERICAN. LET'S KEEP COLORADO AMERICAN!"

Although the *Post* screamed for action, the *Rocky Mountain*

News preached patience and reason. "If the federal government meets this problem squarely and intelligently, there should be no injustice either to these aliens or to Colorado," the *News*'s Valentine's Day editorial read. "But there ought to be a complete understanding between Governor Carr and the government as to methods before the migration is started."

Warren knew the decision would be made by the federal government with little regard for Colorado's feelings. That was what Republican politicians, led by Governor Carr, had been harping about since the beginning of the New Deal. That said, if the migration were to happen, he wanted "to know what positive assurance can be given that the Jap enemy aliens will be sent out of Colorado after the war. What is the guarantee and how is it bonded?"

Warren called for meetings across the state to generate attention for his position. He spoke in Denver to the Native Sons of Colorado. The group was actively trying to "arouse ourselves and prevent these almond-eyed sons of the Orient from being dumped on our doorstep. The Japanese challenge has invaded [our] own home state territory."

The group's literature pointed out how its brothers in California had been warning for twenty-five years of the "yellow peril" that was acquiring agricultural land across that state. It detailed how Japan is one of the most mountainous countries in the world and "all you have to do to make their victory complete in the Pacific is to fortify them back of the Rocky Mountains." It encouraged its members to engage in an "all-out effort to protect your state."

What had started as rumor and innuendo had taken on a greater urgency two days earlier when Colorado's War Board chairman Dewey Harmon told the United Press that the federal Department of Agriculture had asked him to conduct "an official housing survey to find quarters for Japanese who may be removed from some portions of the Pacific Coast." Harmon said the survey would be focused on the state's mostly abandoned Civilian Conservation Corps (CCC) camps. Many of those camps were located in Colorado's produce-raising areas. Harmon said the goal would be to accommodate the "highly-skilled [Japanese] laborers from the fruit and vegetable-growing sections of the West Coast and hopefully alleviate any produce shortage from occurring during the war."

The order had been given by Tom Clark, federal alien control coordinator for the West. He wanted a sense of what states could take which aliens for "useful labor."

"This gives an official tone to rumors that many of these Japanese may be concentrated in Colorado and other Rocky Mountain region states," said Harmon. "We have assurance that any aliens transferred to Colorado will be given close supervision.

"Our own safety and security will be given first consideration if any actual transfer of the Japanese to Colorado is undertaken. This, however, is just one more stern reminder that we are in an all-out war."

All Japanese, German, and Italian nationals had to register with their local postmaster. Failure to comply would result in detention. Each alien would have three pictures taken. One was sent to the FBI, the second to the State Department, and the third was kept in a passportlike book to be carried by the alien at all times.

In Colorado, authorities were expecting some seven thousand enemy aliens to register at one of the state's 643 post offices. More than a score waited for Denver's main post office to open, prepared to return their old alien registration cards and to present their new two-by-two photographs.

But as fear over another Pearl Harbor grew, registration was not nearly enough for many people. National columnists Drew Pearson and Robert Allen reported on February 6 that a congressional committee had "sensational evidence about Japanese subversive activity in the United States." The "front" for the fifth-column activity, according to the committee, was the Central Japanese Association, headquartered in Los Angeles with numerous Japanese American businessmen as members. Included in its files was a cablegram sent to the Japanese War Ministry in the early part of 1941 that read, "We resident countrymen from afar express our wholehearted gratitude to the officers and men of the Imperial army fighting throughout China for the establishment of everlasting peace in East Asia and we pledge ourselves hereafter to exert more and more efforts from behind the lines here in the United States."

"Behind the lines" was a phrase sure to get the attention of those entrusted to protect the country from another attack. Military records showed that naval commanders wanted to clear the coast of those of Japanese descent who couldn't show "actual severance of all allegiance to the Japanese government." In part, that's because General DeWitt told the War Department, "We know there are radios along the coast; and we know they are communicating at sea. They may be communicating with each other."

DeWitt told his superiors in Washington, "The fact that nothing has happened so far is more or less ... ominous in that I feel that in view of the fact that we have had no sporadic attempts at sabotage, there is control being exercised and when we have it, it will be on a mass basis."

Public opinion demanded full-scale evacuation from California. The state's attorney general, Earl Warren, who would later become a civil rights champion on the United States Supreme Court, led the charge. "I believe that we are just being lulled into a false sense of security and that the only reason we haven't had a disaster in California is because it has been timed for a different date. Our day of reckoning is bound to come in that regard." He believed it was impossible to "distinguish between dangerous and loyal Japs," according to *Newsweek* magazine.

The *Los Angeles Times* ran a series of stories with headlines such as: "New West Coast Raids Feared," "Eviction of Jap Aliens Sought," "Californians Seek More Alien Curbs," and "American Japs Removal Urged."

The articles were intense in their distaste for anyone with

an ounce of Japanese blood in them. "Perhaps the most difficult and delicate question that confronts our powers that be is the handling—the safe and proper treatment—of our American-born Japanese, our Japanese American citizens by the accident of birth, but who are Japanese nevertheless. A viper is nonetheless a viper wherever the egg is hatched," wrote W. H. Anderson in the February 2 editions.

When one of the country's more respected syndicated columnists, Walter Lippmann, became a believer, it helped propel the government toward an evacuation. On February 12, Lincoln's birthday, Lippman wrote from San Francisco, "The enemy alien problem on the Pacific Coast, or much more accurately, the fifth-column problem, is very serious and very special. What makes it so serious and so special is that the Pacific Coast is in imminent danger of an attack from within and from without."

His column challenged any naysayers and he scorned those "legalistic and ideological arguments" that were taking place in Washington.

"The Pacific Coast is officially a combat zone," Lippman wrote. "Some part of it may at any moment be a battlefield. And nobody ought to be on a battlefield who has no good reason for being there. There is plenty of room elsewhere for him to exercise his rights."

Los Angeles mayor Fletcher Bowron was also talking about the Constitution on Lincoln's birthday. While Colorado's governor was extolling the virtues of a man who we know today "as a man of strength as well as of tenderness," Bowron's message was dramatically different. He told a radio audience throughout Southern California that he was tired of the "sickly sentimentality" of those worried about doing loyal Japanese Americans harm. Referring to Lincoln, he said that if the former president were alive, he would round up "the people born on American soil who have secret loyalty to the Japanese emperor."

And to those like Governor Carr, who extolled Lincoln's

"tenderness," Bowron said, "there isn't a shadow of a doubt, but that Lincoln, the mild-mannered man whose memory we regard with almost saintlike reverence, would make short work of rounding up the Japanese and putting them where they could do no harm."

A few days later, conservative syndicated columnist Westbrook Pegler jumped on the bandwagon, writing that the fifth-column problem on the Pacific Coast was very serious and that "Japs should be under guard ... to hell with habeas corpus until the war is over," he wrote of the legal principle to safeguard individual freedoms against inappropriate government action.

When the entire West Coast congressional delegation, covering California, Oregon, Washington, and Alaska, sent a letter to President Roosevelt recommending "the immediate evacuation of all persons of Japanese lineage and all others, aliens and citizens alike, whose presence shall be deemed dangerous or inimical to the defense of the United States from all strategic areas," the die was cast. As the representatives and senators stressed to the president, the goal was simple. "No citizen," they wrote, "located in a strategic area, may cloak his disloyalty or subversive activity under the mantle of his citizenship alone and further to guarantee protection to all loyal persons, alien and citizen alike, whose safety may be endangered by some wanton act of sabotage."

On February 19, the day Attorney General Biddle announced that his local hearing boards had reviewed 1,084 enemy alien cases, President Roosevelt signed Executive Order no. 9066. It began, "Whereas the successful prosecution of the war requires every possible protection against espionage and sabotage to national-defense material, national-defense premises, and national-defense utilities," and it concluded by turning over to the secretary of war the power to use whatever "action necessary" to protect military areas on the coast. Media reports at the time labeled it a "step away" from martial law.

The order meant that roughly a hundred twenty thousand

West Coast residents of Japanese descent, two-thirds of whom were American citizens, would be evacuated from their homes. The question then was where they would go.

The majority of newspapers of Colorado sputtered angrily. Many thought the Japanese should be confined, as illustrated by this statement in the *Denver Post*: "The only sane policy of handling the Jap aliens is to round them up and put them in concentration camps under armed guard where they will have no opportunity to stick a knife into this country's back. It may be that some of these Japs are loyal to the United States or that they are not loyal enough to their own country to try to strike a blow for it. But we can't afford to take any chances. Better be safe than sorry.

"While there is war between the United States and Japan, every Jap in this country is either an actual or a potential enemy. They should be treated as such."

But everyone knew that eyes were turning toward Colorado as a place to put them.

The huge piles of mail landing on Governor Carr's office desk in the second half of the month were universally against any movement of either alien Japanese or Japanese Americans to Colorado. Starting the day after Warren's campaign, letters poured in from all over Colorado and from all over the country. The furor spread like wildfire in a dry forest.

George Cheever of Greeley wrote on Valentines Day, "If it is dangerous to have them in California, it is dangerous to have them in Colorado." Charles Krebs of Pueblo echoed that belief: "Let them swim back to where they came from."

A summer tourist, the very type of person Warren hoped to reach, sent a postcard that read, "Are you folks going to be a group of jelly fish and let California dump those Japs off on you? Send them back to Japan."

The next few days unleashed an onslaught, inspired in part by numerous media stories about potential locations of camps.

The state's largest city after Denver, Colorado Springs, sent its share of letters immediately as well. W. B. Venosdel encouraged the governor to "protect Colorado first," and Charles I. Burdick sent a Western Union telegram reading, "We of Colorado Springs protest vigorously against bringing Japs to Colorado." Even state representative Vernon Cheever, who represented Colorado Springs, chimed in with a telegram: "Groups, committees, veterans, individuals urge [that] I protest your office's importation of Japs to Colorado."

Rumors had the West Coast Japanese headed all over Colorado, including to Pueblo, just south of Colorado Springs. Longtime rancher John Bock, in a patriotic gesture, had offered his historic 2,700-acre ranch known as "JJ Ranch" to the federal government.

"We don't want the Japs," Mrs. J. A. Hughes from La Junta wrote the governor. "For goodness sake, don't let the people of Colorado in for anything as ridiculous as playing nursemaid to thousands of Japs."

Another threat of violence came from Mrs. John Bernzen in Boulder. "I have two boys with Uncle Sam and I am afraid I might do something desperate if I saw Japs working in our beet fields."

The governor had not come out publicly on the matter. He had not responded to the request of the *Rocky Mountain News* when the Warren campaign began and all stories were concluding with the fact that Carr had yet to take a position. "Will you not speak definitely regarding the settling of alien Japanese in Colorado?" Alta Cannon wrote from Pine, Colorado. "Even a small population of Japanese is a menace to safety, since 'blood is thicker than water.'"

Groups started to organize across the state and weigh in on the issue. In a sometimes heated discussion, about a hundred farmers in the Hazleton district of northern Colorado voted unanimously to oppose any Japanese labor coming to help with their crops. George Mosler, who acted as the secretary of the meeting, told the *Greeley Daily Tribune*, "Several farmers said they would rather let part of their farm go idle this year than have to use [Japs]."

The *Denver Post* had an editorial cartoon showing a group of men labeled as "Japs from the West Coast" and "Alien Enemies" and "Cheap Labor" in a truck heading down the road toward Colorado. With the state capitol in the background, a large sign in the foreground read, "No Dumping Here ... State of Colorado." The caption at the bottom stated, "And We Don't Mean Maybe."

The contradictions in some of the letters to the governor were apparent as Coloradans were inclined to give the roughly twenty-seven hundred who were their neighbors the benefit of the doubt, while not granting the same accommodations to those on the West Coast. W. D. Neals wrote as "one of your admirers" to Carr to implore him to "let California put them in concentration camps until after [the] war and send them home to Japan or whatever is left of that country after we get through shooting it up."

The letter ended: "Please keep my letter a perfect secret. I have alien Japanese neighbors and I don't want any trouble with them. They are my friends."

It's not as if Colorado's Japanese community was particularly welcoming of others coming from the West Coast. In Fort Lupton, at a labor committee meeting, in addition to the farmers and members of the Mexican community speaking out against any "alien Jap workers," some Japanese residents of the community told the United Press that if "anything happened, it would be [a] reflection upon them in the public mind and they did not wish to see any such risks taken."

The governor received a telegram from a dozen Japanese American families opposing importation of "any Japanese aliens" into the Grand Valley, on the state's Western Slope. "We are law-abiding residents and citizens, thoroughly loyal to the United States, have lived peaceful and useful lives, have many friends here and we wish to do our part in helping the United States to win the war. We feel that consummation of the proposal to bring Japanese aliens here would be most objectionable and would tend to cause suspicions and reflections upon ourselves."

The *Denver Post* actively campaigned against anyone of Japanese descent coming to Colorado. The state's largest newspaper railed against the idea of taking in any more Japanese and even questioned the loyalty of those who had been living in Colorado for decades. This cartoon clearly articulates the paper's position before any decision had been made by the federal government or stance taken by Governor Carr.

This war had neighbor looking at neighbor, wondering if foreign names were some indications of ill will toward the United States and if different accents indicated a propensity toward sabotage. And the concern that these evacuees would be brought in to replace or compete with Colorado farmers was real.

"Are the people of Colorado going to set [*sic*] still and allow the Japanese to come in and take the places of our American farm laborers?" O. S. Sisk wrote after the weekly Monday meeting of Alamosa's Friendship Lodge, No. 134. "If Japs are brought into this part of the country to work in any form, we assure our government that we will not tolerate such a condition."

The Denver Co-Operative Club and the Lions Club followed suit. *No Japanese wanted.*

As the public outcry intensified, reporters finally had the chance to ask the governor for his comment. Carr had always been forthright with the media. He had once volunteered to cover a college football game for the Associated Press in New York after he had been elected and used to joke that the only reason he left the newspaper business was because he wanted to eat "more abundantly." He was usually a reporter's dream to cover because, as Alva Swain put it, "He tells you what he knows with the understanding as to what part may be used in print."

But when it came to the topic of Colorado accepting Japanese evacuees from the West Coast, Carr proved strangely silent. The *News* reported that he was "neutral in anti-Jap row," and that when asked specifically about Robert Warren's campaign to keep them out, he kept "mum on the drive to exclude aliens." The only quotable material from Carr was a phrase he rarely, if ever, used. "I have no comment to make."

The letters, postcards, and telegrams kept coming from all over the state. "Get busy," Lillie Hughes wrote from Evergreen. "Keep the Japs out," R. S. Rasmussen from Hillrose wrote. H. P. Ottosen from Meeker said, "I feel they should be returned to wherever they came from."

The Bent County commissioners approved a resolution "strongly opposed to immigration ... of any Japanese aliens." The Grand Valley Farmers Union Local No. 432 passed a similar resolution. A petition signed by hundreds of people in Conejos County didn't want the CCC camp in their area used for Japanese. More than three hundred members of the Loyal Order of the Moose in Rifle sent a telegram also opposing importation.

There were fears of violence. A Japanese rooming house proprietor was shot and killed by an unknown assailant in northern California, another was wounded by a gang of gunmen. Immediate evacuation was recommended by the county supervisors of one California locality because it was becoming "dangerous for loyal enemy aliens" to stay.

One rancher living near a CCC camp in southern Colorado went into a local sporting goods store and demanded two boxes of .30-.30s. "Going deer hunting?" asked the clerk. "Nope," the mountaineer was quoted by the Associated Press as saying, "Jap huntin', that is if any of 'em wander too fur [sic] from camp!"

A little more than a week after Dewey Harmon had first been approached to look into housing for thousands of Japanese evacuees, Coloradans like Robert Warren could breathe easier. "Plans to Stock Colorado with Japs Abandoned," the front-page headline of the *Durango Herald-Democrat* proclaimed. The newspaper reported that James Henderson, head of the Department of Justice's Regional and Trust division, had been informed by West Coast officials that evacuation plans had been cancelled. The reason for releasing the information was "to ease the fears" of Coloradans and residents of other Rocky Mountain states.

Two days later, a completely different story got out.

"Denver Hears CCC Prepares Alien Camps," was the headline in the *Rocky Mountain News*. Although officials at the Colorado-Wyoming district CCC headquarters would not comment on any preparations for the camps, there were reports that they were being made ready for occupancy. "Large quantities of supplies and other equipment, consigned to various sectors of the state, were moving yesterday throughout Colorado," the paper reported. The United Press in Durango reported that a camp there was being cleaned up and visitors were barred. Sources told media outlets they had seen truckloads of CCC boys from camps moving throughout the state.

The letters, postcards, phone calls, and telegrams began again immediately. "Have we any way of always knowing who are our friends and who are our enemies?" wrote Miss Grace Quinby, a social studies teacher in California. "Since we are so often unable to know these facts, why take chances with any of them?"

As FBI agents arrested hundreds of enemy aliens on the West Coast on February 21, the oldest living inhabitant of Elbert County posed with a Bowie knife in hand, comparing the war of today with the war against Indians that he fought in Colorado in the 1870s. "Japs is just like Injuns," said John Lewis Baldwin. "My old dad always told me to remember a good Injun was a dead Injun. Same way with these here Japs."

At the same time, Coloradans battling the war in the Pacific were making sad headlines of their own. The *Rocky Mountain News* reported that twenty-nine Coloradans were being held prisoner by the Japanese. An airway worker whose parents lived in Colorado Springs had been captured. Samuel J. Millward Jr. was among the forty-six feared taken at the Pan-American port in Manila.

Any movement by Japanese in Colorado resulted in a newspaper story. When eleven Japanese bearing travel permits from Los Angeles authorities arrived in Colorado on their way to pick peas, it made the news. The Associated Press reported that local police chief Robert Peel called the head of the Denver FBI office for permission to let them pass.

Nine-year-old Leo Goto remembered being in the pickup truck with five of his siblings and his parents, coming over Loveland Pass from California to live with aunts and uncles already in southeastern Colorado. Authorities stopped the truck at the top of the pass, asked dozens of questions, and offered numerous skeptical looks before allowing the family to continue. Nine miles and thousands of feet in elevation later in Georgetown, the Goto family realized it had left a family member atop the pass. That's how nervous American families of Japanese descent were at that time.

February 24 brought another denial from West Coast officials in charge of enemy alien control. The United Press story said that widespread reports that Colorado's CCC camps were being prepared for "concentration camps for Japanese [were] positively not true." It did nothing to allay the fears of residents.

"Governor Carr, as a housewife, mother and grandmother, I plead with you to veto any such murderous thing," wrote Mrs. Gilbert Worrell from Colorado Springs. "It is dangerous enough to have them in the lettuce gardens in California. A lady said the other day that she had found glass in a California head of lettuce … [and] a cousin told me she had found glass in a can of canned food. Oh please realize this, and stop any such a move."

"Keep them yellow rats from California out of Colorado," Mr. and Mrs. R. F. Shull of Platteville wrote. "We are buying bonds to exterminate them, not feed and house them." Another resident wrote, "I'll take a pop or two with my old Lion shoot-gun if'n Japs get into our valley."

The American Legion Post No. 6 out of Las Animas followed up on the concept that violence might be likely if any freedom was allowed to those of Japanese descent. Clarence Couch, the adjutant, wrote the governor, "Some morning, some citizens of Colorado will receive a telegram from the Navy or War Department telling of the death of his son, killed in action. These citizens will feel very bitter toward all aliens and his bitterness might cause him to take a shot at the first Japanese he saw. If he did, where would we be?"

The politicians were piling it on, pandering to a demanding public. The secretary of the Loveland Chamber of Commerce said he had letters from Colorado's two U.S. senators and its Fourth District congressman that echoed the sentiments of many Coloradans. A. H. Sampson told the *Rocky Mountain News* that Senator Johnson, Senator Millikin, and Representative William Hill had expressed a "unanimous opinion against an importation of Japanese to Colorado."

Wyoming's governor Nels Smith sent a telegram to U.S. Attorney General Biddle, saying, "The state of Wyoming, while willing to render every assistance in our war program, cannot acquiesce to the importation of these Japanese into our state."

Still Governor Carr remained silent. The unusual politician who liked responding to every piece of mail that came to his office was avoiding the issue. His notes to Colorado citizens weren't always long, they weren't always full of significant detail, but they were always personal, until now.

The governor who had cautioned the state's council of defense against judging a man based on the color of his skin rather than the content of his character the day after Pearl Harbor was mute.

The governor who had reminded Coloradans two days later in a statewide radio address that "we cannot test the degree of a man's affection for his fellows or his devotion to his country by the birthplace of his grandfathers" was still.

But those stands had been taken when the conversation was about Colorado's roughly twenty-seven hundred residents of Japanese descent, not when the possibility arose of anywhere from five to forty times that number could be sent to the state in the name of national security. Few knew how or if that changed the governor's stance.

The reporters weren't backing down. His fellow politicians wanted answers. Most important, the public demanded to know his policy. They'd find out soon enough.

When the governor did make a statement, it was strong and clear.

Chapter Eight
Late February 1942

Ralph Carr's temper was legendary around the office.

His jowls would shake. His face reddened. His voice boomed. Although he was a physically small man, he could make others feel smaller.

"When he got [angry], he scared people," said his secretary Myrtle Graham. "He wasn't kidding."

No politician was too big. No businessman too powerful. No detail too small. Anything could trigger one of those moments that would make his staff whistle, say "whew," and hope the storm blew over quickly.

One time after a football game at the University of Denver, the line of cars to leave the parking lot seemed to go on forever. The governor was an impatient man by nature. He felt a wasted minute was a wasted opportunity. When it finally came time for his car to move, another driver cut in line, blocking the governor's car.

"You son of a bitch!" Carr yelled out the window.

The other driver, built like a Denver bungalow, stopped the car and got out to confront the man who had cursed at him.

Road rage consumed Carr, who didn't hesitate to challenge the man now towering above him. "I called you by your right name, didn't I?" Carr demanded.

The other driver blinked, realizing who he was looking down at. "Yes, you did, Governor," he said. "I made a serious mistake. I'm sorry."

They returned to their cars, and Carr waved at the man as he drove away.

"[The tantrums] lasted but a few minutes," said Wayne Patterson, Carr's personal state patrol officer. "You never had to wonder where he stood on anything. He was governor every minute."

February 19, 1942, provided one of those tantrums. The staff was in the office, some in the chairs surrounding his desk, a couple on an oversized uncomfortable sofa against the north wall, when a telegram from the White House arrived. It was Executive Order no. 9066, allowing the military virtually unlimited authority in security areas up and down the West Coast. It ordered martial law and gave the army wide latitude to oust or bar anyone from military areas. The implied goal was to remove anyone of Japanese descent.

Carr's eyes flashed. The disdain in his voice was apparent. He was furious.

"Now, that's wrong!" he shouted. "Some of these Japanese are citizens of the United States."

He couldn't believe what he was reading.

"They're American citizens."

The more he spoke, the angrier he got. No one dared interrupt.

"Why would a man want to put that kind of an order out? Why would a man want to put those people in jail?"

No one answered.

"I'm not going to do it. They're citizens of the United States."

Someone asked about the alien Japanese, the ones who could be involved in espionage and sabotage. Carr stepped back from his earlier declaration of friendship. The war had taken its toll.

"Yes, I'd put them in [jail] in a minute and be tickled to death to do it, but I'm not going to put any United States citizens in jail. There's some good people among the Japanese, like there is in every race of people.

"If the president wants to put those people in concentration camps, he's going to have to foot the bill. He's going to have to take care of them. I've got a National Guard, but I'm not going to use them to guard United States citizens."

He'd soon have the opportunity to share that message with more than just his staff.

Representative John Tolan, a California Democrat, had flown

out to the West Coast from Washington for an emergency set of congressional hearings designed to study "national defense migration," or, in other words, the Japanese issue. Tolan was set to hear from the western commander, General DeWitt, and California governor Cuthbert Olson. The first hearing would be in San Francisco with others slated for Portland, Seattle, and Los Angeles.

The last Sunday in February brought news of a spy sweep all along the West Coast, with government raids capturing enemy aliens from San Diego to Seattle. It also brought ominous news from Congressman Tolan that residents in the Rocky Mountain states did not want to hear.

"It is practically certain the Pacific coast will be bombed," Tolan said. "It is practically certain that we will have to evacuate hundreds of thousands from the West Coast, and we should certainly set up federal agencies to meet the problem. The Pacific coast is definitely in danger. Danger from attack and danger from [espionage]."

In the next breath, Tolan ruled out using Nevada or Arizona for receiving evacuees because the states had no room. Colorado was certainly in his sites. State officials had estimated that Colorado could hold up to thirty-five thousand enemy aliens on farms, and that didn't take into consideration the virtually empty Civilian Conservation Corps camps throughout the state.

As if Tolan and his fellow congressmen needed further proof about the wishes of the people who lived on the West Coast, California attorney general Earl Warren answered that emphatically as one of the first witnesses to testify at the hearings.

"American-born Japanese are a menace," he said. "Many of them have gone to Japan for a large part of their education and have been indoctrinated with Japanese ideas of imperialism and the religious fanaticism which surrounds the emperor. There are many American-Japanese who speak very little English."

A bizarre and scary incident that wasn't reported in the press but was putting pressure on Warren, Tolan, and California authorities was an attack on the U.S. mainland that had been feared since Pearl Harbor. A Japanese submarine, commanded by a former freighter captain who felt he had been humiliated during an earlier visit to the United States, surfaced near an oil field pier just north of Santa Barbara, California. The sub shelled the pier and the neighboring area; the pier was damaged, but no one was injured. The government was sure it was the first of many attacks.

Carr helped the Council of Defense send out ideas and news statewide about the war and how to win it. By the middle of February, one hundred local defense councils had been established. One of the biggest was in Colorado Springs, soon to be the home of Camp Carson and the thirty thousand men the army planned to train there. One of that council's projects was a window display in a downtown department store that depicted the city under attack, showing what could happen in Colorado.

Coloradans were donating not just men and work to the war effort, they were also buying war bonds in bulk. In the tiny town of Walsenburg in southern Colorado, more than $220,000 in defense bonds and stamps had been purchased since November, more than any other city its size in the country.

As rumors of the humiliating treatment of the Japanese toward captured American soldiers emerged, anger toward the Japanese grew. One story making the rounds told of Marine prisoners of war in captured Shanghai being forced to haul "Japanese war lords around in rickshaws."

"Whether these stories be true or not, they contribute nothing to local calm," wrote the *Greeley Daily Tribune*. "They can be expected to be intensified thruout [*sic*] the war."

Back on the coast, Congressman Tolan concluded that evacuation was necessary, and now he needed to figure out how to make it happen. He sent the governors of the Rocky Mountain states a telegram, hoping to have a number of questions answered for the record.

"Many witnesses here are urging that we send ... all Japanese of whatever citizenship to areas east of the borders of California, Oregon, and Washington," Tolan cabled from Portland on February 27. "What is [the] response of your state to this proposal? How many of these people could your state assimilate? What opportunity would there be for employing these people in useful work?

"Under what plan would you consider such movement feasible? What do you think is the attitude to the people of your state towards such a movement?"

Ralph Carr knew this was the right time to share with Coloradans the speech he had been writing and rewriting all week, one that he had already asked radio stations to broadcast on February 28. His speech would serve as a real answer to the overwhelming number of letters from constituents, letters he simply couldn't respond to.

In a form letter before the radio address, he said, "Instead of answering your letter which comes with hundreds of others, I am broadcasting my views on a statewide hookup … to save time and work. Will you please listen to my statement and I should be happy to hear from you further then."

As he went through the stacks of mail, it was obvious that people were terrified at the thought of anyone who looked Japanese moving to Colorado.

"We are at war with Japan thru no fault of our own and just as their government is treacherous, so is every individual slant-eyed, yellow wasp of their people," housewife Mrs. Roy Puckett wrote from Boulder. "We've been mad since December 7 and are considerably madder at the idea of bringing 3,500 of these yellow devils into this state."

Another woman identifying herself only as "A Mother," wrote Carr, "Why should these dirty rats run around while we mothers and fathers are eating our heart out for our loved ones."

Rumors were carried in newspapers throughout the state about the CCC camps being "rehabilitated as Japanese concentration barracks." Despite the denial from government officials with the

Enemy Alien Control Unit, United Press reporter Willard Hasel-bush wrote, "Reports that Japanese aliens from the West Coast will be moved into Colorado and other states of the Rocky Mountain area for the duration of the war still persisted today."

Numerous papers carried his story, many on their front pages.

It didn't help morale to read stories like the one in the *Rocky Ford Enterprise*: "Jap Aliens Rounded Up in Alaska are Well-Treated." The story quoted Harry Kawabe, a wealthy Japanese man who was placed in an army camp after Pearl Harbor. "The food is fine, of excellent quality and ample quantity," he said. "We are kept in a warm and comfortable dormitory. We have books, magazines, and writing materials."

The Fort Collins newspaper printed a quote from an assistant U.S. attorney in San Diego who said that Japanese residents in the military zone would be sent somewhere east of the Sierra Nevada mountain range in California. The government attorney insisted he had been told "authoritatively" that evacuation orders were being drawn up for anyone of Japanese descent, including those who were American citizens.

Colorado's War Board chairman Dewey Harmon was bombarded with questions by the federal government in the two weeks since his first public comments started the speculation. He said the feds were wondering if the state could step up vegetable production, whether adequate farm labor was available to handle increased production, and "whether the people of the state would have any objection to the importation into the state of Japanese farm laborers, if properly supervised."

He told the *Pueblo Chieftain* that he believed the request indicated plans to send Japanese to Colorado. This contradicted the message Colorado's congressional delegation was getting in Washington. The state's senior U.S. senator, Edwin Johnson, cabled reporters from the capitol that the army would not be confining any Japanese in either the CCC camps or using them in the sugar beet areas as farm laborers. The Associated Press reported that Johnson's opinion was based on the fact "he had [personally] made a careful check of all government departments which might be concerned with the move" and he had found no evidence to suggest it would happen.

What should anyone believe? Uncertainty raised the level of fear.

"[We are] protesting California's Asiatic, almond-eyed, yellow-bellied, sneaking skunks," Mr. and Mrs. Cline wrote Governor Carr from Denver.

An unsigned letter to the governor suggested how to deal with any possible espionage that could result from their importation. "To meet any [sabotage] in Colorado ... we have enough Duck shooters and Deer hunters to amply take care of it."

Carr's secretary went over to 747 Downing Street the last Saturday in February to take down the governor's speech before typing it for delivery later that night. He was alone when she arrived.

The governor had received reports that an overwhelming majority of aliens were registering in Colorado. In Denver, 1,830 subjects of Japan, Germany, and Italy were required to register, and postmaster James Stevic said "less than a dozen" failed to do so. He told the *Rocky Mountain News* that there had been no problems during the three-week registration period and that he "saw quite a few people leave the registration counter and walk around the corner to buy defense stamps and bonds."

However, the governor knew that registering those aliens already living here differed dramatically from the idea that thousands of others could move to Colorado. As he readied his remarks, he cursed under his breath at the huge, front-page story in that morning's *Denver Post*. The paper reported findings from Texas congressman Martin Dies's Committee on Un-American Activities. The article was titled, "Dies Unfolds Startling Report" in small print, and then, in a headline below it twice the size, it read, "American-Born Japs Active Spies."

"A startling recital of years of Japanese spying on American military and naval activities and vital water and oil supplies, combined with careful scouting of the Pacific coastline, was unfolded in a report tonight," the article read. The committee presented maps, pictures, intercepted messages, and testimony to "support its charges that Japanese aliens and American-born, formed a menacing [spy ring] in California."

Congressman Dies told reporters how movement of the American fleet was being watched "by Japanese 'fishermen' who in reality were naval officers." The committee quoted a witness who said, "The fishing crews became totally Japanese as soon as they were clear of the American shore, frequently hoisted Japanese flags, took pictures of the shore lines, and any American naval vessel encountered."

As the governor began dictating his speech, Myrtle Graham found herself "spellbound." The wording was so crisp, the analogies so clear, the message so powerful, his secretary would later call the speech "a humdinger."

The governor hadn't scheduled his speech until 10:15 that Saturday night, figuring more people would be home then. He would be on the radio after programs like *Believe It or Not with Bob Ripley*, *The Green Hornet*, *Cab Calloway's Music Hour*, and the day's news program.

If Carr's mail was any indication, the state wanted to know where he stood, sooner rather than later.

The governor, however, had other business to attend to that night before his talk—namely dinner in Boulder and attending a basketball game at his alma mater. He had tickets to the Big Seven Conference championship basketball game at the University of Colorado field house.

An active supporter of the university and a fiercely loyal fan to its teams, the former sportswriter sat among five thousand fans just hours before the most eagerly anticipated address of his tenure as chief executive. The CU Buffaloes stomped Brigham

Young University, 52–35, to capture their third undisputed conference title in the last four years. Carr hoped the result was a good omen.

Back in Denver, his fifteen-minute address would be carried live on four different stations that covered the entire state. He would take his views straight to the people, just as he had done during the budget crisis and the labor riots. Surely they'd understand. They'd realize the truth in his words. They'd see the wisdom behind his position.

"Pray for me," he told his staff as he got ready to speak. "Pray that I'm making the right decision."

And then Ralph Carr delivered the speech that would define his career.

> People of Colorado:
>
> In answer to the call of our country, Colorado has done everything in her power to uphold the hands of our national leaders in carrying on the battle for humanity, for liberty, and for civilization. Our people have sent their dearest possessions to the ten or a dozen battlefronts where the Stars and Stripes are leading in the fight on savagery, paganism, and the worldwide imposition of servitude upon freemen.
>
> Today, because of a lack of information and perhaps also because of an unhappy interpretation which has been placed upon certain rumors, Colorado as a state is threatened with a charge of a disinclination to cooperate in essential war efforts. A suspicion of a lack of patriotism which is not deserved and which cannot be permitted to go unanswered has been raised.
>
> A few weeks ago rumors came that alien residents of the Pacific Coast states of Japanese origin were to be evacuated and perhaps 3,500 would be sent to Colorado. From some unidentified source came another suggestion, probably born of unfriendly propaganda parentage, that California was attempting to dump a bothersome problem into Colorado's lap. The first inclination

of every Coloradan was one of resentment. There was a feeling that we did not want enemy aliens within our borders who might acquire property rights, who might compete with Colorado labor, and whose presence would be a constant menace and threat to our peaceful conditions of life. Acting on this first impulse, many persons voiced a protest by mail, by telegraph, and, in some instances, through statements in the daily press. Colorado has been placed in a peculiar and embarrassing light. An official request has been made for a survey of our facilities for harboring aliens of all classes—Italians, Germans, and Japanese. Last week, a presidential order was issued directing the establishment of military zones in the United States, from which any person can be excluded. Clearly, this refers specifically to the West Coast.

In the hope that I may assist in clarifying the situation by establishing our position toward this and other national problems and our patriotism and sincerity of purpose, this announcement is made.

Colorado must never be charged with a failure to cooperate in the gravest moment of our nation's history. Three months ago, no American dreamed that the Japanese or any other people could dominate the Pacific by force of arms. Today many strongholds, including the Gibraltar of the East at Singapore, have fallen. Our own ships, our own air forces, our own army have suffered severe losses. The blood of American soldiers stains the soil of nearly every island in the Far East.

Tonight, as General Douglas MacArthur and his glorious band of Americans and Filipinos set new records for bravery and resourcefulness in the Bataan Peninsula in the face of terrific odds, we have finally come to guess the seriousness of the situation. The enemy controls the very conduct of life in every corner of the world since it has seized the countries where essential raw materials are produced.

There can be no question that the attacks on Pearl Harbor and the Philippines were aided by fifth columnists [saboteurs].

The potency of that evil organization has been proved in every European country which has fallen, exemplified by the desertion of France, as Winston Churchill described it, and the rape of Norway and the rest. The overthrow of any nation is assured when the approach of an attacking force is made smooth and paved by subversive activities within.

Along the Pacific Coast there are thousands of persons who are not friendly to those things which we call American. Only Monday night of this week, the beautiful country surrounding Santa Barbara in Southern California was attacked by an enemy submarine which came to the surface and hurled shells at a great supply of gasoline. The enemy has become so confident that he knocks at the very front door of one of the great cities of the world and attacks the mainland of the United States.

Military strategists say that if Java falls, then Australia will constitute the only barrier between California and the enemy. Fifth columnists—our enemies—are within signaling distance of any plane, any battleship, any submarine which approaches our coast. Attacks similar to that one of Monday night, fraught with infinitely more serious consequences, are to be expected any minute.

And if Australia, New Zealand, Java, and Sumatra fall, we know what the next move will be. We will be put to it to protect our shoreline from Canada to Mexico against the most aggressive, the most effective, the most dangerous war machine that has ever been assembled. The defense of California is the defense of Colorado, of the United States of America, of the cause of the United Allies. It is the defense of the very future of that civilization which we value above everything else.

If those who command the armed forces of our nation say that it is necessary to remove any persons from the Pacific Coast and call upon Colorado to do her part in this war by furnishing temporary quarters for those individuals, we stand ready to carry out that order. If any enemy aliens must be transferred as a war measure, then we of Colorado are big enough and patriotic enough to do our duty. We announce to the world that 1,118,000 red-blooded citizens of this state are able to take care of 3,500 or any number of enemies, if that be the task which is allotted to us.

When our boys are facing thousands of them along the battlefronts of the Pacific; when Americans are being cut down by the withering fire of machine guns; when our ships are sunk by treacherous planes while their diplomats sue for peace, when our very shores are shelled by submarines—Colorado will not complain because she is asked to take care of a handful of undesirables whose presence on the coast might prove the difference between a successful invasion and the saving of our country.

We do not welcome any enemy aliens from any country into this state. But by the same token, we do not rejoice that our boys are conscripted. We find no happiness in the daily casualty lists which we scan for familiar names with fear and trepidation. We do not glory in the fact that we have been drawn into the most terrible warfare that humankind has ever invented. There is no pleasure in the sacrifice of great industries and the surrender of private rights for the good of the nation. In fact, there is nothing connected with this war which renders it desirable. But as patriots, as Americans, as Coloradans, we say to the world—we say to our leaders—Colorado will do her part and more.

The people of Colorado are giving their sons, are offering their possessions, are surrendering their rights and privileges to the end that this war may be fought to victory and permanent peace. If it is our duty to receive disloyal persons, we shall welcome the performance of that task.

This statement must not be construed as an invitation, however. Only because the needs of our nation dictate it, do we even consider such an arrangement. In making the transfers, we can feel assured that governmental agencies will take every precaution to protect our people, our defense projects, and our property from the same menace which demands their removal from those sections. And in this connection, I think it is only fair for us to ask in the placement of evacuees that local conditions and the needs of our communities be consulted. Sources of water supply, timber growth, and essential industrial activities should be considered. The protection of wildlife is a major concern in Colorado.

For an understanding of the reasons for the possible evacuation of such enemy aliens, let us hear a story told by an American, a Colorado girl now living in Hawaii. She witnessed the attack on Pearl Harbor. She saw the awful results of those unbelievable assassinations. Many planes, manned by Japanese pilots, were shot down by the American anti-aircraft guns. And the bodies of those pilots shout a warning which we cannot ignore. And when the break came, when Japan loosed its attack on Pearl Harbor, the rings and insignia of the graduating classes of high schools and colleges of the islands and the Pacific Coast of the United States were found on the fingers of many of the Japanese pilots who fell under American gunfire.

All of these educated Japanese are not pilots, however. All of them are not confined to the city of Tokio [*sic*]. Nor do they constitute all of the people who dislike Americans and America. They are to be found wherever there are Japanese, Italians, and Germans—and particularly in California.

In justice and fairness, let us pause here to speak a word in behalf of loyal German, Italian, and Japanese citizens who must not suffer for the activities and animosities of others. In Colorado there are thousands of men and women and children—in the nation there are millions of them—who by reason of blood only, are regarded by some people as unfriendly.

They are as loyal to American institutions as you or I. Many of them have been here—are American citizens, with no connection with or feeling of loyalty toward the customs and philosophies of Italy, Japan, or Germany.

The world's great melting pot is peopled by the descendants of every nation in the globe. It is not fair for the rest of us to segregate the people from one or two or three nations and to brand them as unpatriotic or disloyal regardless.

The coming of these evacuees will, of necessity, give rise to social problems, to business and labor questions, and similar vexing issues. But surely we possess the brains, the resources, the solid American character which will enable us to solve those problems properly and intelligently.

People of Colorado, let us remember that we have a job to do. Answers which would be correct under ordinary circumstances do not apply when all conditions are changed. We are at war. We must realize that.

Let us approach these social and economic problems with a new attitude of mind. Let us get that job done as quickly as possible so that our boys may come home and we may return to our American way of life.

Men of Colorado, if MacArthur and a handful of men can hold off hundreds of thousands of Japanese under the conditions which they face, we can control the conduct of any little group which may be sent to Colorado.

And finally, I urge upon our people the danger of inflammatory statements and threats against these unwelcome guests. The newspapers report that some aroused citizens have threatened force against the approach of undesirables. In my presence the other morning, a young man in uniform quoted a superior as favoring the firing squad as the solution of this problem.

Such reckless statements may bring reactions which we shall always regret. Let it be understood that such conduct is not approved by the code of humanity. Americans have too great a sense of fair play. Let it also be known that we do not hold all the cards and that reprisals would be visited upon our own soldiers, officers, and citizens who will be taken prisoners before this is over.

Let us consider ourselves as part of a great army, engaged in the most righteous war in history. No good soldier interferes with the activities of his superiors.

People of Colorado, let us all be good soldiers. Let us accept the fortunes of war with heads up. This is a solemn affair. We must approach it in that attitude of mind.

A blizzard of calls and letters engulfed the Sunday papers before spreading to the governor's office on Monday. Those who did not stay awake long enough to hear the speech on radio could read it in its entirety in a number of newspapers over the next few days. Not all the comments were negative.

From southern Colorado, the *Pueblo Chieftain* ran a rare page-one editorial titled, "Gov. Carr is Eminently Right in His Stand on Enemy Aliens." It included this statement: "There was profound wisdom in [Carr's] admonition that if the United States did not accord civil treatment to the nationals of our enemy countries, we of the United States could expect unthinkable reprisals toward our citizens who are their prisoners."

From western Colorado, the *Grand Junction Sentinel* published a telegram sent by the city's chamber of commerce directors expressing no "serious objections" to the internment of Japanese aliens in their area. "We consider it our patriotic duty to cooperate in this and all other war measures."

The state's largest paper, the *Denver Post*, disagreed. Throughout many of its eighty-two pages on March 1, it attacked both the position and politician who believed in it. The paper was known as Colorado's leading Republican Party paper, or as John Gunther would later describe it in his travelogue *Inside U.S.A.*, "the most lunatic paper in the United States as well as one of the most conservative." Gunther wrote, "[The *Post's*] presentation of news was often murderously vindictive."

Carr had felt the wrath of the paper during the "shock" and "scandal" caused by the pardons and commutations he granted certain criminals during his first term. However, as a former newspaperman, he realized the importance of cultivating a relationship with the newspaper's leaders.

After the 1940 election, Carr had written editor William

Shepherd thanking him for the paper's coverage. "I think if we were to search through the newspaper morgues in the whole country in the last fifty years, we would find no newspaper which supported any cause more unselfishly, more courageously, and more intelligently than did the *Denver Post* in carrying the banner for the Republican presidential nominee and for myself."

The editor wrote Carr back in equally flattering prose. "I firmly believe that during the next two years, you are going to make a record that will stamp you as the best governor the state of Colorado has ever had.

"I hope you thoroughly enjoy your second term as Colorado's chief executive, and I know you will because you will be eternally fighting for what you know is right; and although they are sometimes discouraging, those are the battles which bring contentment."

Shepherd forgot those words during the early spring of 1942. On that Sunday, March 1, all harmony was set aside. The roughly 273,000 newspapers sold that day declared that the political hunting season for the state's chief executive had begun.

Starting on page one, an editorial cartoon showed a combination Uncle Sam–Governor Carr figure standing over three little boys sitting on a couch with halos over their heads. They were drawn to represent German, Japanese, and Italian kids. A knife sticks out from the pocket of the Italian and a gun from the pocket of the Japanese. Tags attached to the kids' clothing read "Enemy Aliens," "Sabotage," and "Map of U.S. Defenses." The caption read, "Uncle Softheart—I Wonder if They Are Real Angels?" The lead story that day was titled: "Colorado Likely to get Aliens Despite Protests." Readers were told, "Removal in the near future of an undetermined number of Japanese from west coast defense areas to Colorado appeared Saturday to be more than just a probability, despite growing opposition in this state to such action by the government."

Post readers could turn the page and read another editorial blasting Carr's position. "Governor Carr has taken a 'fence-

The day after Governor Carr championed the Constitutional rights of Japanese Americans and said he would not fight the federal government's decision to intern non-American citizen Japanese, the stance was decried on *The Denver Post*'s front page, its opinion page, and many in between. Carr drew on his political hero, Abraham Lincoln, for his belief that the Constitution and the rights of American citizens should not be trampled on, even during a time of war.

straddling' position on the Jap alien question. His statement certainly does not express the sentiment of the people of Colorado. Instead of coming right out and saying, 'COLORADO DOESN'T WANT THESE YELLOW DEVILS AND DOESN'T INTEND TO ALLOW THIS STATE TO BE TURNED INTO A SANCTUARY FOR ENEMIES OF THE AMERICAN PEOPLE,' he makes the announcement that, 'If it is our duty to receive disloyal persons, we shall welcome the performance of the task.'

"The people of Colorado are NOT going to welcome any Jap aliens transferred here from Pacific coast areas. WE DON'T HAVE TO EXPRESS LOVE FOR THE JAPS AND A WILLINGNESS TO PROVIDE THEM WITH HOMES TO DEMONSTRATE OUR PATRIOTISM. Over in the Philippines and down the East Indies, JAPS ARE TRYING TO KILL EVERY AMERICAN THEY CAN FIND. Japs in the United States are just as much our enemies as are the Japs in Japan ...

"The position taken by the governor amounts to a backhanded invitation ... if the government should try to force Colorado to allow a few thousand of these Japs to land and stay at liberty in the state, we might not be able to prevent that. But it certainly should be made plain now that WE DON'T WANT THESE JAPS IN COLORADO. WE WILL NOT WILLINGLY RECEIVE THEM, and with all due respect to the governor, WE DO NOT CONSIDER IT A PATRIOTIC DUTY TO PROVIDE SANCTUARY FOR OUR ENEMIES, even if somebody in Washington does ask that."

On page eight, the *Post* asked nearly twenty Denver residents—some civic leaders, some state and federal officials, some average folks—for their thoughts on the issue. No one came out with anything positive to say about Governor Carr, although a few posited that if Japanese were sent to Colorado, they should all be placed in concentration camps and "kept under strict federal supervision at all times."

Asked his opinion, Denver District Court judge George Dunklee said, "I certainly am opposed to it. We don't want them."

Mrs. Frances Borg, a housewife, told the paper, "We should give the Japanese aliens their choice of getting out of the country or going into a concentration camp. They are not entitled to their freedom."

Business executive R. E. Pate Jr. said, "All Japs not born in this country ought to be shipped back to Tokyo. ... I certainly do not favor bringing any of them to Colorado."

Robert Harvey, Denver's tire-rationing administrator, told the paper, "If the Japanese aliens are a menace to our safety, they are just as much a menace in Colorado as in California."

Maybe businessman J. Nevin Carson summarized the newspaper sentiment best when he said, "Nobody wants them."

Readers turning to the "Open Forum" section of the newspaper, where letters to the editor were published, found more venom directed toward anyone who looked Japanese and more venom toward their governor.

Mrs. Eleanor Schweikhardt wanted hard labor and concentration camps for the enemy aliens. "We Americans," she wrote, "are always afraid of taking away someone's liberty and what have we now." Lula Baker of Denver said, "If California wants to get rid of them, why not dump them in the ocean?" Henry John Demarest wondered, "In the name of the great Jehovah, isn't there anything that can be done to keep the Japanese alien enemies out of our beloved state?"

Back in California, the man in charge of security for the West Coast finally broke his public silence on the topic. General DeWitt said the army was ready to announce an evacuation program based solely on the "yardstick" of military needs. One of those needs was the "exclusion of certain groups" from the West Coast, meaning anyone of Japanese descent.

At his press briefing in Denver that Monday morning, March 2, the governor announced that the state was largely in favor of the

STANDARD TIME INDICATED
RECEIVED AT

Postal Telegraph

Mackay Radio   All America Cables
Commercial Cables   Canadian Pacific Telegraphs

THIS IS A FULL RATE TELEGRAM, CABLE-
GRAM OR RADIOGRAM UNLESS OTHERWISE
INDICATED BY SYMBOL IN THE PREAMBLE
OR IN THE ADDRESS OF THE MESSAGE.
SYMBOLS DESIGNATING SERVICE SELECTED
ARE OUTLINED IN THE COMPANY'S TARIFFS
ON HAND AT EACH OFFICE AND ON FILE WITH
REGULATORY AUTHORITIES.

TELEPHONE YOUR TELEGRAMS
TO POSTAL TELEGRAPH

LA129x   LB115V TWS GOVT PAID 3 MINS=FTLOGAN COLO 1 648P

HON RALPH L CARR GOVERNOR OF COLORADO=   1942 MAR 1 PM 7 22

(DELIVER TONIGHT WHETHER IT BE CAPITOL BLDG OR RESIDENCE)
DENVER COLO=

93 WD YOUR POSITION AS TO THE WILLINGNESS OF COLORADO TO AID IN
SOLVING THE JAPANESE EVACUATION PROBLEM IS A MOST LAUDABLE ONE
STOP I AM HOPEFUL THAT THE GOVERNORS OF OTHER STATES IN THIS
REGION WILL TAKE A SIMILAR POSITION AS IT WILL BE MOST HELPFUL
TO ME IN SOLVING THE PROBLEM=
    J L DEWITT COMMANDING WDC AND FOURTH ARMY
PRESOFSANFRANCISCO.

Governor Carr tried to tamp down the protests by showing reporters this telegram from General John DeWitt, who was in charge of
military operations on the West Coast. Carr would routinely argue
that his position helped the war effort and that those against it were
not as patriotic as he. Despite DeWitt's hopes that other governors
would take "a similar position," they blasted the federal government, threatening to order out National Guard troops to keep Japanese from crossing their borders. Wyoming governor Nels Smith
went so far as to say that if anyone of Japanese descent was sent to
his state, they'd be "hanging from every pine tree."

stand he had taken. He had no evidence to support the assertion, but he was once again trying to dictate how the story was covered. It appeared to work with the majority of newspapers. He told reporters, "I have received only one telegram and two letters protesting my stand. The others upheld my belief that it is a patriotic duty for the state to assist the war effort in every way possible."

The United Press was convinced. "The people of Colorado applauded the stand taken by Governor Ralph L. Carr on the internment of enemy aliens in the state." Carr released a telegram he had received Sunday night from General DeWitt complimenting him on the "most laudable" of positions. "I am hopeful governors of other states in this region will take a similar position," DeWitt wrote, "and it will be most helpful in solving the problem."

Carr had not yet read his daily mail, the slew of letters and telegrams that covered his desk and were uniformly opposed to his decision.

Reporters looking for the other side of the story did not have to go far. Up one marble staircase at the capitol, they found state senator Robert Elder, who earned himself a "Person of the Week" honor in the *Post* with his comments. The World War I infantry captain chastised Carr's "remote generalities" and "sacrificial flag waving," which he felt left Colorado's gate wide open "to whatever inundation of cheap labor and fifth-column sabotage the harassed coast authorities may choose to turn loose on us. For they will find no other governor quite so obliging.

"It is unfortunately up to you as governor of Colorado to clarify the equivocal and disastrous stand you seem to have taken," Elder wrote in a letter to Carr. "It is up to you to move fast and get Colorado out from behind that eight ball.

"If the Japs come to Colorado beet fields, farms, ranches, mines, they're YOURS governor. Not mine."

Elder was right on one account. No other governor in the area was going to be quite so "obliging." Colorado's governor, living in a landlocked state, found himself on a political island.

Telegrams from other governors in the region were released by Congressman Tolan, who was in Seattle for a committee hearing on the topic. Only Carr expressed a full willingness to "aid in solving the Japanese evacuation problem." He realized he had no choice. States' rights gave way to national security. Lincoln and the Civil War had taught him that.

Each western governor was as familiar with history as Carr. They knew the inevitable outcome, yet none risked their livelihood like Carr.

Wyoming governor Nels Smith said, "The citizens of our state are unalterably opposed to such a plan."

Arizona governor Sidney Osborn said, "We do not propose to be made a dumping ground for enemy aliens from any other state. We not only vigorously protest, but will not permit the evacuation of Japanese, German, or Italian aliens to any point in Arizona."

Montana governor Sam Ford said, "From information received, opinion here [is] opposed to importation of enemy aliens into Montana."

Arkansas governor Homer Adkins said, "We are always anxious to cooperate in any way we can, but our people, being more than 95 percent native born, are in no manner familiar with their customs and ways and have never had any of them within our borders, and I doubt the wisdom of placing any in Arkansas."

Kansas governor Payne Ratner said, "The infiltration of enemy aliens into our loyal Kansas communities would distinctly menace the security of our war industries, and would weaken the advantage our state offers to the nation as an area with maximum safety against attack from abroad and sabotage from within."

Nebraska governor Dwight Griswold said, "Your telegram … is difficult to answer as I do not understand just how it is planned to handle them. The people of Nebraska would not want these aliens released in this state."

South Dakota governor Harlan Bushfield said, "The people of South Dakota do not want evacuated aliens within our borders."

Idaho governor Chase Clark said, "[It would] be [a] serious mistake to send enemy aliens to the Idaho area on account of opportunity for sabotage of reservoirs."

Nevada governor E. P. Carville said, "People here do not want enemy aliens coming into [a] state promiscuously or being allowed to drift to all parts of [a] state without proper surveillance and supervision."

North Dakota governor John Moses said, "Our state cannot assimilate any of these people."

New Mexico's acting governor, C. R. Quintana, said, "As [a] border state, New Mexico may become [a] strategic area and we therefore oppose such [alien] migration."

Meanwhile, the telephone rang continuously that Monday morning in the Colorado governor's office in response to his Saturday night speech. No other issue, no other topic, had aroused as much public interest, Carr said, since he became governor.

The *Denver Post* attacked again on Monday, slashing both Carr and the federal government's position. "Army to Ignore Protest in Evacuating Coast Aliens" was the page-one headline.

One page later, the paper's editorial writers complimented governors like Smith in Wyoming and Osborn in Arizona for their stand. "IF THESE ALIEN JAPS ARE SO GREAT A MENACE TO CALIFORNIA, FOR EXAMPLE, THAT THEY HAVE TO BE MOVED OUT, THEY ARE TOO MUCH OF A PUBLIC MENACE TO BE TURNED LOOSE IN COLORADO OR WYOMING OR ARIZONA OR ANY OTHER STATE."

The *Post* was not the only paper highly critical of Carr's stand. The *Rocky Ford Daily Gazette-Topic*, a paper serving a largely agricultural audience, wrote, "Spreading [the problem] thruout [*sic*] the nation by putting little bands of aliens all over the west to organize larger bands seems to be inviting trouble. ... Refusing to give farm boys a deferment and then importing enemy aliens to do the work is a more illogical decision than hiring fan dancers to entertain us while we are in air-raid shelters."

Carr knew the citizens of Colorado weren't happy, but he sincerely believed it was a matter of time before they came around to his way of thinking. He wrote Congressman Tolan in Seattle, "The attitude of the people will change in a few days after this broadcast. I do not offer this in an egotistical manner, but I believe the people's patriotism and sense of justice will react favorably to such a suggestion as I am trying to make."

Still, the mail poured in. International Machinists representative W. B. Jordan wrote a polite note, "I trust you will pardon the intrusion, but your statement ... on the west coast Jap situation does not meet with my approval." Mr. and Mrs. John Cook wrote, "We think you have been a great Governor and we have been proud of you and are sorry that we cannot agree with you now. We think you are absolutely wrong."

"By accepting the Japs we have brought the war into our sleepy Eden. Let's hope we wake up," wrote Gertrude Tracy.

A letter signed "A Mother" said, "Sunday, March 1, in Colorado was a beautiful morning, the sun shining bright ... but waking up here one had the same feeling that I imagine you have waking up in Germany. In Germany, the MASTER speaks—the masses have to do his bidding; in Colorado, Governor Carr has spoken and we had the JAPS crammed down our throats whether we liked it or not. Put yourself in the place of a Mother who is sending two boys to fight the JAPS ... you can't change human nature; you can't make we people who have never come in contact with these people before like and associate with them while our loved ones are fighting them."

Not surprising, many notes came from residents on the West Coast, complimenting Carr for his "courageous," "progressive," and "patriotic" stand. "What more than pleased me about your position in the matter was its breadth of understanding, its human and Christian spirit. It just did my soul good to listen to your words," Josiah Poeton wrote from Claremont, California.

"Perhaps if we had more governors like you, our National unity would be more real," wrote Cathleen McAliney from La Jolla, California. A former Coloradan now living in Oregon wrote, "I wish to thank you for the courageous stand that you have taken ... these Japanese do make a dreadful problem."

Carr received some support from within Colorado. The curator of the State Historical Society, LeRoy Hafen, wrote, "Never before, in the eighteen years I have looked across the street, have I seen the gubernatorial chair so ably filled." From Boulder, Benjamin Galland handwrote a note to the governor in which he said the speech "was as high-minded and fine and patriotic an utterance as I have ever heard or read. Thanks for being such an American and such a Governor."

Ralph Carr had more mail waiting in the outer office, representing more views, more opinions, and more anger from Coloradans.

He didn't need the *Rocky Mountain News* to tell him that his statement "proved a shock to a number of persons who were busy organizing against the evacuation plan." People including his cabinet officer and friend Robert Warren.

Carr held to his views; he had found his voice on this topic and trusted it.

The piles of letters would have to wait for a response. He had a meeting with the state Republican Party to attend. This seemed an awkward time to talk politics, but the party hierarchy wanted to know if he was going to run for the U.S. Senate or reelection as governor or anything else in November. It was the beginning of March, still eight months from the election, but they'd want an answer from the governor because many aspiring candidates were looking to "get their campaigns under way before the flowers bloom."

Despite their wishes, he would leave another group unhappy. It was becoming a pattern.

Chapter Nine
Early March 1942

Ralph Carr strode into the elegant Brown Palace Hotel in downtown Denver on an unusually brisk March afternoon, the cold, gloomy weather matching the nation's dismal mood as the war increasingly engulfed the world. News had just come that the country's largest warship in the Far East, the *Houston*, had been sunk, killing hundreds of sailors. At this point in the war the Japanese Navy dominated the seas, and there seemed to be no stopping the Japanese Imperial Army as it marched toward regional domination.

Inside the hotel, Carr was met by warmth from the hotel's massive fireplace. Ladies sat in the luxurious open lobby, enjoying afternoon tea and listening to piano and harp music.

The lobby walls, slabs of onyx installed with mortar made with imported sea sand, reached up eight floors toward the stained-glass ceiling. Looking up, visitors could see more than seven hundred iron grillwork panels ringing the lobby from floors three through seven. Two of those panels had been hung upside down. One was to serve the tradition that man, imperfect by nature, must put a flaw into his work; the other was snuck in by a disgruntled worker.

Walking through the Brown Palace lobby, Carr walked where kings, emperors, and presidents had—the nineteenth-century hotel was considered by many Coloradans to be the nicest hotel in the state. On this day, in Room 235, the Colorado Republican state central committee waited to hear from its governor about his future plans. It was the Republicans' first major gathering of 1942.

Party business had to be attended to before the speeches. The Republicans affirmed that they would hold their convention in July and the central committee voted to increase the number of delegates who could attend to just over thirteen hundred. William Lloyd, an attorney from Pueblo and former state senator, was named Republican Party chairman without opposition. He replaced Arthur Sheely, who had been drafted into the army as a lieutenant.

Lloyd offered his opinion that party politics could still play a role while the war was on. He laid out what he thought the Republican Party strategy should be in the November 1942 elections. Government would go on, he said, whereas an officeholder may not. He said citizens should only support the officeholder if he's devoting 100 percent of his effort to winning the war. This was an obvious reference to their plan to defeat Democratic candidates who were only interested in perpetuating big government, he believed.

When the governor rose to speak, most assumed he would announce his intentions for the fall. The Democrats had shown their hand early, already lining up many candidates for the November election when a full slate of jobs would be on the ballot. The papers reported that the Democrats would be launching "an all-out drive to end GOP superiority." State treasurer Homer Bedford would run for governor. Democratic senator Edwin Johnson would run for reelection, but might face a primary challenge from the wing of his party that felt he did not support President Roosevelt enough. Democratic heavyweights George Saunders and Byron Rogers, swept out by the Carr-led Republican revolution of 1940, wanted to recapture their jobs as secretary of state and attorney general, respectively.

Carr had already told his close friends he truly did not know what he wanted to do, although before the war began, he had been intrigued by the idea of running for the U.S. Senate. A potential battle with "Big Ed" Johnson didn't daunt him. The thought of doing battle with Roosevelt's New Deal philosophy and its "power-grab policies" was appealing. Carr took great pleasure in promoting his pragmatic western pay-as-you-go values as a good solution to the complex budget problems the country was facing.

He also loved running the state. He openly told reporters it

Senator Edwin C. Johnson, known as "Big Ed" and Colorado's most powerful Democrat, puts his arm around Governor Carr in his Capitol Hill office. Johnson was known as the best vote-getter the Democrats had in Colorado, while Carr was the Republican's best candidate. The two would square off in November 1942 in a Senate race where their policy differences were as obvious as their physical differences. Johnson wanted Carr to call out the National Guard to stop the Japanese from coming to Colorado, reminding voters that when he was governor in the 1930s, he had called out the troops to physically remove "Mexican aliens" from the fields during the height of the Depression. Courtesy of the Colorado Historical Society was the best job he'd ever had because it gave him the chance "to do something" for his state and his nation.

Columnist Alva Swain wrote about the pressures facing the governor. "There is great pressure being brot [*sic*] to bear on him to stay where he is and run for the governorship for the third term. It is claimed that he knows more about the details of the office as they will unfold during the next two years than any other man in the state. On the other hand there are many who think he can wrest the seat in the United States Senate from Edwin Johnson and they want him to try for it. Each group is honest in their convictions."

As Carr rose to speak to the gathering, no one quite knew what to expect. He hadn't prepared a formal statement, choosing to speak to the group from his head and heart, a method he had perfected during the numerous jury trials he litigated as a country lawyer.

"My friends have been asking me what I intend to do this fall," Carr told a hushed crowd, pausing for effect. "The plain answer is I don't know. I don't know what the next three or four months will develop and it is the next three or four months that will determine my course. Things might shape themselves during the next few months that I might not be a candidate for any office.

"All I can say now is that I am going to continue to be the kind of citizen that I want to be and say what I believe in saying and I'm going to call the shots as they come."

His speech would be reported the next morning as an "announcement or lack of it." Whether Carr was using strategy or he was genuinely uncertain, his friend, Pueblo judge Harry Strait, saw it as the right direction to take. He expressed approval of Carr's "giving no indication of what you might do politically until May when all matters concerning the nation will crystallize, politically and otherwise. ... [Your indecision] has made it certain that you really don't know what you want to do and let your enemies keep sniping at you for the record later on."

Carr's frankness had always stunned those who didn't know

him well. Many in the room, who had put their own campaign plans on hold awaiting Carr's decision, chafed at their leader's impudence. With no campaign news to report, Carr quickly shifted to a topic that Swain and everyone in the room knew "without doubt" would be a major issue in that fall campaign—his stand to accept Japanese aliens into Colorado.

"The United States—and not any individual state—is fighting this war, and I believe every state should give the government its unqualified cooperation," Carr declared. "This is the most serious situation this nation has ever known, and we as state residents cannot determine the strategy of the commanders of our armed forces."

Not even this roomful of people in his own party were swayed. Many became angrier by the minute. The Republican faithful knew the impact this decision could have on the party statewide, especially if its symbolic leader was seen as the driving force behind it.

Carr had received letters from "loyal Republicans" protesting his stand. Magdalene Blosfeld of Denver wrote, "I cannot understand your attitude regarding this matter ... you are simply inviting trouble if you do this thing. Now, Governor Carr, I hope you will give this your deepest and sincere consideration in not allowing the Japs to come into our dearly beloved Colorado, which has been such a grand privilege to live in and to live for. I am a taxpayer and a loyal citizen for 40 years. I, and my people way back, have been staunch Republicans, but I could never honestly give you my support again if you allow this to our state."

Carr was unapologetic. As he left the hotel and a bewildered, frustrated group of Republicans, Carr told reporters, "I've stuck my neck out on matters of policy but I'm making no apologies because I believe I am right. Colorado leads the western states in its position on this."

When responding to letters, Carr stressed that accepting the enemy Japanese aliens from the West Coast was patriotic.

He made that point to General DeWitt, who ran the Western Defense Command, telling him again, "We will cooperate with you in every way." While offering the state's cooperation, Carr suggested that the needs of local residents be considered. He knew the people, problems, and geography of Colorado and said he could advise them where to relocate the evacuees.

"Please understand that I am not trying to dictate any terms to the Army," he wrote. "It is assumed that all who are evacuated will be under government supervision and surveillance and in the event that they are not, then I wish to be advised so that I may attempt an organization which will protect our people. Many are so hysterical and full of panic that only the very strongest assurance can bring them to the point where they will welcome the unwelcome guests."

The governor's incoming mail indicated many Coloradans were not yet at that point. The "unwelcome guests" remained, by and large, unwelcome.

Raymond Winters from Howard, Colorado, wrote, "I firmly believe if it were left to a vote of every citizen of this State that you would find out that we don't want the yellow devils."

William Beard in Colorado Springs accused the governor of falling victim to "another fast political move" from Washington. "You gave your Colorado people, NO CHOICE. We must be either SLACKERS OR SUCKERS. If we receive the Japs, we will certainly be a bunch of SUCKERS. If we don't take them then you picture us as a SLACKER state. I can not agree with you as neither is true or necessary."

Ruth Porter wrote from Colorado Springs, "We are told that protests of public officials and civic organizations can not be heeded, and that Colorado must be infested by the Jap virus."

On personalized stationery, Mr. and Mrs. Milton Young of Boulder quoted Corinthians and Psalms and then added, "Do you realize what is going to happen if you let these alien Japs into our state to settle down? Wives and mothers whos [sic] husbands and grown sons who have to go to fight will not feel safe to go to bed at night for fear of these Japs breaking into their homes. Attacks with intent to kill, rape, robbery [*sic*]."

Hundreds of people wrote, called, or cabled the governor's office to complain. Emotions ran high. The FBI reported that in its raids on enemy alien homes and businesses, it had taken possession of enough dynamite from Japanese homes on the West Coast to destroy bridges, dams, buildings, and defense factories. FBI agents, under orders from Director J. Edgar Hoover, had arrested more than fifty-three hundred Japanese, German, and Italian nationals since Pearl Harbor, and seized enough firearms from their homes to equip a regiment. Those were the people everyone feared would be coming to Colorado.

The McNally family said it had no desire to "take care of a flock of yellow-belly Japs. We don't want them and we don't mean maybe. Read the *Denver Post*, this is the people's thoughts."

W. B. Butler wrote in from Victor, where the governor used to edit the local paper. "These people are traitors and spies," Butler insisted. "They have accepted the advantages of our country for many years … unless the authorities place ample guards upon them and are severe, [our] lives and safety in Colorado will be destroyed."

George King from Denver pled, "Please regard this letter as a vigorous protest against any of those damned Japs being sent to this state except under strong armed guard."

Supporters from the West Coast came to Carr's defense. The *Portland Oregonian* wrote an editorial commending him on his decision and sent it to him. Carr responded to its editor, "I have kicked up a big quarrel because of this statement, but I think that every thinking American must agree with me."

That would become a main staple in the Carr defense for his position: "Every thinking American must agree with me." He wrote one man back, "I think I made myself plain enough for anyone to understand."

The governor would stress it was Colorado's duty, its role in "the most awful conflict in all history," and its citizens had to understand this is what it took to win the war. "Can't we be unselfish enough?" was a regular question he asked. Carr was not above a guilt trip.

Every hour, dozens more protests were filed with his staff. Every day, hundreds more letters arrived at his office. Every week, thousands of Coloradans grew more fearful, with continuous reports of bad news coming from the Pacific. The sheer volume of the correspondence overwhelmed Carr. He traveled daily with a Dictaphone that he plugged into the cigar lighter of his 1940 Cadillac to answer constituent mail at any time. He couldn't keep up.

"Colorado has not invited the army to bring Japanese into this state," he would tell anyone who listened. "It has simply been suggested that if the best interests of our country demand it, Colorado will obey orders.

"I am advised that it is the invariable practice in such cases for the army to hold such persons under guard and close supervision. This may have to be done in order to assure us a place to live when this war is over. It is certainly better to harbor thirty-five hundred Japanese under control than to receive an army of them bent on conquering our people.

"Can you imagine how a man with MacArthur on the Bataan Peninsular in the Philippine Islands tonight would feel if he knew that the stay-at-homes in the interior of the United States were protesting the guarding of a few Japanese?"

Carr sent hundreds of these letters to angry constituents. His biggest problem, though, was that numerous Japanese were already coming to Colorado, and they weren't under guard as he had anticipated. Both Japanese Americans and Japanese aliens moved to Colorado to join the twenty-seven hundred people of Japanese descent already living in the state. Each day in early March, that number grew, and many Coloradans blamed their governor.

California governor Cuthbert Olson wanted "wholesale

evacuation of the Japanese people" from his state. The military planned to comply. Many Japanese didn't wait for any official evacuation orders. They simply packed up and went where they thought conditions would be most favorable.

Newspaper reports indicated that the Japanese Americans and Japanese aliens living on the West Coast felt Governor Carr's stance was a welcoming one. They began packing up and heading east. They hoped to live with family or friends in Colorado and get work on farms.

Carr distinguished between the two groups. Patriotism called for Colorado to accept guarded noncitizens if that's what it took to win the war. But patriotism was also his reason for standing up for Japanese Americans, who, he continued to assert, should not be imprisoned without proof. What's more American, he'd say, than the constitutional rights afforded to its citizens?

However, Coloradans did not distinguish between Japanese Americans and Japanese aliens. And the unchecked migration terrified the people of Colorado. The state's newspapers fanned the flames of hysteria.

The *Fort Collins Express-Courier*, in northern Colorado, reported on its front page on March 5 that aliens in the San Diego area were looking to come to Colorado. Assistant U.S. attorney Ed H. Law told the Associated Press that "numerous Japanese" were seeking travel permits to head east.

On March 6, the *Rocky Mountain News* had a front-page story about yet another Japanese war victory. Right alongside this bad news was a story headlined: "Jap Vanguard Said Heading for Colorado." An Arizona highway patrol captain told a reporter that most of the vehicles he stopped along Highway 66 because they had Asian drivers were "headed for Colorado ... heavily-laden with household equipment."

The *Pueblo Chieftain*, in southern Colorado, ran a story from San Francisco, saying that "thousands of enemy aliens and American-born Japanese were packing their belongings" with a reported destination of Colorado. The *News* followed up its Arizona story by reporting that Colorado had no operating ports of entry and that "alien Japanese could thus pass into the state without official notice."

Everything was uncertain. Rumors were rampant. America appeared to be losing the war. The movement of anyone with Japanese heritage got front-page coverage, especially in Colorado's smaller towns.

In southeast Colorado, the La Junta newspaper reported that six carloads carrying fifteen Japanese, with travel permits signed by an assistant U.S. attorney from California, were coming to town. Crowley County sheriff John Armstrong immediately dispatched deputies to "meet the Japs and accompany them through the [county]," the paper reported. "They were to be carefully checked for contraband and [County Sheriff] Armstrong said none would be allowed to remain here if it could be avoided."

The migration story appeared just above a story that told of a raid of enemy alien homes in Albuquerque, New Mexico, where authorities found "a shortwave set capable of reaching around the world" and a small arsenal of firearms. Afterward, one Navajo Indian truck driver said that if Japanese were sent to his state, "there would be fresh scalps in the hogans."

The *Post* had a field day with the stories. "CAN YOU IMAGINE AMERICANS MOVING AROUND IN JAPAN LIKE THAT? WHEN IT COMES TO THE JAPANESE WE SHOULD MAKE IT UNANIMOUS. ONCE A JAP, ALWAYS A JAP. WE CANNOT AFFORD TO TRUST ANY OF THEM."

Carr knew the state must have order. Coloradans were worked up over the unchecked borders, so he assigned the highway patrol to fix the problem. Carr told patrol supervisor J. J. Marsh that the goal was to "trace" any Japanese aliens, but not to imprison them.

Officers were instructed "to stop all cars and trucks entering this state containing Japanese aliens, to trace their itinerary and find out where, if at all, they plan to settle within this state; also, to determine if they have on their person or within their belongings any shortwave radios, photographic equipment, guns, or ammunition, and if any of these articles are found with the belongings of these Japanese aliens, you are to hold the article or articles, and individual or individuals, and report the same to the Denver office for further action."

All patrolmen were required to investigate the settlement of any alien Japanese in the parts of the state they covered. Marsh told his staff that all aliens were to be registered with the U.S. Attorney's Office. If they chose to move outside of their immediate locality, they must first receive written permission from the aforementioned office. Every piece of information was to be sent back to the Denver headquarters.

Marsh's marching orders from the governor were clear: Stop and detail enemy aliens or noncitizens, but Japanese Americans were to be treated differently. Citizens could travel freely into and throughout Colorado.

Besides the continuing deluge of letters from Coloradans offering opinions on what he was doing or not doing, Carr received petitions from Japanese Americans on the West Coast seeking permission to come and live in Colorado.

The Yamagawa and Kaneshi families of Los Angeles enclosed two self-addressed stamped envelopes with their request to Governor Carr.

"I, Kitaro Yamagawa, wish to leave the state of California, to evacuate to the state of Colorado. I am requesting the honor of a permit, submitted by you or your equal, allowing or permitting my family to enter the state, Colorado. The family consists of six members ... our destination is Route 1, Box 30, Littleton, Colorado, the home of Mr. Geneyi Miyasato, who has consented to house and employ us on his farm.

"Mr. and Mrs. Chuschchiro Kaneshi, also of Los Angeles, California, request the same honor asked above."

The governor found himself in a difficult position, insisting in many of his responses that federal authorities were monitoring everyone of Japanese descent. He stressed that his earlier comments were only directed to Japanese aliens evacuated from the West Coast. When it came to Japanese American citizens, he insisted they "have the right to travel through America and to earn their way as they see fit."

The courtesy patrol was told to "keep a watchful eye" on the borders for enemy aliens, although no instructions were given on how to tell the difference between the Japanese aliens and the Japanese Americans.

Meanwhile, the concept of evacuating all Japanese from the coast was described by Japanese national radio as "diabolic savagery … seventy thousand American-born Japanese will be ejected forcibly from areas where they have spent their entire lives," the Tokyo-based report stated. "Neutral observers said obviously the constitutional rights of those American-born Japanese have been ruthlessly trampled upon in the heat of resentment aroused by American political and military errors.

"The viciousness of the American government in persecuting a helpless, strictly civilian, and manifestly innocent minority will remain in history as one of the blackest crimes ever committed by the so-called great powers."

Having the Japanese government sharing his position did little to boost Carr's standing in Colorado. He knew the issue wasn't going away until the government decided precisely how those who looked Japanese were to be treated. He also knew that public sentiment against them would rage as long as the Japanese military continued to win battles in the Pacific.

Carr wrote to his friend Ferd Lockhart in Los Angeles, "Since I stuck my neck out on the Jap proposition … I have been three times as busy. I'm getting many letters … which fairly take the hide off."

It was the lowest point of the war for America and its allies.

Pessimism and worry dominated the headlines as battle after battle in faraway destinations ended poorly. British troops were forced to evacuate Rangoon in Burma. Dutch soldiers surrendered to the Japanese in the East Indies and the emperor's forces invaded Salamua and Lae on New Guinea. The battles to prevent the seemingly inevitable Japanese invasion of Australia were futile. The Allied forces could not stop the Japanese offensive.

A depressed Carr wrote to a friend, "It's the first time in my life that I ever thought it was possible for the United States of America to lose a war. Tonight, I am fearful that just that thing can and is apt to happen."

Colorado newspapers covered the war closely, depressing readers both with news of Japanese military victories and stories of "alien Japs" moving into the state. Every day in mid-March brought news of another caravan, of more families coming to Colorado.

In northern Colorado, the *Greeley Daily Tribune* reported that Japanese were "moving into the county in small and unescorted groups." In southeastern Colorado, another newspaper reported that "a Jap caravan" of two trucks, seven cars, and dozens of "transient Japs" coming to the area. Two days later, the paper reported that thirty more "Japs" arrived. They said that they were part of a group of two hundred Japanese, roughly half of whom were citizens, who had been given travel permits to Colorado by California authorities.

It was the fourth month of the war, and Americans were being called on to sacrifice for the cause, buy war bonds, fly American flags, and do their part to win the war. Men were encouraged to apply for jobs at the weapons plants in its cities, the union bosses telling them, "We need a lot of bullets to put the Japs in their place, so go to it, boys."

Pamphlets were distributed statewide reminding people that "Loose Talk Loses Lives." The Council of Defense handout reminded all Coloradans that "the enemy is listening. ... Keep it bottled up by keeping your mouth shut. Everyone can spy, everyone must spy, everything will be found out—that is modern espionage."

Colorado's twenty-seven hundred Japanese residents were being watched especially carefully.

The United States Forest Service warned about the danger if Japanese aliens were housed inside one of the state's fourteen national forests. "While it is not the intention of the forest service to become excited or unduly alarmed, at least until we know how many Japanese will be evacuated to Colorado or under what restrictions they will be kept," Arthur Brown, chief of the forest fire control told the *Denver Post*, "still we must recognize in advance that the setting of forest fires is the easiest possible form of sabotage."

Colorado may have been a small state, but its citizens served overseas with honor and dignity. Thousands were fighting, and dozens had already died.

Carr was a wordsmith who was never known to place noun to verb without creating his own memorable sentences, yet he felt inadequate conveying the state's sympathies to parents whose son had "passed to his glorious reward in the service of his country and of humanity recently."

"On behalf of the people of Colorado," the governor wrote, "may I extend the sympathy of the entire state. There is little which I can say at a time like this which will offer condolence. Let us hope that the years to come may relieve humanity of future suffering and misfortune such as has been visited upon us in the last few months, and let us hope that his life may not have been given in vain."

As a parent whose son would likely soon enter the war, Carr knew the fear and agony parents of servicemen endured. Besides his personal worries, and the anxiety he felt because the United States was at war, Carr remained concerned that the war was being used as an excuse by the federal government to take big bites out of the U.S. Constitution.

More regulations were imposed and the government centralized some operations for efficiency. But often the feds ran roughshod over the states with little understanding of what was appropriate, in Carr's strong opinion, and he wasn't alone.

As Colorado State College president Dr. Charles Lory put it in a note to the governor on March 16, "If some of our officials in Washington would investigate before they order, we would have less trouble and more confidence in their judgment."

One example of the federal government interfering in state matters with no understanding of the consequences was a ruling by the War Production Board (WPB) prioritizing the type of metals needed to win the war. It denied machinery and equipment to mines with complex ores running more than 30 percent in gold and silver. Carr believed it would result in the shutting down of more than a thousand Colorado mines and put thousands out of work. For a governor who grew up in a mining town, it was akin to an attack on his hometown.

Colorado Mining Association vice president LeRoy Burkett said the ruling "brought chaos, discouragement, broke our morale, and put fear into the hearts of every miner in our state."

Syndicated state capitol reporter Alva Swain thought the mining issue would take the attention of the state away from "the Jap alien question." Swain wrote on March 8 that "the people are far more interested in the mining industry than they are in the shipment into Colorado of Japanese."

Swain was wrong. He hadn't seen the governor's mail.

An anonymous letter writer expressed "righteous indignation" that the governor had signed off on bringing aliens into Colorado. "FDR must be paying you a huge sum of money to get you to do this."

Pueblo native M. J. Sanders described Colorado as perfect prey for the "despicable yellow vermin." He worried about the "beautiful forests to burn, pure waters to pollute, wild game to destroy, cabins to loot, American women and children to annoy.

An ideal spot for irreparable damage."

The governor had restrained himself after some of the more inflammatory statements hurled in his direction. However, when a Mr. Haines of Denver insulted his integrity and motivation, his legendary temper surfaced. "Frankly, I am ashamed of any Coloradan who writes such a letter as yours. If you would like to talk it over with me, why don't you come in and look me in the eye."

Carr chose not to challenge the *Denver Post* directly as it continued its assault on his evacuee policy. "One trouble with these Japs is that there is no certain way of telling that they are not enemies. Even thos [*sic*] born in the United States, they still may be loyal to Japan—our enemy," the *Post* wrote in its "That's That" column of March 9 before launching into the point it shouted at its readers. "NO WORSE THING COULD HAPPEN TO COLORADO THAN TO TURN IT INTO A SANCTUARY FOR JAP ENEMIES." The next day, the paper again pounded on the governor, calling him a "sappy sentimentalist ... Jap aliens in the United States are cut from the same racial 'cloth' as are the Japs who have been ravishing women and slaying men who fell into their hands with the capture of Hong Kong. Jap enemies in the United States will be just as ruthless and barbaric, if they get the chance."

When a legislative committee gathered to plan a fundraiser for the war effort, the governor tried to tamp down the rhetoric. Carr acknowledged he had received numerous protests against his position on the evacuees, but he told them that he wasn't backing down. He vented to his friend Dr. Lory.

"I didn't take this job to feel the public pulse or to follow the popular demand. I think it is up to a person in my job to direct public opinion rather than to follow it."

Colorado's "non-politician" wanted to lead, but Coloradans did not seem inclined to follow. Less than a week later, in a news section, the *Post* ran a story titled "Japan had army of spies ready to take over Pacific Coast area." An editor's note before the column by Far Eastern expert James Young read, "Colorado is about to be visited by an influx of Japanese, American-born, naturalized citizens and aliens. Some of the latter undoubtedly are capable of sabotage."

The paper also ran numerous angry letters from citizens in its "Open Forum" section that same Sunday. "The governor says that if the federal government wants us to take the Japanese we must do so," writes A.T.M. from Denver. "When the Japanese in Bataan told General MacArthur to surrender he did not answer that he would if the government wanted him to do so. He bluntly said NO."

Finally, Congressman Tolan's committee on National Defense Migration issued its initial report recommending the creation of the War Relocation Authority. It would be in charge of evacuating the estimated 92.5 percent of the Japanese in the country, who lived in California, Washington, and Oregon.

The March 19 report stated, "The tragic events of Pearl Harbor have created in the public mind a consciousness, whatever the character of the evidence, that the dangers from internal enemies cannot be ignored." The committee determined that the character of the evidence was far from convincing, but did not choose to take the same stand as Governor Carr. Filled with a "profound sense" of the constitutional challenges it was presenting to Congress and the president, members urged the establishment of temporary reception centers and the humane treatment of the evacuees.

"We cannot doubt," the report read, "and everyone is agreed that the majority of the Japanese citizens and aliens are loyal to this country. The innocent ten in this time of war will perforce suffer for the guilty one."

Chapter Ten
Late March 1942

Pollster Harry Field's assignment was to test America's isolationist views during this critical time in history. He had no client and only hoped to complete a poll to get his name and new firm some public attention.

Field figured he already knew how it would come out—anybody who read the newspapers and listened to the radio would. Yet, he would conduct it with the highest-trained interviewers working in the industry.

His firm, the National Opinion Research Center (NORC), the third-largest polling firm in the country and the newest, was headquartered at the University of Denver. He had a ten-thousand-dollar annual stipend from the school with the charge to give people a voice in political, economic, and social decision making. He wasn't beholden to corporate interests like the majority of the pollsters during that time, but offered research at cost to nonprofit organizations and university educators.

The first survey was national, with a goal of looking at whether Americans' approval of isolationist politics had changed with the onset of the war. In doing so, they'd also study the American reaction to its enemies.

Twenty-six hundred people around the country were asked about their attitude toward the people who live in Germany and Japan. The results showed an American public not interested in an imperialistic policy (only 13 percent wanted to capture as much new land as possible), but in favor of a magnanimous one (80 percent were in favor of feeding starving foreigners after the war).

Field wanted to know if Americans distinguished the European enemies, Germany and Italy, from its Asian enemy, Japan, or were they seen as one unit? Were they feared and loathed equally?

When the results came in, the results were uniform across

the board. Men and women, young and old, rich and poor, those with lots of education and little education, all believed that there were many more problems with Japan than with Germany.

Field took a second survey in the Rocky Mountain region. His researchers asked the same questions and used the same methods on the twenty-five hundred respondents living in Arizona, Colorado, Idaho, Montana, New Mexico, Nevada, Utah, and Wyoming.

The western participants scored even higher than the national average on whether they thought the Japanese had an aggressive nature that couldn't be curtailed. They also showed far more benevolence toward the Germans than the Japanese. Field found the same attitudes over and over. He concluded the obvious. "A significantly large proportion no matter where they live, are more favorably disposed to the Germans as a people than they are towards the Japanese as a people." This was before any hint of the Holocaust had surfaced.

It was clear to Field that Americans made few distinctions between Japanese American citizens, Japanese who lived in America but weren't citizens, and Japanese soldiers.

Field's mentor, George Gallup, had also taken a poll on the public's perception of the Japanese. Seventy-three percent of the Americans surveyed in his research described the Japanese as "treacherous" and another 63 percent labeled them "sly."

Governor Ralph Carr had copies of both polls sitting on his desk in mid-March 1942. They both illustrated empirically what he had learned anecdotally—people were particularly distrusting of anyone Japanese.

Milton Eisenhower, whose brother Dwight D. was serving as general in the European theater, had been appointed head of the War Relocation Authority. Governor Carr thought this was a step in the right direction, but it didn't directly address the issues he was most concerned with. He wanted to know what, if anything, was going to be done with the carloads and truckloads of West Coast residents of Japanese descent currently migrating to Colorado.

Pressure continued to build as public opinion raged. Coloradans could pick up their newspapers and see this foreboding type of headline found in the *Fort Collins Express-Courier*: "Japs have won first-round—Navy chief indicates."

Everyone wanted revenge. Even high school girls were showing up at recruiting stations "for just one shot at [the] Japs." Lucille Smith, a junior at Denver West High, and one of her "comely" friends from the school's girls' rifle team, wanted to enlist with the marines for "active duty where the Japs are thickest." As the headline in the next day's *Rocky Mountain News* read, "Regretful Marines reject girl sharpshooters."

Meanwhile, West Coast evacuees flowed in. Another seven cars and two trucks made their way into southeastern Colorado, according to press reports. The Otero County sheriff was told to expect seventy-six more the following week, all looking for work in the sugar beet fields.

"It seems that the Japs are making our county the center of their migration and there is little we can do about it," Sheriff Armstrong told the *Rocky Ford Enterprise* on March 20. "All the authority seems to be in the hands of the federal government and local law enforcement officers have little to say about the matter. Until I get further orders, I will just have to sit still and let them come into the county in any number they see fit."

The following day, a Saturday, the first formal evacuation of Japanese from southern California began. The Associated Press reported "few smiles, a few tears, mostly set resigned faces" as the first group of "alien and American-born" Japanese left from downtown Los Angeles for a "relocation camp" located in eastern California. The group included plumbers, painters, cooks, bakers, nurses, and waiters. Larger groups were soon expected to leave from the Rose Bowl football stadium in Pasadena.

Anyone who looked Japanese was required to leave the West Coast.

"A Jap's a Jap," General John DeWitt said from Western Defense Command Headquarters in San Francisco. "It makes no difference whether the Jap is a citizen or not." The same attitude was reflected by his aide Colonel Karl Bendetsen. When the head of a California orphanage asked Bendetsen about the fate of American-born Japanese kids, Bendetsen said, "I am determined that if they have one drop of Japanese blood in them, they must go to camp."

That Saturday, inside a shack on the Colorado border, Highway Patrolman Raymond Peterson reported seeing "one of the largest groups of Japanese" he'd witnessed enter the state. Twenty Japanese, eight of them noncitizens, all carrying legal travel permits, were searched for weapons, cameras, and shortwave radios before being allowed to enter Colorado. All of the citizens spoke English, but Patrolman Peterson reported that the Japanese aliens could not.

In an emergency meeting that morning, the thirteen members of the state's American Legion Executive Committee met to discuss the problem its leaders had seen "blowing up for the past month and steadily so." The committee sent their unanimous resolution to all 126 posts. In it, they remembered Pearl Harbor with bitterness and said it was made possible by "aliens" that the United States had allowed to move about freely.

The group's recommendations were twofold: Demand action for the "immediate imprisonment" of Japanese aliens in "humanely conducted concentration camps," and urge Governor Carr to call a special session of the Colorado General Assembly to enact laws to cope with the presence of Japanese aliens already in the state.

"It's simply sane thinking in the field of national defense," wrote M. L. Lyckholm, who ran the Legion's Colorado delegation. "American citizens are NOT wandering alone, or in twos or threes, loose and unrestrained in either Japan, Germany or Italy. If any of us were permitted to roam freely in any Axis country, we would, as good American citizens, do all the damage we could—

and help the United States. Japanese, German and Italian aliens surely are at least half as smart as we are. Let's quit kidding ourselves. These enemy aliens belong in concentration camps."

Ironically, the national Legion Executive Committee had two and a half years earlier passed another resolution condemning intolerance toward people of different races, religions, or political beliefs. "This attitude presents a constantly increasing danger to the rights of these [people] and to the democratic form of government under which they live in the United States," the September 1939 resolution read. Obviously, the war had changed attitudes.

The strong public comments by the American Legion—a well-respected veteran's group—made a big splash in newspapers all over Colorado. Many of the stories quoted members of Colorado's congressional delegation who supported the Legion board's demand for concentration camps.

"Further concentration [of Jap aliens] in Colorado might lead to trouble," said Senator Edwin Johnson (D-Colorado), who filed an official protest with the War Department for not doing anything to stop the current migration into the state. Johnson told army officials that the only way Colorado wanted any more evacuees was if they were "placed in concentration camps within the state and guarded and herded by military forces."

Representative William Hill (R-Colorado), the governor's former secretary and one of his biggest supporters, sided with Johnson. He saw the direction the political winds were blowing. "I don't want a one of them unless it's absolutely necessary to the war effort."

Governor Carr took another chance to convey his strong philosophy to his constituents the night of March 20. He would talk to a navy rally in Durango, in southwest Colorado. The navy headquarters in Washington, D.C., had just announced that another ship had been lost in the Pacific. The 1,270-ton gunboat *Asheville* was thought to have 185 men on board when it went down south of the island of Java. Casualties were not known.

There was news as well from Tokyo, where the Japanese Navy commanders charged that the "United States and Britain since the start of the war in the Pacific had waged 'extreme warfare based on retaliation and hatred' and declared that Japan would reciprocate," according to the Associated Press.

That night in Durango, Carr would share a platform with Mayor John Fankhauser, listen to the high school band, watch the Boy Scouts pass out programs, smile for Frank Stapleton, who was taking pictures, and thank Martha Carman, a high school senior learning to be a stenographer who had taken down his earlier speech at the Strater Hotel. The rally was a time to talk about how Coloradans could help the war effort, specifically by enlisting, but the earlier public banquet at the historic nineteenth-century hotel was a time to talk about the enemy alien question. It was his first speech on the topic since his statewide radio address.

Inside the restaurant of the opulent, redbrick, four-story Victorian, the guest of honor told those gathered, "If I don't speak the feeling of the people of Colorado in my office as governor, then I haven't any right to be there. I'm telling you this. That if the people of Colorado, knowing these facts, are unwilling to cooperate with the army of the United States and with our leaders in Washington in taking care of their share of the burden, then I don't want to be your Governor!"

Carr laid down a strong challenge in as forceful a tone as he had ever used.

"Let's have no more loose talk. Let's have no more threats of what we would like to do to the Japs. For every idle threat that gets publicity, a hundred Americans may suffer. For God's sake, shut up!"

The crowd was stunned.

"This is real, this is serious. You would be astonished to see the letters I receive from people who, I know, are just as sincere as you or I. They will buy bonds and stamps, will give their sons, will pay their income tax with a smile. They think they are being patriotic when they say, 'Don't bring those Japs in here. Let them stay in California.'

"What is California? It is the outpost of American civilization at the present time. California is the line of defense which will serve Colorado and you. California is the place where your boys may meet death if every precaution is not taken to protect and defend it. And so if California goes, Colorado is going too … if Colorado's part in the war is to take care of 100,000 [aliens] then Colorado will take care of them."

The response was polite silence. Carr realized that it was not the type of speech to get a crowd on its feet, applauding. The topic was too somber. Yet, he always felt that if he had the chance to give the facts and make his case, reason would always win. As Carr took the noon train back to Denver, he knew the stories of unchecked migration would continue. His policy so far was to monitor these newcomers to Colorado; this only assuaged the public concern so much. He was complimented by a number of West Coast newspapers, including the *San Francisco Examiner*, which said: "It is nice to know that we Pacific coasters have got Colorado and Governor Carr with us." But that wasn't going to turn public opinion at home.

His hate mail continued at a brisk pace. An unsigned letter from Denver asked the governor, "We don't want Denver overrun by the yellow race, unless you officials want the whites to move out to California to leave you officials and Japs here."

Florence Doty, who taught American-born Japanese at a Long Beach, California, high school, offered these words of warning: "DO NOT LET ANY JAPANESE GET ESTAB-LISHED IN THE MOUNTAINS. Every American-born Jap is a Nipponese. His heart and soul is in Japan. He has attended Japanese schools from his babyhood and he doesn't know anything else. DON'T TRUST ANY OF THEM."

Mrs. George Fisk wrote from Greeley in northern Colorado that she was confused. "I can hardly believe your patriotism would allow you to endanger the lives of the citizens who raised you to the position of trust you occupy, to consent to such an unheard of move."

The governor asked U.S. Attorney Thomas Morrissey to alert federal authorities about the seriousness of the situation in Colorado. He had already met personally with Morrissey and Colorado's attorney general Gail Ireland, but he wanted a paper trail with the federal government. Carr told Morrissey that it was a problem that involved "many persons, both American citizens and Japanese nationals who ... are coming to Colorado seeking a haven where they may earn a living and support their families during the war."

This was the type of tourist or new neighbor few in Colorado wanted to see. Despite Carr's insistence that he had not invited anybody to Colorado, the reality was that more and more people who looked like the people who had bombed Pearl Harbor were coming to the state. Coloradans wanted Carr to deal with them, but he believed that it was the federal government's responsibility.

He explained his plight to Morrissey. On one hand, there were a few letters from residents wanting to rent or donate their land to the newcomers. Then, there were those evacuees who sought to buy property. There were also notes from companies that needed men to fill jobs. On the other hand, there were demands for immediate imprisonment, regardless of citizenship.

The treatment of Japanese American citizens remained a major concern of the governor. Carr thought it violated the U.S. Constitution to imprison American citizens simply because they happened to be born to Japanese parents.

"This state bows to those principles of American government which give to American citizens the right to move freely from place to place, to earn a living as they deem fit or as circumstances allow, unhampered in their movements as individuals," he wrote Morrissey. "The suggestion that an American citizen should be seized, deprived of his liberty, or otherwise placed under restraint without charge of misconduct and a hearing is unthinkable.

"But for the protection of our public utilities, water supplies, munitions plants, of training schools and military establishments, as well as our people and their homes—for the protection of these very persons they should be induced to stay in places where their activities may be supervised and guarded. Under such an arrangement, all people, all property, every activity would be secure."

He asked for help "immediately and definitely. These persons have the right to enter our state and to live here, but our present residents must be protected." Inaction, he wrote to Morrissey, could lead to an "emotional explosion" no one wanted and to a situation where those of Japanese descent would soon be coming "in such numbers" that the problem would be magnified.

As he finished the letter, he picked up the *Denver Post*, which featured an article on "Why American-Born Japanese Can't Be Trusted With Nation at War." The story was written by a former wire service bureau chief in Tokyo.

That paled in comparison to the poem printed by the *Pueblo Chieftain* the next day entitled, "Woe, Nippon, Woe." Written by George Smith, its first two stanzas left no doubt as to the vengeance many Coloradans wanted to enact upon any Japanese, American-born or otherwise.

> Woe, Nippon, woe for on thy head
> Thy crimes shall all be visited
> Distance nor thy vaunted power
> Shall protect thee in that hour.
> "The vengeance of an outraged race
> Shall smite thee on thy cruel face,
> Revenge as hot as molted lead
> Shall be poured upon thy head.
> But in fair fight and not upon
> The prisoners gained by battles won.
> For on our name no blot shall sit.
> That in the future, we'll regret.

When Carr returned from the Durango meeting, he learned of more problems.

Federal government surveyors planned to work on a northern Colorado highway the next day, looking at the landscape for potential roads leading to a potential labor camp. He had neither been consulted about the work of the crew nor asked about the location they were scouting. The *Greeley Daily Tribune* reported that the Farm Security Administration (FSA) had an option on an eighty-acre farm, known as the James Graham farm. FSA officials told the paper that war conditions would not interrupt construction of labor camps needed with the scarcity of farmers. The FSA found time to meet with reporters, if not the governor.

More alarming, the paper also quoted a federal government official worried that the county unemployment office could be overrun by the "mass exodus of Japanese from California areas." Despite the fact only two evacuees had applied for compensation benefits since arriving in Greeley, U.S. employment manager Jerry Hamilton said that the importation of Japanese to Colorado "is bringing with it various problems."

Out in eastern California, a group of eight hundred evacuees had made it to their initial destination. The evacuees found thirty-eight completed barracks and seventy-six partially completed ones at the Manzanar Reception Center. The 6,020-acre site in the Owens Valley was once, thanks to irrigation, fertile land conducive to growing vegetables. However, it could only hold 10,000 evacuees and there were 110,000 more who would need places to go.

Any question of that was cleared up by General DeWitt's comments. He was quoted by the Associated Press as saying, "Let me make it perfectly clear that evacuation has started and will continue until all Japanese and Japanese Americans are removed from the critical areas and zones as quickly as possible. This is a final warning to the Japanese and Japanese Americans within the areas to be evacuated that they must immediately cease wishful thinking that there will be exceptions or delays of departure."

Carr called Senator Millikin in Washington, hoping to build on what he had written to Morrissey. Ironically, the governor who was critical of the White House for overstepping its bounds and infringing upon states' rights was now looking for an immediate federal government intervention. Millikin met with Major General Allen Gullion, the provost marshal general in Washington, who was DeWitt's liaison with Washington. General Gullion told Millikin that there were "no present plans for locating alien detention camps in Colorado." Millikin also took up the Carr protest of wanting to make sure if "in the future Colorado is considered for the location of such camps that we be given advance notice and advance opportunity to offer our views on whether such plans would provide protection [for] Colorado's proper interests."

In his two-page telegram to the governor who had appointed him to his Senate seat, Millikin wrote, "General Gullion agreed that such notice and opportunity will be given." When it came to talk about the relocation of the American-born Japanese who were flooding into Colorado, Gullion sent Millikin to Eisenhower's War Relocation Authority (WRA).

After conversations back and forth with Eisenhower's assistant, he was assured the WRA did not favor the voluntary, unrestricted movement of Japanese Americans. Maybe more important, Millikin wrote Carr that he was told "the army within [the] next day or two will issue a freezing order which will end uncontrolled volunteer movements of such evacuees."

The order could not come soon enough. Finally, the governor felt like he received what he needed to remove some of his state's worry. The former journalist knew he needed to spread the word immediately. The news could not wait for one of his two daily briefings with the press.

He called the reporters into his office.

Carr told them that Millikin's telegram was a victory for his position. There was a definite assurance from the federal government that it would not only supervise all movements of Japanese evacuees, but take complete responsibility for them.

"There is no need for hysteria over the coming of some Japanese into the state at this time," the governor told the Associated Press. "The problem is going to be dealt with by the federal government. The thing for us to do now is to keep calm."

His words did little to soothe many communities. Both the Greeley City Council and its Realty Board held emergency meetings after it was revealed that one Japanese American had shown up at a local real estate office saying he represented seventy-five Japanese families, each of whom wanted to rent or buy places to live. The *Greeley Daily Tribune* reported that another Realtor said that a Japanese man had entered his office, wanting to rent every house listed in the entire city of Greeley and that he was "able and willing to pay reasonable rent."

Other Realtors passed along rumors that thirty-five hundred Japanese were heading their way.

Despite the fact they could make lots of money from a spike in sales and rentals, the Realty Board unanimously passed a resolution preventing its members from doing any business with anyone of Japanese descent without the "sanction of the board of directors … and the concurrence of the Greeley defense council."

The City Council would unanimously pass a resolution opposing the evacuation of any Japanese to Greeley on the basis that the city could not provide police protection "for both the persons evacuated and the people of the city." Mayor L. L. Wilkinson said that he saw outbreaks of violence in the city's future if it didn't act immediately and forcefully to prevent evacuees from coming there.

"The point is that when we begin to get casualty lists that include the names of local boys, there may readily be trouble," Wilkinson said.

Carr didn't back down. To a *Rocky Mountain News* reporter who assumed he believed all Japanese evacuees should be jailed regardless of their citizenship, he said, "I don't insist that every man be placed in a concentration camp. Many of these people are American citizens and you can't put an American citizen in jail for no cause without violating the law."

Greeley was not the only city opposed to this policy. The mayor and town board in the tiny town of Lyons in Colorado's Front Range wrote to Carr, "It is a safe assumption that not even all of our present Japanese population are to be trusted. We have every reason to feel that these newcomers would be wholly devoted in their hearts to the cause of the Japanese Empire in the War."

The governor also heard from a number of the town's residents, including O. J. Ramey. "It looks like Americans must defend themselves from their Rulers while fighting a bloody war abroad," he wrote. In response, Carr showed resolve. "I still claim the right as Governor to express my thoughts when I think my people are wrong."

He expanded on those thoughts to members of a local union from his former hometown of Antonito. "We must be careful not to try to imprison American citizens without charge of misconduct and a hearing," he wrote to the group. "That would be against all of our ideas of Americanism and in violation of the Constitution. We must preserve the rights of all men under the Constitution."

As northern Colorado witnessed an influx of evacuees, so too did the arid plains of southeastern Colorado. The most serious threats to evacuees came from the Lower Arkansas Valley. Unlike the area upriver, once called home by famous western gunslingers Doc Holliday and the James-Younger gang, the folks from the towns of Rocky Ford, La Junta, and Swink were mostly farmers. The influx of anyone looking like the enemy had residents terrified.

In the sparsely populated counties, the faces of Japanese were rarely seen. In Otero County, with 23,571 people, there were 175 citizens of Japanese descent, 67 of whom were noncitizens or aliens. Neighboring Crowley County had even fewer minorities. A county with 5,398 people contained only 62 Japanese residents, 17 of whom were aliens. Roughly 1 percent was still considered too many.

Earlier in the month, the governor had received a note from the Arkansas Valley Cultural and Educational League, whose executive committee was largely made up of Spanish-speaking people. Members of the league feared the economic conditions if the Japanese were to take the jobs of the "hundreds of Mexican citizens that work and live in this community.

They wrote: "It certainly will not help the feelings of our boys now in the armed forces of our Country to know that, while they are fighting the Japs across the ocean; Back home his Father, Mother, little brothers and sisters, are being thrown out of the best agricultural places, to make room for those same Japs."

The *Pueblo Star-Journal* reported that in neighboring Crowley County "residents are not excited over the influx of Japanese." Although the county had registered only twenty-five new aliens since the war started, fifteen of Japanese descent, the paper wrote that "citizens of the county are of one opinion … that any suspicious action should be dealt with dramatically." Any previous hints that the area may have been interested in an influx of Japanese evacuees to help with an impending labor shortage "are unfounded," the writer added.

That was followed by an even more intense display of emotion by the two hundred-plus Swink residents who attended a town meeting on the night of March 18. Six more Japanese had reported that day at Otero County sheriff John Armstrong's office and it was estimated that would mean roughly two hundred new Japanese residents in the county in less than a month.

That more than doubled the number of Japanese already living there.

Swink mayor G. E. Kimble formed committees that would tell those Japanese already in the community not to invite any more friends and relatives to join them. The committee began phoning residents immediately after the meeting. But it was the resolution they passed unanimously that quickly got the attention of U.S. Attorney Morrissey, Governor Carr, and the others they sent it to.

Their telegram stated: "It was the unanimous opinion that this influx of Japanese will upset the economic balance of the community and result in a condition that may well lead to open violence …

"It shall be our purpose to resist the encroachment vigorously."

A reporter at the *La Junta Daily Democrat* called it, "open protest," and said that there was a "strong antagonism" against the new arrivals. The authorities saw the resolution as a direct threat against the safety of a number of people, many of whom were American citizens.

Morrissey immediately cabled a response to each of the Swink residents who signed the resolution. After he told them that he would have the FBI investigate their concerns and that he would forward their protests to the War Relocation Authority, he made this point: "All alien enemies are thoroughly investigated by the FBI before travel permits are granted. Many Americans of Japanese ancestry have been inducted and are serving with the U.S. Army.

"Do not let hysteria control your actions. Injury to Japanese might result in retaliation by Japanese on those they now control. Surely you do not want this. As patriotic Americans, it is your duty to abide by the laws of the U.S. I know you will do it."

The governor felt he needed to go to Swink, to the lower Arkansas Valley, to explain his position. The threats were getting out of hand. Carr followed Morrissey's telegram with a letter of his own to each of those who had signed the resolution sent to him. He wrote, "[This] can be handled sanely and without trouble.

"There seems to be a lot of misunderstanding of my policy and many people are misquoting me through ignorance, I hope. I don't think there is a man in Swink, when he knows the facts, who will disapprove of the stand I have taken. I didn't invite them here. We're simply saying that we'll do our part as Americans and I know that the people of the whole Arkansas Valley will stand behind me in this."

He wanted to make that point in person. Coincidentally, La Junta had planned a town meeting for the following Thursday, March 26, with the Colorado Council of Defense to talk about "The Arkansas Valley Japanese Problem," and the governor was invited. Chamber of Commerce Manager Jack Lacy invited "every interested resident of the Valley."

In Rocky Ford, citizens from Swink, La Junta, Ordway, Manzanola, and all over the Valley gathered days before the mass meeting. Swink Mayor Kimble shared a telegram he'd received from New Mexico's governor saying that they had "alien Japanese … interned under guard." It wasn't true. It was merely a wish, but it sent the message that Colorado was weak in its preparation to handle the issue.

One paper cautioned readers to remain calm leading up to the mass meeting, with a crowd expected to be in the hundreds.

"How many times have you gone over and over the evacuation problem in the past few days?" asked the *Rocky Ford Daily Gazette-Topic* in an editorial called "Be Calm." "Probably as many times as you have been with another person. You have grown hot with the hot-headed, and have tried to calm yourself when you were fortunate enough to meet someone who wanted to look at the matter reasonably …

"No one in Rocky Ford wants to incite a riot or to cause a greater problem than may exist here. We want to be fair and honest in the matter, but many honest people are too gullible or mentally lazy to analyze plausible statements or to examine their sources. Others are too driven by their emotions to withstand inflammatory appeals."

The next day, the paper asked its readers to listen to the governor before getting emotional. "Bringing the matter out in the open at a town meeting where everyone will have a chance for discussion is better than shutting up ideas, and brooding over them until they emerge tinged with the blackness of our fears."

La Junta chamber officials sent Carr a three-page list of suggested conversation topics for the meeting set for that Thursday. Among the proposals was a statewide police radio system to improve communications and allow officers to better track Japanese evacuees. The group also recommended a plan to use fingerprinting to help identify people and the appointment of federal marshals to monitor "sore spots ... [to] prevent an uprising of either the Americans or Japanese."

The governor knew there was anger; he would travel to the region with a state patrolman for protection. The meeting's organizers tried to ease the governor's security concerns by telling him, "The feeling of the majority [is] that no American rights should be encroached upon; there should be no 'witch hunts,' 'vigilantes,' etc., but instead a sane, practical plan of control adopted to ease the minds of not only our Colorado citizens but also the minds of our new residents."

Governor Carr woke up that Thursday morning to great news out of San Francisco. It appeared Senator Millikin was told the truth by the War Relocation Authority officials. General DeWitt would be signing an order that morning forbidding any Japanese to leave for new homes until they had been officially evacuated by the army. The order would be effective that coming weekend. Carr would have his own verbal ammunition at the town meeting. The caravans would not be entering Colorado any more. He would tell the meeting it was proof that "there is no need for hysteria in Colorado."

Carr would bring with him to La Junta, U.S. Attorney Morrissey, local FBI chief Gordon Nicholson and Thomas Clark, alien control cocoordinator for the Pacific Coast. Clark was sent by General DeWitt to personally deliver this message of a "freeze" in voluntary migration to Colorado.

As the governor and his group drove into town, past the Fox

Theater, showing "You're in the Army Now" with Jimmy Durante, and "Far East Command," the story detailing the Allied strategy in the Pacific, they feared there would be trouble. The chamber had warned that if some plan was not put into effect, mobs could take the law into their own hands. The governor had heard that vigilante groups were forming and threatening to hang all Japanese in the area from telephone poles.

The crowd spilled out onto the Courthouse Square. More than five hundred people came to the event. They came from Rocky Ford, ten miles to the west, and from Las Animas, nearly twenty-five miles to the east. The meeting was originally going to be held in a small adobe building known as the "Chamber kiva," but they quickly ran out of space and moved to the nearby junior high school auditorium.

The local paper described the governor's goal at the meeting as "[pouring] the oil of appeasement on the troubled waters of the Valley Japanese situation." The governor's worst fear was that he and his colleagues would end up drowning.

Carr spoke first. He had worked on this speech for days. He remembered growing up in Cripple Creek where "Scar Faced Mag," a woman with unsightly burns, was not always treated humanely by her fellow citizens because of her appearance. He remembered he had been called a "sissy" as a child. He had long, blond, curly, girl-like hair and his mother dressed him in Little Lord Fauntleroy velvet robes. His older brother taught him to box, to stand up for himself, and in doing so, earn his confidence back.

He remembered how when "the cold embers of disappointment and frustration" would set in throughout the mining camp, "human life experiences a falling market as emotion supplants reason and violence takes the place of neighborliness and fair dealings." Each time a black or Hispanic struck gold and a white did not, bitterness and backbiting were common.

He remembered how few of his initial law clients in Antonito could speak English and couldn't pay fees with anything other than

© Colorado Historical Society

As a little boy, Ralph Carr had long, curly hair, and his mother dressed him in clothing more suited for London, England, than the mining community of Cripple Creek, Colorado. He was picked on mercilessly for his appearance, and developed empathy for those "poor devils" who just needed a pat on the back. His belief in the Golden Rule—"do unto others as you would have them do to you"— guided his stand toward Japanese Americans as much as his belief in Lincoln and the rights spelled out in the U.S. Constitution did. Courtesy of the Colorado Historical Society vegetables or farm animals. Yet, the man they nicknamed "Rafaelito" would give them the best legal representation he could.

Ralph Carr did not believe in turning his back on anybody. For the governor, this speech was personal.

"You can't believe I would jeopardize your rights," he began in a booming voice. "You know that I have battled for the protection of Colorado's water rights and the state's interests in many other matters. [The evacuees] are not going to take over the vegetable business of this state and they are not going to take over the Arkansas Valley." The five hundred-person crowd sat silent, caught up in Carr's emotions.

"But the Japanese are protected by the same constitution that protects us. An American citizen of Japanese descent has the same rights as any other citizen. He has the same right to run for governor as I have, provided he meets the residential requirements.

"If you harm them, you must first harm me. I was brought up in small towns where I know the shame and dishonor of race hatred. I grew to despise it because it threatened the happiness of you and you and you," he said, pointing at three different farmers in the crowd.

He concluded, "In Colorado, [they] will have full protection."

The next day, Carr told reporters at the capitol that the meeting had been "a complete success." He said that after everyone had been allowed to say what he wanted to say, "the differences were all ironed out and the crowd went away satisfied that the state, the federal government, and the county officials are all trying to do what is right by every one.

Ralph Carr prided himself on being able to take the political pulse of the average Coloradan. Rarely had he so misread a situation.

Three days later, lower Arkansas Valley residents Earl Norris, Elmer Sapp, and George Pence sent the governor a telegram. It read: "Rush 250 doses of Jap soothing salve to Swink. ... Last Thursday did not take."

Chapter Eleven
April 1942

Ralph Carr was no stranger to physical threats.

On May 11, 1929, the day before he was selected U.S. attorney, top law enforcement officer in the state, the major headline in both Denver dailies was about a "bloody gangland war between rival mobs of bootleggers and hijackers." The last person to "squawk" to federal officials had been shot multiple times and dumped six and a half miles north of the city limits. Federal officials were being threatened as well. The end of Prohibition was only four years away.

Instead of shying away from the liquor war between Joe Roma, the bootleg czar of Denver, and the Carlino family of southern Colorado, which was looking to expand its territory, Carr got right in the middle of it. Shortly after taking office, he picked up the phone and warned "Little Joe," a soft-spoken, five-feet-one-inch man who had eluded prosecution for the better half of the last decade. "Joe," Carr said, "I'm not going to prosecute you until I get a case against you."

Little Joe, who was also known as "Little Caesar," reportedly replied in his heavy Italian accent, "Meester Carr, do me another favor will you? If you want me, don't send policemen to my house, just telephone me and I'll come in."

Carr hired people to infiltrate Roma's world, people like George Bahl, who went by the name George Stuart. He worked undercover for two years, earning the position of lieutenant in Roma's gang and earning his trust along the way.

Carr also brought on board Lawrence Baldesarelli, otherwise known as Baldy, to infiltrate the mob and pass along information directly to him, the U.S. Attorney. No one knew who was on the take, which police officers or which politicians were being bribed, so Carr felt it best to have Baldy skip any middle men and

Ralph Carr is sworn in as U.S. attorney for Colorado in 1929. He became the state's top prosecutor enforcing Prohibition. It brought him into direct contact with organized crime leaders and the realization that numerous law enforcement officers were also on the take. However, no one ever accused Carr of being corrupt. In fact, one of the former bootleggers he sent to prison would later help his campaign for governor, saying that Ralph was the only public official they "weren't able to buy. Now I'm an honest businessman and I want another [honest man] in office." Courtesy of the Colorado Historical Society come to his house on Downing Street whenever he had evidence of a crime that had been committed. He specifically asked Baldy to bring the weapons.

Baldesarelli would stand on Carr's small patio late at night and throw pebbles at his rear bedroom window. "I would open the window and Baldy would pass the gun or guns up," Carr said. "I would have them tested. Dozens of guns came to me in that way and they went back out the window to Baldy. We found many clues to gangland murders through those guns."

For four months, nearly every night, few stones in Carr's backyard would go unturned.

Evidence was mounting against the biggest mobsters of the day. Then, Baldy was gunned down by thugs with sawed-off shotguns, the penalty for the ultimate snitch. But the work he did before he died helped nail the case.

Carr soon picked up the phone once again to call his adversary. "Better come in Joe," he said.

Roma was later convicted and sentenced, but was freed on bond while his case was being appealed. Just before his day in court, three men appeared at his house and "liquidated" one of Denver's most feared mobsters. As U.S. Attorney, Carr would quash two other major liquor gangs in Colorado, enduring threats to himself, his wife, Gretchen, and their two kids. He was offered bribes, power, women, liquor, everything a man could want, and what many men of that era accepted. Any man, that is, who didn't have the integrity and determination of Ralph Carr.

"The power of money, the power of rotten politics, the power of organized crime, and the threats of the underworld have broken many men—and pretty good [men]," said a supporter of Carr's before his first election. "Find a man who has served his term … in a large city—who has come through unscathed by offers of wealth and power and threats of personal ruin and even of loss of life and the lives of his loved ones, and you will have found a man who has stood the fire test of integrity, impartiality and courage.

Such a man is Ralph Carr."

When he became governor, Carr got used to receiving abstract threats of violence, in connection with his stand about the Japanese. "They would holler and call him a Jap lover, but he waded right in the middle of it," said Wayne Patterson, who worked for the Colorado Courtesy Patrol in 1942. "He appointed me his driver, but he needed a bodyguard."

Carr himself described the atmosphere as one of "wild times" in a letter to his friend Jim Lockhart in California.

"There are those who think I am Japanese, others who think I am merely in love with them and they shout and rip and tear as if this were a time of peace instead of war," he wrote.

In a letter to the editor of the *Grand Junction Daily Sentinel*, he described the Japanese situation as "dynamite. From every corner of the state came protests ... the chief trouble is that [people] arrive at judgments with only part of the information."

Carr's concept that when "thinking" people stepped back from the emotion of the debate, they'd understand there really was no choice to be made, actually seemed to be working with some of the state's newspapers, if not with its readers.

From the leading Democratic-leaning paper on the state's Western Slope, the *Grand Junction Daily Sentinel*, came an editorial acknowledging that "of course, Colorado and Coloradoans would prefer not to have California's Japanese population evacuated to this state. But the fact remains that many such evacuees will be here. ... Even if you can't feel kindly toward enemy aliens in our midst, on general humanitarian principles, have consideration for the sake of those Americans who are or may become prisoners of war."

From one of the leading papers in southern Colorado, the *Pueblo Star-Journal*, came a suggestion to its readers to ease up on Governor Carr "because of a condition OVER WHICH HE HAS NO CONTROL IN ANY LAWFUL MANNER. He is simply permitting the enforcement of a regulation ISSUED

BY THE PRESIDENT OF THE UNITED STATES for the removal of these people and we can find no reason why [Governor Carr] should be censured for doing what the president says ALL governors should do."

Politicians meanwhile continued to criticize his position. Senator Edwin Johnson, in a telegram to the Denver dailies, suggested if he were governor, he would order out the Colorado National Guard to keep the state free of any Japanese. He also requested that the federal government round up the evacuees, who had already come to Colorado, or at the least, maintain strict surveillance over them. He charged that Governor Carr's statements on the topic served as an invitation to Japanese residents of California.

"I have protested against the Japanese whether considered harmless or otherwise coming to Colorado," he wrote from Washington. "I have pointed out that we already have a comparatively large Japanese population and a further concentration of them might cause trouble."

He sent a letter to Milton Eisenhower, head of the War Relocation Authority: "Hundreds of Japanese migrants recently have entered Colorado and have taken up residence throughout the state without permission from anyone," Johnson wrote. "Most certainly we ought not to be made the dumping ground for the Pacific Coast states." No evacuees ought to be allowed, Colorado's senior senator believed, unless approval was first given by the county commissioners of the area, a proposition in the current political climate that was never going to happen.

Other states' governors were still opposed. Nevada governor E. P. Carville said that despite the president's directive, "I have not changed my attitude." Wyoming governor Nels Smith showed no sign of backing down either, sharing his position both publicly and in his correspondence as well.

"I could very clearly visualize the West Coast Japanese percolating into our State, a few at a time, gradually taking over jobs which by right should be done by our citizens; becoming public charges and an added burden upon our state and county Welfare Departments; purchasing farms and gradually crowding from our most fertile districts our own Wyoming farmers and ranchers, and at the conclusion of the war remaining with us and creating for us a Japanese problem similar to the one the West Coast states, particularly California, now have," Smith wrote to a local county attorney.

Kansas governor Payne Ratner ramped up the rhetoric even further, telling the Associated Press, "Japs are not wanted and not welcome in Kansas." He instructed his state highway patrolmen and port of entry employees to carry out his warning and physically turn back any Japanese trying to enter his state. "We don't want them here."

The deadline to freeze the movement of evacuees to Colorado could not come soon enough for Carr, but before it arrived a story out of Phoenix and the Associated Press reported, "Most of approximately 1,000 Japanese and Japanese Americans who crossed Arizona last week were on their way to Colorado, Supt. Horace Moore of the [Arizona] state highway patrol reported. Moore said that those bound for Colorado reported they were going there because they believed Gov. Ralph L. Carr had assured haven in Colorado for Japanese evacuees from California."

The same day, Colorado Public Welfare director Earl Kouns announced that through a survey of county welfare directors and with the help of federal officials, he had determined the number of Japanese evacuees who had arrived in Colorado to be approximately four hundred people, with significantly more than half of them American born. He said that they ranged in age from two months to seventy-six years old and that the migration had been confined "almost entirely to agricultural areas where other Japanese have settled.

"We will receive constant reports on the persons they contact and on the work they are doing," Kouns told reporters in Denver. "We plan to conduct our activities in the closest relationship with federal social security and other agencies concerned with the Japanese evacuation or migration problems."

According to the Weld County welfare director in northern Colorado, two hundred and fifteen of the Japanese refugees had settled in his area, fifty-two of whom had registered in the last week alone. Press reports out of Colorado Springs described a party of seven adults and a baby who were on their way to Greeley as well, in three cars (two with trailers) and two trucks. As if to prove the heightened level of concern in Governor Carr's state, the group of California Japanese told local police "they had been stopped in almost every Colorado town through which they passed and that little attention had been paid them in other states."

The Young Women's Christian Association (YWCA) and its American-Japanese members announced they would open an information center for the seventy West Coast evacuees who had come to Denver. The YWCA set up a special committee to help "the group find answers for the many problems which are expected to arise."

Among those problems were lack of housing for people of Japanese descent. Realtors refused to do business with them, and neighbors were loath to welcome them. There was talk of holding a special legislative session to pass a measure denying Japanese the right to own property in Colorado. It stemmed in part from reports by Alva Swain in his "Under the Capitol Dome" column where he said, "Letters have been coming to many Colorado real estate men from Japanese on the Pacific Coast asking if it would be possible to purchase large tracts of land in this state for settlement purposes by the Japanese." Swain wrote that the letters indicate some two thousand families would come if they could buy land.

A newspaper advertisement reading, "Japanese family wants to rent a farm or five-bedroom bungalow with garage," drew the following response from Elizabeth Blank. "Wonders never cease," she wrote to the *Rocky Mountain News*. "I trust that the FBI is still functioning."

The anger was shared around Colorado as well. The *Fort Collins Express-Courier* reported that one Boulder theater sold "Slap-a-Jap" cocktails at a dime each in an effort to raise money for defense stamps. From Denver, T. Y. Northern wrote the *Rocky Mountain News* that he felt contempt for Governor Carr, who would "court the friendship of a race of people who have, for ages, proven themselves treacherous, conscienceless, and unappreciative ... nor would I consider making friends with Jap aliens since the Pearl Harbor incident, any more than I would seek the friendship of rattlesnakes."

The deadline for those living on the West Coast to move freely arrived and U.S. Attorney Morrissey told the *Denver Post* that he expected the influx of evacuees to slow down tremendously.

"The only Japanese emigrating now are those who received travel permits before the deadline," he said. "There is no reason to expect a sizable influx from now on."

Few believed him.

Three days after the March 29 deadline, Morgan County sheriff Rufus Johnston revealed at a mass meeting in his eastern Colorado community that he expected between four and five hundred evacuees to settle in his county in the next week to ten days. "I was not warned in advance that they were heading this way," Johnston told the crowd. "I have heard and today received proof they would settle in this county.

"We are going to organize so that we can keep them under surveillance and check any movements of a suspicious nature."

Colorado's Ports of Welcome chief Edward Reilly and U.S. Attorney Morrissey discounted the sheriff's estimates. "It's ridiculous to expect such a number of Japanese to settle in any one county," Morrissey told the *Post*. Reilly meanwhile reported that Wednesday, April 1, was the largest single day as far as evacuees coming into the state, with nearly a hundred entering Colorado within the last twenty-four hours. Reilly said he expected that to be the peak of the movement, as no more migration would be allowed without permission of California authorities.

Aside from three shortwave radios being confiscated and Fort Collins police being instructed to catch three cars full of Japanese evacuees who didn't know they were supposed to stop at the port of entry, Morrissey said that most of those coming to Colorado were "bending over backwards to stay out of trouble."

Among the new residents of Denver was Walter de Havilland, father of the famous actresses Olivia de Havilland and Joan Fontaine. He and his Japanese wife of fifteen years, Yoki, were forced to leave Los Angeles. They asked for a good place to go outside of the military zone and were told by a California official, "Denver." He said neither of his daughters would have anything to do with him because of his Japanese wife, who, he said with a wink, "gives her word not to blow up any bridges."

Eisenhower was busy trying to formulate a permanent solution to his overwhelming problem of evacuating more than 120,000 people of Japanese descent but having nowhere to put them. The current temporary evacuation centers were not satisfactory and he needed help from the inland states. He cabled the governors, attorneys general, state war board chairmen, and state farm directors to attend a meeting, "executive and confidential in nature," the following week in Salt Lake City to talk about the problem.

"I wish to do all I can to assist in having evacuees contribute the maximum to useful production during the War, yet at the same time it is obvious that I cannot meet hundreds of individual requests for Japanese relocation without consuming precious time that must be devoted to the larger problem," Eisenhower wrote. "Our policies on relocation are only now being developed."

A more immediate concern were press reports that evacuees would be earning fifty dollars a month to build the centers that would house them. Even with the recent vote in favor of Senator Johnson's measure to boost pay for an army private to forty-two dollars per month, the media and the public jumped all over the plan.

"Just think of that!" the *Post* screamed. "MILLIONS OF AMERICANS ARE BEING TAKEN AWAY FROM THEIR HOMES AND FAMILIES... AND THEIR GOVERNMENT IS PUTTING THEIR ENEMIES TO WORK AT $50 A MONTH."

The policy was quickly changed, and two separate federal agencies announced no Japanese evacuee would receive a greater cash wage than any soldier. No set amount was determined for the evacuees who would work to help the war effort, but it would not be more than the American enlisted man.

Carr was struggling; he felt physically and emotionally spent. Sometimes he would turn to his aide George Robinson for space to think and relax. "Let's go over to your house, George," Robinson remembered him saying. "He laid down in my house and my wife looked scared to death. I said, 'What's the matter?' She said, 'What should I tell him?' I said, 'Don't tell him anything. Let him rest.'"

He would lay down in the house of his black employee for fifteen or twenty minutes. "That did me more good for the governor of Colorado to have that much confidence in me," Robinson said. "I tried all the harder to do something for him."

Other friends tried to support him as well. Jim Lockhart, who was serving as an air-raid warden, wrote him from Los Angeles. "Was there a time when a conscientious man in public life was entirely free from torments of narrow-minded, uninformed selfish bigots whose technique well could be borrowed from the well-known ubiquitous yapping fist," he stated to his college friend. "Your offer of aid to another state in this dark hour of danger, when state lines, party lines and selfish prejudices should be eliminated, and for the time forgotten is magnificent. Even your harping critics one day must realize that."

To that letter, the governor responded, "You almost make me happy to be Governor of Colorado."

He sincerely believed that if he had the chance to share the full story, and to explain to people what really was at stake, the situation would become a nonissue. It was so obvious to him that his stand was the patriotic one. At a conference held in the state house chambers at the capitol, he urged Colorado's police officers to work with the FBI when it came to the topic of Japanese evacuees from the West Coast.

"Control of our enemy aliens is just a very small part of the entire war effort," Governor Carr told the crowd of two hundred fifty, which included sheriffs, deputies, police chiefs, highway patrolmen, and a reporter with the *Rocky Mountain News*. "The war effort is a federal matter. You local officers should work in the closest cooperation with the FBI, any army military police authorities which might be designated and the office of the U.S. district attorney. I have confidence they know what they are doing."

To ease concerns, Morrissey reported to the group that since the voluntary evacuation had been frozen, Japanese influx into Colorado had "slowed to a trickle … and is expected to cease entirely within a few days."

The governor had spoken at eight or nine places on the topic before arriving at the University of Colorado, his alma mater, to deliver a talk on Thursday night, April 3. Inside the State Preparatory School building at Seventeenth and Pearl streets, Carr saw the largest crowd at a talk he'd ever seen before in Boulder.

The nineteenth-century high school auditorium was packed, probably a thousand people in all, full of Boulder residents and University of Colorado students and faculty members, for what was labeled a "Victory Rally." Flags donated by the school's booster club lined the room, and local musician Patricia Stone played two violin solos before the Star Spangled Banner was performed and Governor Carr walked onto the stage. His topic was Colorado's role in winning the war, and at the top of his list was his belief that the state must accept evacuated Japanese from the West Coast if that's what the military asked the state to do.

"I have no right to question the wisdom of any general of the

United States Army while we are at war. Every state in the union should be eager to comply with orders for evacuation of Japanese aliens into their areas.

"It is my conviction that it is our duty to take in these aliens in time of war. I have been assured that any [Japanese] moved here will be under close guard and will not be permitted to compete with labor. It is simply a question of Americanism and patriotism. We are Americans and must do what the government desires us to. ... This will be my policy as long as I am governor."

On the topic of those evacuees already in Colorado, he was equally defiant. "I can assure every man, woman and child in Colorado that the Federal Bureau of Investigation is barely asleep and that every precaution is being taken. There is nothing to fear. There is no cause for alarm."

Carr challenged the audience to realize that America was at war and that the average person needed to focus on what they could do to aid the war effort instead of wondering with greater interest "what was the basketball score?" They should concern themselves with the future of democracy in the United States and how to treat those evacuated from the West Coast who were United States citizens.

"If we put American-born Japanese in concentration camps, we abrogate their constitutional rights. Further if we put them in camps or physically injure them in any way, there will be reprisals against our soldiers later. ... If I'm right, let's stop making threats against the Japanese. If I'm wrong, you can oust me at the next election."

The wire services reported, "Governor Ralph Carr is willing to stake his entire political future on his conviction that Japanese evacuated from Pacific Coast defense zones should be permitted to enter Colorado." That political future and the speech offered pundits the chance to speculate about the governor's plans.

Since he had spoken to the state party a month earlier and declared he had made no decision, he had remained noncommittal, writing to one friend, 'The things which are going on in the Pacific will determine my course more than any plan or intention of my own."

The speech in Boulder offered a clue at least that the governor was planning on running again, although he did not amplify his remarks about any campaign.

"Many political observers regarded the Republican chief executive's statement as significant because U.S. Senator Edwin C. Johnson has been outspoken in criticism of the Governor's policy toward Japanese migrants," reported the Associated Press. However, two paragraphs later, the wire service noted, "The governor's statement … gave added indication that he is considering running for reelection as governor instead of for the Senate."

The Japanese attacked American troops at Bataan with intense fighting, and casualties were reported to be heavy. It was the long-awaited final push to capture the Philippines and force the surrender of the roughly twelve thousand U.S. soldiers stationed there. Men had been on half-rations for months, and all reports brought dark and sobering news.

That Easter weekend, state officials reported what to the public must have seemed like a sharp spike in the number of Japanese evacuees from the West Coast. Although the number at the end of March hovered at approximately four hundred, state welfare director Kouns said that his latest calculations, with the help of the counties, put the number more likely at twelve hundred. Over the last week, nearly two hundred had arrived in Denver, in fifty-seven different cars, according to the city's point person on the evacuees, S. C. Becker.

Becker told the *Denver Post* that they all showed proper paperwork at his office, travel permits signed by the U.S. district attorney in Los Angeles, and that some of those documents were stamped "Never to return." He said most were staying in hotels in the city's lower downtown area and that one family that tried to rent a house had backed out after concerns were raised by neighbors.

"They seem to be scared," he said. "They are cooperative and they seem to have money so they are not likely to become welfare cases."

One evacuee family in southern Colorado had been arrested because they did not have appropriate travel permits. They had paperwork to allow them to travel to Longmont in northern Colorado from California, but they were not permitted to leave that area. Because they did not have that authority, federal officials put Ichiji Udo, his wife, Toki, and their seven-year-old daughter into custody at the Pueblo County jail.

Before attending the largest Army Day procession ever to pass through the streets of Denver, Carr made an informal appearance before a Defense Council committee on education and public information. Not surprisingly, most of his talk turned to questions about his stand on the issue of the Japanese evacuees. He said that Coloradans needed to think "intelligently" in order to help emerge victorious.

"We are at war and there are no state lines when we are at war," he told the committee members. "This is a war order to avoid fifth-column activities on the West Coast."

The public outcry continued as it had every day for months. More letters, more telegrams, more phone calls. Carr's staff wanted their boss to say, "Enough already, I get your point." But, he wouldn't. So the venting continued. He could not escape it.

Wheat Ridge resident Fred Beniger wrote a letter to the editor of the *Rocky Mountain News*: "I am not willing to have the Japanese settled in our state. The best citizens here would be glad to get rid of them as they do not become a part of the white race." Another letter writer from Denver chimed in, "Too bad we don't see eye to eye with Governor Carr, but he is not talking our kind of patriotism." Ira Francis from Jarosco wrote directly to the governor, "No one is going to feel at ease until they are restricted in some way or the war is over."

Carr stood for two hours on the reviewing stand next to the

Army Day parade marshal, Colonel Thomas N. Gimperling. A thousand soldiers from Lowry, fourteen hundred men from Fort Warren in Cheyenne, Wyoming, forty bands, and every civic organization and educational group in the area marched by. Fifteen thousand participants in all walked through downtown Denver on its way to where dignitaries at Civic Center Park would speak. People were literally hanging out the windows of buildings along the way, towering over a crowd estimated at one hundred fifty thousand, almost half the entire population of the city.

"I think it will not only lift the morale of the people but at the same time will impress upon them the enormity of the job," the governor told reporters at the start of the parade.

Spirits were generally high. The good-looking brunette on the United Service Organization float had scores of requests for her telephone number. She laughed it off and told the *News* she didn't have a telephone. The goal of showing "a demonstration of unity, preparedness and of deep faith in the cause of free peoples and their coming victory," was accomplished, according to parade organizers.

They sold twenty-five thousand tickets for a dance at the city auditorium that night to raise money for the war effort. Hollywood star Mary Martin sang "My Heart Belongs to Daddy," a Carr favorite, and then he got to introduce British Academy Award winner Charles Laughton to the crowd.

"Some people have said [he] looks like me," Carr wrote to his friend Jim Lockhart. "How in the name of heaven did he ever get into the movies if that's true?"

This small amount of levity couldn't erase the impending clash of ideas set to take place the next day in Salt Lake City when Milton Eisenhower gathered the representatives of the ten western states to talk about Japanese evacuees.

Carr himself could not go, as he had a speech planned that he did not want to cancel.

He asked his trusted friend Judge John O'Rourke to represent Colorado at the meeting. O'Rourke was a Durango Democrat who served on the state's water conservation board with Revenue Director Ferry Carpenter and who had known the governor through their work on irrigation issues for decades. Dewey Harmon, the state agricultural agent, whose remarks in mid-February had first alerted Colorado that evacuees might be coming, was also in attendance with a few others representing Colorado's state's farmers and ranchers. However, it was O'Rourke who spoke on behalf of Governor Carr.

As the one hundred or so men from Arizona, California, Colorado, Idaho, Montana, Nebraska, Nevada, Oregon, South Dakota, Utah, Washington, and Wyoming descended into Salt Lake City, their cars had to dodge more than pedestrians as they made their way to the downtown Newhouse Hotel. Heavy snow in the mountains had driven thousands of Rocky Mountain mule deer into the city center and the herds went about nipping at buds at the state capitol, subjecting them to cars, dogs, and game wardens who were unsure how to solve the problem.

The men met in the heart of Salt Lake City's "little Wall Street." On the southwest corner of Main and 400 South streets, the grand hotel sat just west of the city's Stock Exchange and Commercial Club buildings. The representatives of the states were set to do some commodity trading of their own—with the lives and future of tens of thousands of American citizens and their Japanese-born parents. No media representatives or outsiders were allowed to attend.

Thomas Clark, envoy from the Department of Justice and alien control co-coordinator for the Pacific Coast, told the group that they had been gathered to "thrash out some of the problems that are confronting the army and the War Relocation Authority (WRA). When we understand each other's problems, we can decide on a course of action that will be best for all of us."

From the beginning, however, it appeared to the westerners that the meeting was all about solving the army's and WRA's problems with little concern for their own. Further, the feds were patronizing.

Clark said the group would have a "little *Quiz Kids* program" afterward, giving the impression that he and the others from Washington thought they were more intelligent than the state's representatives. *Quiz Kids* was a popular Wednesday-night radio program at the time where a host "as clueless as the kids were bright," according to one historian, would fire questions at some of the sharpest young minds in the country.

After Clark, Colonel Karl Bendetsen, the youngest colonel in the United States military, spoke. As the assistant chief of staff to General DeWitt, he was required to carry out the evacuation program on the West Coast. He explained to the group that in war, "There is a Home Front and a War Front. The war front involves our young men and equipment, their supplies. It involves getting them to the theatre of war fully equipped and ready for fighting. The emphasis of the army must be in that direction, not on resettlement, but to do battle and kill. The army should not be asked to undertake the difficult problem of resettlement. It could, but the responsibility of the army is to win the war."

Just in case the people in the room didn't understand what he was saying, he said it again. "We have had requests from some places that if we would furnish labor under army supervision they would be received to work on farms. Ladies and gentlemen, the army cannot provide that kind of supervision. You don't want it, nor do I, nor does anyone. If you disburse your army and your soldiers, your fighting men and their equipment, to do that you are not going to win the battle. ...

"Therefore, it must be understood that so far as they're going out voluntarily to work from where they are assembled by the army, the army cannot provide federal troops, and the responsibility must rest with the state and local governments."

Eisenhower went next, stating that his goal was to "handle this problem in a way to set a model for the rest of the world."

He talked about how emotional the issue was, telling the group he had received a telegram "from Colorado and it was a very violent telegram." He also addressed Senator Johnson's request that all the evacuees who had settled in Colorado be rounded up and interned like those who were now frozen on the West Coast. "I have searched my knowledge of the American Constitution and I don't know how they can go and take those citizens who reside in Colorado and bring them into the War Relocation Authority."

He described a work program he wanted to establish where workers could clear weeds and work on conservation and flood control. The hope was to avoid prolonged idleness, which could lead to declining morale among the Japanese population, which could then lead to trouble. Eisenhower told the group that he didn't want "Japanese labor to displace normal labor," but that he hoped to create self-supporting communities for the evacuees. That way, he could assuage certain agricultural interests that had asked for help planting and harvesting the crops to provide the food for the armed forces and the American public.

Eisenhower described "reception centers" for the Japanese, which would be qualified as military areas if needed. Those would be controlled by the army, but any leaving of the military area would pose problems. "Obviously, when an American citizen leaves a military zone, he is just as free as you or I to go any place he pleases," Eisenhower said, pointing out numerous times that two-thirds of the evacuees were American citizens. "About all we can do is handle this problem as decently and humanely as possible in the American way."

The incredulous faces of those gathered must have tipped off Eisenhower, Bendetsen, and Clark about what they would hear next. "The governors literally began shouting at me," Eisenhower said later.

Utah Governor Herbert Maw stood up: "I don't know what you want today. Do you really want frank statements or do you want us to say that everything is OK," he said, not waiting for an answer before continuing. "I am tremendously disappointed with what we have received today. I can't say that we have received anything. We don't know what our program is and we are here asking you to work it out for us."

The WRA note-takers in attendance would say the gist of Maw's comments were that "the federal government is completely at sea on the problem of handling the Japanese and has no program to offer."

For the next couple hours, the governors of Utah, Wyoming, Idaho, and Nevada, as well as representatives from the rest of the states in attendance, laid out what they wanted to happen. It was summed up by the governor whose state was hosting the meeting. "If you will turn over to the State of Utah one tenth of the money you are going to spend in the program and let us handle the problem and give us one-tenth of the Japs you have to evacuate. ... We want them where we can guard them, where there are not permanent settlements and when the war is over, they move out," said Maw. "That is what the people of the state of Utah want."

Idaho governor Chase Clark followed. "I would hate it," he said, "after I am dead, to have the people of Idaho hold me responsible at a time like this for having led Idaho full of Japanese during my administration. ... When this war is over. ... I don't want ten thousand Japs to be located in Idaho."

Stenographers took down the remarks from Wyoming governor Nels Smith: His chief concern, they noted, was that "the Japanese would overrun his state if given the opportunity. People in his state have a dislike of any Orientals."

Nevada Governor E. P. Carville was somewhat less emphatic than his counterparts, but articulated a similar position. If the evacuees would not be guarded by army soldiers, he could not see a situation where they could be allowed into the fields or into any industry to work as his state did not have a National Guard. "If the Japanese are spread over the state there is the chance for them to commit sabotage."

When it was Judge O'Rourke's turn to speak, he acknowledged that likely everyone in the room knew his governor's stand on the issue, that Colorado was willing to accept the "responsibility" for taking evacuees if that's what the military deemed necessary. "We can't take the shortsighted view of this situation," he said.

When they adjourned four hours and fifteen minutes later, the governors and attorneys general had taken up all the time allotted and the farmers and ranches didn't get a chance to speak. Any chance was gone for "establishing small inland camps on the model of Civilian Conservation Corps camps which would serve as staging areas for the evacuees as they were moved into private jobs as soon as possible." Any widespread dispersion in the inland states for agricultural or industrial purposes was unpopular, as was any program that did not call for complete military control. WRA plans to encourage the evacuees to "fan out" from the centers to either individual homes or to colonize uninhabited areas would be scuttled.

Eisenhower said afterward, "We asked for frankness and we got it." He later described it as "the most frustrating experience I ever had." He recommended to Congress that large sites be selected for evacuees with work opportunities twelve months of the year. All sites would be located at a safe distance from strategic points. Finally, each "reception center" would be declared security zones, and thus, guarded by barbed wire, machine gun turrets, and military police.

As Japanese troops made gains on the Bataan peninsula in a "furious around-the-clock assault," New Mexico's governor, John Miles, who wasn't invited to the conference, said he would use "emergency police powers, if necessary" to prevent any Japanese Americans from being evacuated to his state. "In my opinion, they are likewise aliens, holding allegiance to the emperor of Japan," he told the Associated Press.

The mayor of Albuquerque, New Mexico, supported his governor. "This is no place for Japanese to be running around loose," said Clyde Tingley. "I don't trust any of them since Pearl Harbor."

Back in Colorado, the three major universities in the state followed the moral compass of their governor and agreed to accept evacuated Japanese American students from schools on the West Coast. The University of Colorado, Colorado State College, and the University of Denver were among only fourteen inland higher-educational institutions in the country willing to accept some of the three hundred students who needed to leave the military zones. The students needed to be American-born, well-qualified academically, hold a certification of character from their old institution, and be able to pay nonresident tuition.

"Letters from the presidents of the universities of Washington and California and Leland Stanford University assure me that these American-born students are intensely loyal to the United States, eager to continue their studies so they may be of greater service to this country in war or peace," said CU president Robert Stearns. "We have checked with navy authorities since naval units are situated on our campus and have received their approval of accepting such transfer students."

The high level of antagonism had not waned. B. Butler implored the government to send Japanese Americans to a remote "island." S. E. Jones wrote from Denver that he had noticed "of late an alarming number of Japanese on our streets—man, woman, boy two and one half years old, baby in buggy? What will be the result of allowing these Mongolians to come here and multiply," he asked Governor Carr. "The Japanese should stay on their side of the Pacific. They are a designing, crafty race. If we allow them to remain and multiply we shall have a grave problem on our hands."

S. B. Simmons from Platteville wrote to the *Post*'s Open Forum complaining about the "menace" he had seen in the state's vegetable district from Adams City to Greeley. "One frequently sees new Jap faces in this district," Simmons wrote. "But Governor Carr says the Japs are native born and entitled to their rights under our laws. The plain fact is no matter where a Japanese is born, he is never a loyal citizen at heart, never develops our ways and customs. He remains an alien enemy and should be disposed of in some manner from our society."

Despite the pleas of some state lawmakers and the American Legion in Colorado, the governor rejected a plea to hold a special legislative session on the topic. Besides the fact it would cost thousands of dollars to do, Carr believed any changes to Colorado's farming, industrial, and labor laws needed to wait until the draft of men between forty-five and sixty-four was completed as the state's needs would not be known until after then. Also, he did not want the rhetoric dialed up even higher.

"Whenever it appears there is an emergency, I will always move in an effort to meet it," Carr said. "Our people are somewhat emotional now and legislation should be the result of calm reasoning and intelligent argument."

Calm reasoning was in short supply after the fall of Bataan. The Japanese were one location—Corregidor—away from capturing the entire Philippines, and the American forces, despite valiant efforts, had shown little ability to stop the physical onslaught. Scores of Colorado men were feared to be casualties.

The *La Junta Daily Democrat*, reporting on the continued tensions in its area since the public meeting with the governor and the federal officials a few weeks earlier, wrote, "Since Governor Carr spoke here reassuring the county that the Jap transient situation would soon be under control by the federal government, the number of alien and citizen Japanese in Colorado has increased from about five hundred to twenty-five hundred, according to John Armstrong, Otero County sheriff."

Fears of where they would live and what they would do remained palpable. A group of Pueblo County farmers hired an attorney to try to keep out some three hundred Japanese families who were being evacuated to the Ingersoll Ranch, east of town, only to be told by the governor the matter was out of the state's hands and all demands would have to be taken up with the federal government. That was what Carr had wanted all along, telling a Victory Day Rally in Pueblo, "It has been said that no state in the union has been as prompt as Colorado in following out the national administration's orders in this war. It will be that way so long as I'm your Governor."

Yet, the numerous expressions of patriotism could not prevent the verbal onslaught against the governor's position from continuing, primarily from Senator Johnson.

"Who would have thought one year ago that Governor Carr and Senator Johnson would be in a debate over the bringing by the federal government of Japanese into this state," wrote Alva Swain in his "Under the Capitol Dome" column of April 9. "Such a thought would have been ridiculed by even the most advanced thinkers on political questions. And yet, that subject is before the people, through the position taken by each of the two men and it is going to be one of the debated questions of the coming campaign."

Johnson's reelection campaign had been attempting to return to its populist roots since the war started; that included support for the president at all costs, attacks on Carr for favoring Japanese and publicly refusing outside help. For example, Johnson was asked by his fellow Democrats in the Senate what they could do to help. He turned them down flat. He told reporters, "[I'll] rest my case with the voters of Colorado without any interference."

Johnson believed he would be running against Carr, even though the governor had given no indication as to which office he'd be a candidate for. No matter what position Carr took, Johnson would advocate against it.

"Senator Johnson, who perhaps should be busy in the Senate providing ways and means of protecting the people against the domesticated Japs, appears to be very active urging resolutions by public bodies on the subject," wrote Joe Thomas to his former Antonito neighbor. Thomas told Carr that Johnson wrote a letter to the local newspaper editor suggesting he propose a resolution at the Antonito Chamber of Commerce demanding the internment of all Japanese evacuees who recently came to Colorado.

"I think," Thomas summed up to his friend, "if you have a way of influencing the army people, this Jap question should be solved as soon as possible. It is just the kind of a silly thing that can be used 'by knaves to bait a trap for fools.' It is being ridden as hard as possible while it is still warm."

As the Young Republican League of Colorado gathered for its biennial convention, Weld County Republican Walter Bain announced in the welcoming address he hoped to persuade the governor to be a candidate for the U.S. Senate. Bain said that the campaign was moving quickly among the three thousand people in attendance to "draft" Carr to take on Johnson in November. The move was criticized by the *Pueblo Star-Journal*: "Many Republicans will agree that in Governor Carr they have a splendid political asset and an excellent public servant and for that reason among many other reasons we do not think [the Young Republicans] should crowd him into coming to a decision before he is fully ready to do so."

Colorado Republican Party Chairman William Lloyd decided that Johnson's attacks on the governor could not go unanswered. He sent a letter to the coordinators of the local defense councils around the state, attaching a *Rocky Mountain News* editorial criticizing Johnson for his position on the alien evacuation, and writing, "We thought you might be interested in their slant on this important issue." The editorial addressed a statement Johnson had recently made encouraging Coloradans to "stop bellyaching and start doing something ourselves to win the war."

"We'll tell you who's bellyaching. It's shilly-shallying politicians such as Ed Johnson who are bellyaching," the editorial sent to the defense council coordinators read. "The federal government asked Colorado to handle a number of Jap evacuees from the coast. Governor Carr agreed with stipulations and the people of this state accepted the necessity as part of our war effort. But not Ed Johnson. ... If Ed Johnson did as little bellyaching as the people of this state during these days of sacrifice, he would have a much brighter reputation for integrity."

Johnson accused Carr and the Republicans of "boldly, brazenly, and without shame" politicizing the war effort. He demanded the party "cease such outrageous prostitution of the defense agency dedicated by the people of Colorado to a high and patriotic purpose." He turned a copy of the letter over to the federal government to investigate "this wicked thing." Lloyd apologized and promised not to send anything more to defense council coordinators.

Governor Carr did not comment. Possibly because he had heard from Senator Millikin that, as Alva Swain reported, "The Japs Are Coming." Three thousand were set to be in the first wave, according to what Millikin was telling friends, and they would be located near Alamosa, coincidentally just down the road from Carr's home in Antonito.

"According to the Senator, the federal government will take complete charge of their coming and of them, while they are here," Swain wrote. "They are to be kept in camps, but whether they are to be allowed to work for themselves, work for others or stay in the camps is not yet known."

The governor knew the translation of that meant there would still be concern, there would still be rumors and innuendo floating around Colorado.

This issue simply would not go away.

Chapter Twelve
May to June 1942

Roy Davis was waiting by the phone that May evening, expecting his friend to call. It was the night of an execution and Davis knew a fellow Rotarian, Governor Ralph Carr, would be suffering.

One time they had walked all night, the governor in the "dumps" because a man was set to die in the gas chamber at first light. Carr couldn't pardon the man because a jury of his peers had spoken and because "he was a vicious criminal" and he didn't want to turn him loose on society. However, morally, the Christian Scientist was tormented.

"And so," Davis remembered, "we walked and walked until we were both ready to drop in our tracks. Cement sidewalks can soon make your legs and joints stiffen up until each step causes some degree of pain."

The convict that night was Colorado State Inmate No. 21410, known in the papers as thirty-five-year-old hospital janitor Martin Sukle from Colorado Springs. Sukle, who was convicted of killing his wife's lover, had his case go through the courts twice. During his visit with the governor inside his Cañon City cell, he could give no evidence why his life ought to be spared. So, although Carr had "made many pardons that were not popular with the folks," this time he would not interfere with Sukle's execution.

"That was the most tortured part of being governor for him," said his son, Robert. "It angered him.

"He was always trying to find some excuse to commute sentences although legally he didn't have much basis to do such. Any time there was an execution slated, he'd take no appointments at that time … so if anything developed at the last minute to give him cause to commute the sentence, he'd be available."

He knew Lincoln had once been chastised by his own secretary of war, Edwin Stanton, for pardoning men Stanton thought should be shot. Lincoln pardoned more men than any other president before him. Carr enjoyed the story of Lincoln's boys, Willie and Tad, who sentenced their toy soldier to death for sleeping on guard duty, until their dad stepped in. "The doll Jack is pardoned by order of the President A. Lincoln."

Carr believed men could be rehabilitated. Like Lincoln, he had seen justice up close and believed dearly in what Lincoln said: "I am not bound to win, but I am bound to be true. I am not bound to succeed, but I am bound to live up to what light I have. I must stand by anybody that stands right, stand with him while he is right and part with him when he goes wrong."

During his days as U.S. Attorney, Carr spent many hours in Cañon City, visiting with death row inmates, even those he had put behind bars himself.

Ralph Fleagle was a farmer-turned-bank robber who had killed a couple of people during a holdup in Lamar back in 1930. Carr prosecuted him, pushed to have a strong sentence, and then, spent the last night of Fleagle's life sitting with him as "they recounted their whole lives and everything that had led up to what happened," his son remembered. "He felt even though they were bad characters, they were still very much human beings and that was why he was opposed to the death penalty. That no matter how rotten they'd been in many respects, when he talked to 'em, he saw the other side to 'em, the human side."

Fundamentally, the governor believed human rights were not the creation of the state, but the result of the divine. His parents hadn't associated with any particular Christian denomination when he was growing up. His mother had once told the *Denver Post*, "There were so many times when I needed to feel the closeness of God that [all] I could do was to go up into the hills or into a silent corner of my home. Lift my heart, open my ear and know His presence.

"Then, too, I realized, as I lived and thought and learned, that He couldn't be encased within the walls of any church. So I sought and found Him in my own way and tried to so pattern my life as to reflect His will."

The governor found his first religious home within the walls of the Boulder First Church of Christian Science. In his study of its founder, Mary Baker Eddy's, work, Carr came to believe God's nature could be found through the synonymous names for God used or intimated in the Bible. Names like *Mind*, *Spirit*, *Soul*, *Life*, *Truth*, *Love*, and *Principle*. The governor was known to say, "Principles are as true as truth and will live as long as God's creation."

He found a nonjudgmental faith that offered ways to deal with every aspect of human experience. Unlike Catholicism and many other Christian faiths, Christian Science did not teach that man is fallen and sinful from the outset, but instead freeborn in the likeness of God, with the ability to learn from one's mistakes through prayer. Both his father and older brother had been alcoholics and died young, so the church's teaching on temperance appealed to him. He didn't want to end up like them.

The rigors of being a politician did not make the personal, intimate relationship with his faith easy. He acknowledged as much in a letter to childhood friend Edith Clark when he said, "I have been a Christian Scientist ever since I was in the University. I'm not a good one. I don't know why, but I just ain't."

Perhaps he was thinking of a problem that had surfaced during his first gubernatorial campaign in 1938. His law partner, John Shippey, who traveled with him everywhere, noticed he was drinking lots of liquid, dropping weight, and having trouble with his eyesight. Because he was a Christian Scientist, he resisted going to the doctor, believing he could look to prayer and spiritual means for healing. He lost thirty-five pounds and went through three new eyeglasses prescriptions before his campaign staff selected Myrtle Graham to have a talk with him about his health.

Carr's wife, Gretchen, had died suddenly of complications from diabetes in 1937; Shippey, whose dad, Orland, was a veteran family-practice physician, felt the signs were similar for her widower. Carr had two young teenage kids already without their mother and Graham convinced him that he must see the doctor.

"He realized all he had to do was watch his food and take insulin," said Graham. "He ended up being very good about it and very healthy."

Yet, he had broken with the teachings of Eddy, who felt she had discovered the art of healing that Jesus himself spoke about through prayer. If Carr truly believed that God controlled all, as his church taught, he would have believed the functions of his body were not random, not subject to failure, but able to be managed through a clear understanding of God.

Because he never spoke publicly about his decision to receive medical treatment, a group called the Colorado Welfare Committee actively used his faith against him during his first gubernatorial campaign. Members distributed a flyer reading: "Ralph W. [sic] Carr is a member of the Christian Science Church and is, therefore—personally opposed to medical treatment. This fact ... brings us to the question; what would then become of the health, school and the welfare programs of the state of Colorado? In the interest of the entire medical profession and your own future ... defeat Ralph Carr."

After being elected governor, he was faced with another troubling conflict between his faith and his profession. The legislature had passed a bill requiring blood tests for marriage, which as a Christian Scientist he was against, but he signed it into law. "My personal belief is otherwise," his son remembered him saying. "It was a troubling thing for him, but he listened to the doctors and to the health department who were in favor of it."

He regularly called Gordon Comer, his spiritual mentor or "practitioner" in the Christian Science church, to talk over troubling issues. Comer served as Carr's confidante, a spiritual help in trying to understand and overcome life's problems. It would have been difficult for the Colorado National Bank executive to continue to serve as Carr's practitioner if he had known the governor took insulin daily, but he would not have condemned him. He could still have been a friend to help Carr through the ethical minefields of his job and his life.

Carr had no trouble resolving his faith with his stand on the issue of Japanese evacuees. In Eddy's "Science and Health with Key to the Scriptures," the script that helps explain the Bible for Christian Scientists, she wrote "The question, 'What is Truth' convulses the world. Many are ready to meet this inquiry with the assurance which comes of understanding; but more are blinded by their old illusions, and try to 'give it pause.' 'If the blind lead the blind, both shall fall into the ditch.'"

Carr had no desire to fall into the proverbial ditch or to let Coloradans fall, if at all possible. He spoke regularly about Matthew 7:12 and Luke 6:31, more commonly known as the Golden Rule, or "Do unto others as you would have them do to you." In fact, he regularly surmised that the framers of the United States Constitution had these principles of goodwill to all in mind during their convention in Philadelphia.

"It seems to me that the whole answer is to be found in whether or not we can really believe in the Constitution and Bill of Rights," Carr wrote to the *Christian Century* magazine for its May 20 issue. "The whole answer is one of patriotism and if you want to go a little further as I do, it is the application of the Golden Rule to a very trying problem of life. If we do not extend humanity's kindness and understanding to these people, if we deny them the protection of the Bill of Rights, if we say they may be denied the privilege of living in any of the forty-eight states and force them into concentration camps without hearing or charge of misconduct, then we are tearing down the whole American system.

"If these people are not to be accorded all the rights and privileges the Constitution gives them, then those same rights and privileges may be denied to you and me six months from now for another just as poor reason as the one which is now offered against the Japanese."

He found friends through faith.

Methodist clergy wrote him: "If there were more Americans like you who demonstrate their Christianity and their Democracy with deeds, I would not fear for the future of our country," wrote A. W. Munk, a pastor from Bloomington. "It makes me proud of being a former Coloradoan and of being a minister of Jesus Christ to find such attitudes being taken. God bless you for it," Minister Harold Olson wrote from Sterling, Illinois.

The Baptists offered to help in the resettlement. The Denver Council of Churches and Religious Education issued a resolution commending him for his "fine statement on the Japanese situation."

Carr received letters from Christians in Tennessee, New Hampshire, Washington, Connecticut, California, and Oregon. H. T. Tyler complimented Carr on his "splendid" position despite what he correctly assumed was intense pressure to do otherwise. "I do not doubt that there will be many who will severely censure you for speaking out so boldly on this issue." Martha Johnson told Carr that for his humanness and understanding, she "shall always love" him. "Here after, I shall always think of Colorado as the state with a soul—and you as a true proponent of the teachings of Christ and Lincoln."

There could be no greater compliment for Governor Carr, whose favorite phrase, included in most of his correspondence of the day, was a tribute to both of his inspirations. "The Constitution includes all people," he wrote to the Rev. DeWitt Talmadge Alcorn in Coffeyville, Kansas, and numerous others. "We must preserve its principles for every man or we shall not have it to protect any man."

The praise and compliments were welcome—and rare. As emotions about the war swirled, Carr knew the majority of citizens disagreed with his principles.

Anger toward the evacuees and those who shared their race continued, inspired in part by FBI data released to the public showing that from February through May, it had seized 2,592 guns, 199,000 rounds of ammunition, and 1,652 sticks of dynamite. In addition, they had recovered 1,458 radio receivers, 2,914 cameras, and 37 motion picture cameras. So underwhelming was the haul that Department of Justice officials confided in a private memo to the president, "We have not found among all the sticks of dynamite and gun powder any evidence that any of it was to be used in bombs. We have not found a single machine gun nor have we found any gun in any circumstances indicating that it was to be used in a manner helpful to our enemies. We have not found a camera which we have reason to believe was for use in espionage."

Still, Carr's friend Byrd Fuqua wrote from Nathrop, on Colorado's eastern plains, "Jap Grape-vine talk is growing around here, wish you could make another Radio talk. You MUST be our next Governor and we can't afford to loose [*sic*] any Republican votes around these here parts."

Camp Carson, in the recently designated military area of Colorado Springs, held its "battle cry" contest to come up with a slogan befitting the fight ahead. "Sap the Japs with Hammer Raps" was a possibility, as was "A Punch for Tokyo with every Hammer Blow." Also considered: "Man to Man We'll Whip Japan" and "Don't Nap—Beat a Jap." The winner turned out to be "Nail the Planks—Here Come the Yanks."

Nerves were short. Local papers like the *Rocky Mountain Herald* were running stories advising people how to make smokeless gun powder, known as nitrocellulose or gun cotton, in case Colorado were invaded. The paper reminded them in the process: "DON'T LIGHT ANY MATCHES IN THE VICINITY, because what you have is good medicine for Japs."

The National Rifle Association (NRA) was lobbying Governor Carr and the State National Guard to train Colorado's "civilian rifleman" because a raid by enemy forces met "by the fire of ten sporting rifles delivered at 5:00 is likely to be more effective in disrupting a raid than the fire of fifty rifles which do not arrive until 5:45."

The group sent out "The Fifth Column Strikes Tonight," a fictitious story about a large defense plant in the state approached by three trucks with fifty saboteurs apiece, dressed as soldiers. According to the story, the saboteurs herd up the plant employees before "methodically [mowing] them down." They then plant explosives, and in less than half an hour, "Their work is done. … THIS CAN HAPPEN TO YOU—TO YOUR PLAN—ARM YOUR EMPLOYEES—BE PREPARED TO MEET THIS ATTACK."

Being prepared to the federal government meant rationing across the country without regard to local opinions.

Tire rationing was in place, and sugar rationing was coming. Gas rationing was being advocated as well by many in Washington. A special congressional committee was set to take up the March mining priority order, designed to deny machinery and equipment to Colorado's gold and silver mines that authorities felt did not produce the complex ores needed to win the war.

In early May, the president called a federal-state conference at the Commerce Department to talk about how states could continue to lift "legal restrictions to the war effort." In a message he sent to the governors and state officials in attendance gathered at a Washington hotel, Roosevelt told them that various building codes, weight restrictions for highways, and employment laws in their states had "imposed a heavy toll on the national war effort." His cabinet members and their staffers used the same message for the next two days: Do away with needless state regulation, so America could win the war.

From Carr's perspective, the conference was an unmitigated disaster.

"I hate to say it, but it is true nevertheless," he told reporters afterward. "The people who spoke to us and they were at the heads of many of the important departments, are just totally ignorant of the things they were trying to discuss."

The governor asked what Colorado laws were causing problems to the pursuit of victory. He wasn't the only governor asking that question. Time after time, none of the major cabinet-level federal officials could cite how a specific law in any of the states was causing problems.

Finally, the feds stated that inspectors at ports of entry were "trade barriers." Yet, those were the very people Carr used to track the migration of Japanese evacuees, a problem that the federal government had not taken care of as promised.

"After they had talked to us for hours, they would send us to small rooms where we met a bunch of clerks," Carr described. "The first day, when we went in the room that had been assigned to Colorado, we found a girl about twenty years old. She said, 'You folks collect a wheel tax on trucks, do you not?'

"I told her we did on private trucks. She said that we must repeal that law. I asked her why and she replied, 'I don't know but they told me to tell you it had to be done,' and that is as far as we got with her."

He was chaffed about a plan making it a federal offense to exceed the speed limit. Carr could understand encouraging residents to save rubber by driving at slower speeds, but to turn federal courts into traffic courts seemed the ultimate case of a federal power grab. He told the United Press that to acquiesce to this policy would be to "surrender the last vestige of local control to the national government."

His disdain for the administration's policies was expressed in both public and private.

His contempt truly manifested itself when it came to the topic of the Japanese evacuees. Senator Millikin called Carr's office to warn about the placing of a center for evacuated Japanese. Then, Senator Johnson said he had received a request for a suitable location from Milton Eisenhower himself. Johnson told the Associated Press that he had been assured that the "colony would be under armed guard twenty-four hours daily." Eisenhower preferred that the five or six thousand Japanese evacuees be located on public land or on land "requiring a great amount of labor to improve."

The question of location continued to vex Coloradans, including its chief executive. Rumors circulated about a site near Alamosa. Putting a site on the Pine River in southwestern Colorado was bandied about, as was the renovation of CCC camps in Sterling in the east and Grand Junction in the west. The governor had not been consulted, which angered him greatly.

Casualty reports were starting to come in, making front-page news throughout the state, every day bringing worse news. The Japanese had occupied Mandalay in Burma, Tulagi, in the Solomon Islands, and most important, Corregidor, the last bastion for American soldiers in the Philippine Islands. Every day, the navy and the army released reports listing Coloradans who were dead or missing in action.

Simultaneously, numerous reports of mistreatment of Americans at the hands of the Japanese were revealed. Both coasts of the United States were warned about the possible use of poisonous gas in an attack. Pictures showing the "horrors of gas warfare" reportedly from the Japanese against their Chinese enemy were printed in the *Rocky Mountain News*.

In that climate, local FBI chief Gordon Nicholson created more confusion by making contradictory statements to the press and releasing different numbers about how many Japanese evacuees had come to Colorado. First, he told the United Press for an article that would be printed in numerous statewide papers, that there were approximately five thousand Japanese now in Colorado, nearly double the number who had lived there before the migration began in February. He told the wire service that "many" of the evacuees had been arrested, would have hearings before the enemy alien hearing board, and that the agency would continue to be most interested in "those whom we have come to suspect as questionably loyal to this country."

But just one day later to the *Denver Post*, Nicholson pulled back on his numbers and his tone by saying that it appeared the number of Japanese in Colorado had only gone up 40 percent since the migration, not 100 percent. He also told the *Post* that the evacuees had been "well-behaved ... we have encountered only minor difficulties with them."

Whatever the truth, the governor continued to hear about concerns and problems with any proposed relocation center in Colorado. Local Union No. 5990 wrote from Ramey, Colorado, that its one hundred eleven members were against any settlement. "They were one hundred percent against Japs settling here and they would like for you to be against them also. So if you would ban Japs settling here this local would feel one hundred percent better."

Florence Andrews, a Republican committeewoman for the last decade in Weld County, was angry about the influx of evacuees in her community. "I am wondering, like many others, just what assurance we have that these newly arrived Japanese are not a menace to our person and property?" she wrote the governor. "Within a half mile of my home is a house now occupied by more than one Japanese family. They are most impudent and bold whenever we pass the house."

The head of the Phillips County Republicans on Colorado's eastern plains wrote to voice opposition to the government buying ten to twelve thousand acres for the placement of up to six thousand Japanese. "There is an awful objection to this," Ed Owens wrote. "We took a vote on this proposition and there were 79 people present, the vote resulted in 78 opposed to it and 1 for it. I think I can safely state that if this proposition was put to a vote in this County that at least 95% of the people here would vote against it."

Carr continued to receive more requests from many Japanese seeking to buy land in the state. As Colorado was one of the few states in the region that did not prevent noncitizens from owning property, and because the governor turned down requests for a special legislative session to consider such legislation, the state had become a destination for many evacuees hoping to find a home someplace. E. R. Fryer, the regional director of the WRA, wrote the governor that his agency was "receiving many requests from Japanese Americans, for permits to investigate land opportunities in Colorado."

A group of farmers in Pueblo were concerned enough to hire an attorney to lobby the governor against the sale of the Ingersoll Ranch near the city to Japanese evacuees. Their worries had a good basis. Carr was being lobbied by federal officials in California, who sent him a telegram: "Understand that local Japanese people wish to settle in your state. Have cooperated with this office in this emergency wonderfully. Integrity and ability unquestioned. Will highly recommend them to you."

The positive message was also being sent by the Colorado Division of Agriculture. Its director, W. C. Sweinhart, had written numerous Californians looking to purchase land in Colorado that "while there is [a] tremendous amount of publicity and agitation against increasing the land-owning Japanese population, we feel that much of it is due to temperamental animosity. ... This office has many contacts with very high-class Japanese and we hold them in the highest esteem."

The biggest and most infuriating problem for Carr, however, was that he didn't know what the government's plans were for the evacuees. He had met with Eisenhower during the trip to Washington and got the sense that the army had taken over the issue, with reception centers to be built containing schools, farming opportunities, social contacts, etc. "It would be folly for me to suggest some place in Colorado for you to attempt to go when the Army is planning to take care of the whole problem," he said in a letter to Kay Nishimura.

However, when it came to making a policy about whether or how Japanese could leave a center to go to work, the army

passed the buck. Colonel Bendetsen wrote Carr with the following information: Japanese could leave the West Coast to settle
inland as long as there was an approval designated by a joint statement in writing in each case of private employment, signed by the
governor, the county attorney, the county sheriff, the chairman
of the county board, and the employer. The rules and regulations
spelled out on the written contract included an agreement by the
state and local authorities to "maintain order and to prevent any
direct action" as "no federal troops will be available for protection
or supervision" for the evacuees.

The very concern Carr had, when President Roosevelt had
issued the directive essentially removing anyone of Japanese
descent from the West Coast, was being realized. He would not
use his National Guard troops to guard American citizens. He
envisioned the work he had put in all over the state, to assuage
citizens they would be safe despite their leanings toward hysteria,
going for naught.

He gathered sixty Colorado representatives from the law
enforcement and the farming communities for a meeting at the
capitol. They gathered and talked for the better part of two days,
eventually coming to the same conclusion as the governor. When
he told reporters the consensus of the meeting, the entire group
voiced support of his decision, according to journalist Alva Swain.

The sentiment shared by all was that the "handling of the Japanese as individuals is a federal and not a state problem." The governor wrote General DeWitt and told him that he could not agree "to
receive Japanese evacuees into Colorado under those terms."

Everything he had told Coloradans from the beginning of
this process was crumbling.

"The FBI and the Army are believed to be supervising the
movement and the conduct of all such people. This has rendered
it possible for me to keep the people calm and in a fair frame
of mind. The feeling of insecurity was dispelled. Should it now
be announced that the United States has ceased to exercise this

vigilance. … The problem would be magnified. The whole picture would be distorted."

Tensions, as Carr predicted, remained high. State senator Averill Johnson wrote the governor asking for help in solving the labor problem in his eastern district, but said, "There is still considerable opposition to the Japanese labor question." School districts in counties like Otero and Weld, which received large numbers of children of Japanese descent, were debating whether they would be forced to raise taxes to pay for the additional students.

More serious, the first reported violence against an evacuee took place in Pueblo. Kenneth Togo was severely beaten, with injuries to his face and head, and his home was set on fire because, he said, of his nationality. The *Pueblo Chieftain* reported that Togo told police he met the men at a tavern on Northern Avenue and shortly after that he was beaten. He also told authorities that he had been beaten up several weeks prior under similar circumstances.

In this atmosphere, things began to happen quickly.

Carr received a phone call from Colonel Bendetsen in San Francisco on June 2 informing him that a site had been selected for a relocation center. The rumors would now end. The site was known as the X-Y Ranch area in Prowers County, close to the town of Granada, in the very southeast part of Colorado. It was a windy and dusty spot on the state's high plains.

The governor's reaction was included in a letter he wrote to the head of the Colorado River Water Conservation District. "They did not ask my advice or approval," Carr wrote. "So be it."

Carr knew this would happen and so, too, did his neighboring governors. Although they benefited politically because of their rhetoric, they still ended up with internment camps in their states.

Wyoming governor Nels Smith, who had earlier said that if Japanese were sent to his state, they'd be "hanging from every pine tree," saw the Heart Mountain internment camp opened that summer. It would eventually hold more than 10,700 people of Japanese descent.

Arizona governor Sidney Osborn, who had said, "We not only vigorously protest, but will not permit the evacuation of Japanese, German, or Italian aliens to any point in Arizona," ended up with two camps and a total of roughly thirty thousand internees.

Arkansas governor Homer Adkins had said, "I doubt the wisdom of placing any [Japanese] in Arkansas," but witnessed the construction of two camps, housing nearly seventeen thousand people.

Idaho attorney general Bart Miller, who wanted to keep his state "white man's country," saw a camp constructed for almost 9,400 internees.

Utah governor Herbert Maw, who had complained that, "the army and the WRA [are] much too concerned about the constitutional rights of Japanese American citizens," could do nothing to prevent a camp housing 8,130 internees.

California officials, from the governor to the attorney general to the mayor of Los Angeles, all of whom had campaigned to move the "menace" from their midst, were powerless to stop the erection of two camps in the eastern part of the state where nearly thirty thousand internees were held.

In all, a hundred and twenty thousand people of Japanese descent would be sent to internment camps that summer.

The day the Granada camp was announced to the Colorado public, the Japanese bombed a military base at Dutch Harbor in Alaska, dropping high explosives and incendiary bombs, killing thirty-five Americans. Planes circled back for a second run the next day. It was the first attack on American soil since Pearl Harbor and it engendered much of the same hysteria and paranoia that took place after the Hawaii bombing. A "flash bulletin" telegram went out within two hours from the Colorado Council of Defense to the one hundred thirty seven local councils around the state from the head of the 7th Defense Region at Omaha, Nebraska.

"Two attacks on Dutch Harbor by Japanese planes are direct notice to you that cities in your state are in immediate danger.

Token raids in the Midwest must be anticipated soon," Regional Director Joseph Scholtz wrote. "We must be ready. This means that training of all local units of citizens defense corps must be completed in shortest possible time so that they may be ready to function efficiently in emergency. Delay plays into the hands of the Japs."

The *Rocky Mountain Herald* reported, "Denver was to have been bombed ... according to two sober bets we recently learned of. The Japs over Alaska didn't quite get here. The argument goes something like this: Successful invasion of America is out of the question, but bombing is possible: inland bombing would be psychologically more useful," the story said. "Denver, the argument goes, would be an ideal target—across only one state from the Mexican border ... with the big ordnance plant shining like Orion on New Year's Eve."

Residents quickly learned about "yellow messages," which meant preliminary caution to air-raid wardens. A "blue message" indicated that the enemy was approaching and to be ready for blackouts, and a "red message" would set off air-raid sirens and include a full blackout. The Denver Defense Council was given a chart of the potential bombs that could be dropped on the city during a raid, complete with weight, size, potential targets, and their explosive abilities. Members were reminded that "to date no known agent has been found that will extinguish a magnesium bomb."

Residents also began to let the governor know their unhappiness over the location of the 10,150-acre relocation center.

"Although it is true, you offered our State of Colorado as a refuge for Jap evacuees, you surely did not intend for the best land in the Arkansas Valley to be confiscated for their use," wrote Mrs. Fred Kennedy, who was losing her home to the camp. "Please think of the sacrifices of many of us who have already given up our Sons to defend our land and our American way of living. Will it not seem to our Sons, as well as ourselves that it is none less than an insult added to injury to be subjugated in this manner into giving up our beloved homes that these Japs, our potential enemies may have the best."

The business leaders of the community chimed in. Carr received a letter from the head of the American State Bank in Granada, disapproving of the location of the camp. "It does not seem fair that these people should be forced out of their homes to make room for a bunch of Japs," wrote H. E. McKeever. "I can not believe it is necessary for our Government to condemn good producing land and set adrift a lot of good American farmers in order to find a place for our Jap enemy population."

Eisenhower, and his soon-to-be successor Dillon Myer, believed "Some inconvenience would be caused but we knew of no other site satisfactory for a center which would not have caused greater inconvenience." Half of the land was already irrigated and an additional one thousand acres were irrigable, leading to hopes of producing sugar beets, alfalfa and small grains. Up to seven thousand evacuees were expected to be housed there, with barbed wire surrounding the facility, and a twenty-four-hour guard.

The governor reiterated to those concerned that he had nothing to do with the decision, nothing to do with the location, nothing to do with this whole problem, but he continued to have trouble convincing them. "Would suggest," Margaret Smith wrote, "that the Japs be exchanged—two for one if necessary—for our boys in Japan and all of them, regardless of the place of their birth sent back to their native land."

Lamar attorney Wilkie Ham, whose city was located close to the camp, wrote: "It is reassuring to have some one in public office that has the courage to take [a] stand in the spirit of patriotism rather than what might be popular," Ham stated. But before Carr could take solace in knowing he had an ally, Ham continued, "I make the above statement not because I happen to agree with the sentiment that you have expressed but because I feel that you were inspired by something more patriotic than politics."

At least he understood the governor's position, unlike so

many others. The most recent statistics from the state Highway Courtesy Patrol showed there were now 1,605 Japanese who had moved to Colorado since the war started, an increase of nearly 60 percent over the population before Pearl Harbor. The anger toward the Japanese was so real that even Dr. Seuss, the noted children's author, had developed an ad campaign encouraging people to buy war bonds and stamps that showed a Japanese man smiling with the caption, "Wipe that sneer off his face!"

So when the governor and his driver were driving back one night to Denver from Pueblo, they were understandably cautious when they noticed they were being followed. Threats had been a part of life for the governor since he took a stand regarding the Japanese evacuees. The car trailed closely for miles, slowing down when the patrolman slowed down and speeding up when he sped up.

Carr knew they had to stop. As he pulled to the side of Highway 85, the other car pulled to the shoulder as well. Without waiting for his driver, the governor flew out the back of his Buick, right up to the driver's side window, and demanded, "How come you keep following us?" The driver, embarrassed, stammered, "Good gosh, Governor, I did not know it was you I was trailing. … I was just lonesome. I thought I would stay right behind you for protection on this lonely road."

Not all experiences for the governor worked out so well. He and Senator Johnson had both been asked to provide statements for the Colorado Federation of Labor on their positions regarding the Japanese evacuee situation. To a group that generally aligned itself with the Democratic Party, the governor knew the challenge, yet he did not fear it. "Few questions of such comparatively minor importance have seized the attention of the people and have evoked the discussion and heightened the emotions as the question of the reception of Japanese into the inland states after evacuation from the Pacific Coast," wrote the governor.

He told them the state's economic structure had not been

upended and wouldn't be. There had been no crimes committed by any of the evacuees and he hoped there wouldn't be. He explained he was standing for the very principles America was fighting for in the war. "[The] Constitution starts out by saying, 'We the people of the United States.' It doesn't say 'We the people, who are descendants of the English or the Scandinavians or the French.' It says, 'We the people.' ... When it is suggested that American citizens be thrown into concentration camps, where they lose all the privileges of citizenship under that Constitution, then the principles of that great document are violated and lost."

Johnson took the other side, urging the governor to "close the borders to wandering Japanese migrants, whether citizens of the United States or not." Further, he challenged Carr's stance that his was the patriotic thing to do. "Instead of Colorado being patriotic and helpful to the federal government, she was the only state that acted contrary to the federal governor's wishes by encouraging these frightened Orientals to flee from their homes in the night. Colorado handicapped the orderly handling of this very delicate problem for selfish purposes. General DeWitt finally was forced by Colorado's underground railroad tactics to put a stop to flight-by-night escape."

When Carr spoke to the group at its annual convention, he challenged its members, that they, as men and women of organized labor, should understand the principle better than most. They, as minorities at times, should not be forced to subjugate their rights to employers, simply on whim.

"When a man occupies a place in public life, as I see it, it is his duty to protect and preserve the rights of all. ... A man is an American first with everything that term connotes. He is an American in every ideal and hope and plan and duty and obligation.

"I am talking NOT on behalf of Japanese, of Italians, or of Germans as such when I say this," he implored the group in Colorado Springs. "I am talking for you, working men of Colorado, for the farmers, the industrialists, the executives, for all American people, whether their skins be white, brown, or black and regard-less of the birthplaces of their grandfathers, when I say that if a majority may deprive a minority of its freedom, contrary to the terms of the Constitution today, then you as a minority may be subjected to the same ill-will of the majority tomorrow. If we do not protect and preserve the Constitution and the Bill of Rights for all men today, it will not serve as a protection for any man six months from now."

The rhetoric polished, the position stabilized, it was time to announce his political plans for the fall. For months, the governor had feared that any announcement would cloud the public's per-ception of any decision he would make. For example, he had given a speech in early June in Greeley where he once again stressed how the rights of the individual were paramount in any govern-ment Americans would elect, saying, "As long as I am governor, and that won't be long—six months, I am going to work with the people of Colorado toward the goal of retaining the kind of gov-ernment our boys are fighting for."

Political speculation about what Carr was going to do domi-nated the news coverage, rather than what he said about policy. Columnist Alva Swain reported, "For the last six weeks a rumor has been started at the capitol about Wednesday that Governor [Carr] was certainly going to announce what he intends to do the next Sunday. But the next Sunday, and the next and the next could come and go and the Governor would not announce."

When it finally came, the announcement itself was some-what anticlimactic. Governor or senator? Senator or governor? The political gossips had talked about it since before the first of the year. Would it be Carr versus Johnson for the senate? Would it be Carr versus a Democrat for governor? Would it be Carr going back to what he always wanted to do, practice law?

Hours before he left to attend a governors' conference in North Carolina on June 19, he sent a forty-word statement to William Lloyd, the party chairman. "This is to advise you, as chairman of the Republican state central committee, of my candidacy for nomination for the long term in the United States Senate, subject to the will of the Republican voters at the primary in September."

There would be no primary though. No one would challenge the Republican Party heavyweight, who would then challenge Colorado's Democratic Party heavyweight, Ed Johnson.

"I have known for four years that Governor Carr would be a candidate for the Senate, so this announcement comes as no surprise," Johnson told the Associated Press from Washington.

As if to remind him of an issue sure to be mentioned on the campaign trail up to November, the governor once again was being deluged by requests from Japanese to move to Colorado just as construction work was beginning at the Granada relocation camp. The army engineers had arrived in neighboring Lamar to set up their temporary headquarters inside the state armory building, but Japanese were hoping to settle in Colorado in places other than the Granada camp.

"Would you be interested in a group of people on your farms," wrote Kiyoshi Okamoto, from the Santa Anita Center, on Tenth Street, Block 9, Unit 4.

The retired chief of police from Berkeley, California, wrote on behalf of George and Rindge Shima. "I have known them since infancy and can certify that they are loyal and good citizens," stated August Vollmer. "Please grant their petition."

Kiyoto Uriu submitted the names of three PhD professors from San Jose State College as witnesses to his character and that of the ten family members he wished to move to Brighton, Colorado, where the local sheriff had already given permission.

John Hada was seeking a letter from Governor Carr to rejoin his parents, who lived in Keenesburg, Colorado.

All these requests to the governor made him feel helpless. He simply could not fathom interning American citizens because of their race. Even when the notes came from Mesa County sheriff

H. E. Decker certifying the character of two Japanese on the West Coast, he could do nothing, as it was in the hands of the federal government. He could only reply, "I cannot offer you either advice or encouragement."

Thomas Kido, an American-born Japanese living in Brighton, Colorado, wrote: "In peaceful times we were called fine people, fine Americans," Kido wrote. "In wartime we are now called, en masse, a suspicious, traitorous, and dangerous element. Must we have white faces to be Americans at all times?"

Carr was beside himself and replied, "I want to urge upon you is that you do not become embittered, no matter how great the provocation. Please know that if you keep your thinking straight, you are going to find many, many more people who will look upon you kindly and treat you graciously than the other type. It takes years—and sometimes generations—to wipe out prejudices and ill-feeling. But those who believe as I do will carry on the battle for the rights of all men."

Chapter Thirteen
July to August 1942

The University of Colorado that Ralph Carr attended back in 1910 was much different than the one his children attended in 1942. Instead of worrying about war, death, and the future of democracy, Carr and his fellow students worried about hazing.

Sixteen students, "clad in nothing but the rare Colorado atmosphere," were suspended in the fall of 1910 for taking part in an event that had freshmen running around Woodbury Hall naked. When it had been completed in 1890, Woodbury was labeled the best men's dormitory west of the Mississippi River, as it was "heated with steam, lighted by electricity and supplied with hot and cold running water."

On the late October evening in question, the steam heat and hot running water would be needed. Tradition called for the freshmen in the building to receive, as the *Silver and Gold* campus newspaper reported, "the regular initiation into the 'dorm club.'" The first-years "voluntarily stripped, took two laps around the building barefooted and then, took a hot shower bath."

University of Colorado president James Baker seized on the incident to abolish hazing on campus and immediately suspended four students for one full month and twelve others for two weeks. He said the unusual leniency he had exhibited in the recent past was gone, and even though the freshmen said the run was voluntary, the suspensions would stand.

The students immediately called a campus-wide strike to protest the suspensions, and refused to go to classes until their grievances were heard. A committee of student leaders was appointed to meet with President Baker and faculty members to ask for the reconsideration of the suspensions. Ralph Carr was appointed to that committee.

He was a first-year law student who had received his bachelor's degree from the school earlier that year. As hundreds of CU students protested outside many of the university's rural Italian-style buildings built of Colorado sandstone and red tile roofs, Carr was inside meeting with President Baker.

He emerged unsatisfied and foreshadowed his future candor with the media during his political career. "[We] had been completely ignored," he told a *Boulder Daily Camera* reporter. "[Our] usefulness was at an end." Ever practical, Carr recommended students return to classes.

In 1942, the classes being offered to his son and daughter on the Boulder campus were dramatically different, many geared to help the war effort. Men were signing up or being called to fight in the war in droves. Women and those who couldn't fight were expected to contribute to the war effort. It seemed that the halls of higher education might echo with emptiness.

However, the president of the University of Colorado, Robert Stearns, came up with a creative solution he thought would serve both college students and the larger community.

From Pearl Harbor on, the college "keyed its research and teaching activities to the program of national defense."

The Boulder-based school created and expanded facilities to train aviators, offered courses in engineering defense, technical studies in physics and chemistry, and enough training opportunities for naval officers that it was called "Annapolis of the West." At the start of the war, Stearns knew there was room to increase contracts with the various service branches "many fold."

The army surgeon general directed an expansion of both the medical school's general hospital and the school of nursing. The navy meanwhile established a program through the School of Business Administration to train men for administrative positions currently occupied by line officers needed elsewhere. It also signed a contract with the school for the training of naval radio operators, to help train hundreds of men in the concepts of receiving and sending messages by telegraph. One course was dedicated to radar detection.

As comfortable quoting Benjamin Franklin as he was the Sermon on the Mount, Stearns walked in the footsteps of his predecessor George Norlin, whose motto was "Who only knows his own generation remains always a child." CU's president advocated ending discrimination against the school's black and other minority students. "Nothing is more duplicitous," he once said, "than the utterance of fine phrases without a willingness at least to struggle for the attainment of the ideals which they express."

When it came to the topic of bringing Japanese Americans to campus in 1942, he knew he had a supporter in fellow University of Colorado graduate Governor Ralph Carr.

Carr and Stearns were good friends, having developed their relationship after Carr moved back to Denver from southern Colorado, allowing him to attend alumni functions. Aside from Carr, Stearns was one of the rare voices right after Pearl Harbor preaching calm to the student body and tolerance toward the Japanese in the university community. "I've read your statement to the students and think it is the best I have heard since this difficulty came on," Carr wrote him. "I know it had a wonderful effect, as reflected through the statements of my own children."

Courtesy of a five-to-one vote by the board of regents, Stearns brought American-born Japanese students to Boulder who had been evacuated from the West Coast. In the early summer, he was presented with another opportunity dealing with American-born Japanese. It was an opportunity made possible by the stand of Governor Carr.

Since 1922, the navy had required its officers stationed in Tokyo to take a three-year course in Japanese. Yet, by the end of 1940, only about sixty-five had been trained in the difficult language, and of those, only twelve were regarded as completely proficient in spoken and written Japanese. Out of more than two hundred thousand enlisted officers and men, only a dozen were conversant in the language of the country that loomed as a potential enemy.

By December of 1940, classes weren't being taught in Tokyo because of strained diplomatic relations between the two countries, so programs were set up at the University of California at Berkeley and at Harvard University in Massachusetts. The goal was to produce officers "thoroughly competent in reading, writing and speaking Japanese in quantity and quality sufficient to anticipate the demands which might be made upon the Service for such persons, particularly, in the event of war between Japan and the United States."

The curriculum was intense for the college graduates who applied. They went to classes fourteen hours a day, six days a week, fifty weeks per year, and were tested frequently, taking two hundred fifty hours worth of examinations by the end of the year-long course, far more than any university student completing a four-year degree. Grammar, syntax, phonetics, linguistics, and "all academic theory" were scrapped for practicality and time's sake. Teachers focused on the "how" to speak the language, not on the "why" things were done the way they were.

All classroom discussions were conducted in Japanese, with no English whatsoever. Assignments might be: "Discuss for twenty minutes in Japanese the economic relations of Japan and the United States for the last 50 years." Outside the classroom, students were given records, bulletins, and daily newspapers in Japanese and were encouraged to talk with their classmates in the foreign language.

"Treat the students for what they are," the manual outlining the program read, "college graduates, mature, conscientious, serious, single-minded, and top-ranking scholars from America's best universities."

By the end of fourteen months, each student was expected to be able to read and write roughly two thousand Japanese characters and have a spoken vocabulary of eight thousand words. They should be able to easily read a newspaper in Japanese, listen to a radio program in Japanese, or simply have a conversation in that language. In the early part of 1942, it was decided to significantly increase the student population in the course that had only fifty-six enrolled. However, with the evacuation of the West Coast, the Japanese Americans, who were serving as instructors at the University of California facility, were forced to leave. Naval Intelligence, which ran the Japanese Language School, thought it would be able to facilitate exceptions for its faculty, but General DeWitt ruled against it.

The University of Colorado "had been kept in reserve as a potential location to meet this eventuality," according to the program's commander A. E. Hindmarsh. However, the Japanese Language School would be unlike any of the other naval contracts signed with the Boulder campus, because of the faculty required to come along with it.

At a time when Colorado was protesting the importation of any Japanese into its borders, the navy suggested placing numerous American-born Japanese in the city of Boulder, population 12,958. As Hindmarsh described it, "The University of Colorado and the city of Boulder were thus called upon to meet a most unusual situation."

To put a school like this in a state where its governor disapproved of Japanese Americans would have created an untenable position. The navy needed to locate somewhere quickly where they had a relationship and where the politics of the move would not be a hindrance.

That place, thanks to Governor Carr and President Stearns, was the University of Colorado at Boulder.

Stearns signed the contract with the navy, and by July, the Harvard part of the program had been cancelled and the first of what would eventually be hundreds of prospective translators, code breakers, and interrogators, descended upon Boulder with their stated goal to "fight this war of the Pacific with words instead of bullets."

Having men who spoke and understood the Japanese language became more important because it was clear the Japanese were using English in an effort to confuse Allied forces. The *Rocky Mountain News* reported that "most Japanese officers speak English and the radio is used in attempts to start false rumors in Australia." An example was given to the newspaper by a Dutch pilot who was attempting to return to a naval base with a limited amount of fuel when he called what he thought was the field control station.

"Hello, Charley, this is Tommy. Can I come in now?" the pilot asked.

"Hello, Tommy, this is Charley. Don't come in," was the response.

A few minutes later, the pilot tried again, worried he'd run out of fuel. "Can I come in now?"

"Not now, Tommy, there's a Japanese raid going on here."

He looked for cover in the clouds and waited a few more moments before trying again.

"Hello, Charley, my fuel is almost exhausted. Must come in soon."

The reply, "Don't come in Tommy. The Japs are still bombing here."

With only fumes left in his tank, he landed to peace and quiet. No bombing raid, no Jap attack, and no communication with the control tower.

As Japanese Americans were being invited by the navy to live in Boulder, the army was still telling others along the West Coast that they could move to Colorado with the permission of the governor. Carr continued to receive "large numbers" of requests from relatives and friends of those wishing to live in the Rocky Mountain state.

Army Private Saburo Yamaguchi was stationed at Camp Carson in Colorado Springs when he wrote the governor to request a permit "for my folks and family to move to Denver." His mom was sixty-eight years old, his dad, seventy-three. His brother and sister, who were both American citizens, believed that their parents were "too old to (survive) a Assembly Center

Camp life which they will be required to go (to) in the later part of this month."

Kaoru Helen Negi wrote Carr that her fiancé was at the relocation camp in Arizona, while she was in Colorado. The WRA officials suggested that she get an assurance from the governor so they could be married and help the war effort in whatever capacity they could.

William Reuter Jr., a letter carrier in Oakland, wanted a transfer to the Longmont, Colorado post office because his wife was an "American citizen of Japanese ancestry."

Carr wrote everyone back. To Mabel Parker in Colorado Springs, he said, "I have already been put to no little embarrassment and trouble because of a lack of understanding regarding this evacuation problem." To Ruth Haines at the University of Washington, he wrote, "I am making it clear that Colorado's borders do not offer a bar and at the same time, it is up to the federal government to withdraw its own restrictions to which I did not approve in the first place."

He felt compelled to once again ask the federal authorities working out of San Francisco what was going on, why people were assuming he had control over their movements when every statement from the WRA had been to the contrary. To Major Herman Goebel, the governor wrote, "Throughout the time since the evacuation order, it has been the undeviating policy of the government that it controlled the conduct of these persons and their movements ...

"Transfers are peculiarly within the jurisdiction of the United States and no Governor has the right to deny to any American citizen or to any other person living in the country legally the right to enter or to reside in or to cross his state. The state, by some rule or regulation, has not been clothed with the powers of an immigration board."

The conflict once again made headlines. Alva Swain wrote, "[Carr] takes the position that they are under the care and supervision of the federal government. That he has no way of knowing who are good citizens and who are not. That he might sign a request for one of the Japanese to enter the state and that later the chap might commit some crime and the governor would be blamed forever and a day for it."

Less than a week later, a telegram from the army officers on the coast arrived saying, "Military authorities no longer require Governor's approval." However, they did require the approval of the local police before they authorized sending anyone to any part of Colorado. It's what the governor had been arguing for all along, refusing to use the National Guard to watch American citizens. As Swain reported, "Governor Carr was wearing quite a smile Monday morning. He had just been notified that it would not be necessary for him to sign applications to have Japanese enter the state."

People continued to write, though, and ask for his help. Ichiro Ishida, Colorado native and farmer, asked for aid in getting a friend of a dozen years out of the Oregon internment camp and into Colorado.

Dr. Louis Gaspar asked for permission to have his wife, three children, and their "trusted maid," Fumiko Yoshimura, move to Colorado Springs.

Richard Iwata's parents were living in Delta, Colorado, but he was stuck in California.

To all, the governor made the point he had made since February, that he had "absolutely no objection to the reception of people whether they are first to leave by order of the President or the Army or whether they come voluntarily under legal pact. I still cling to my old position and say that they have the right as American citizens to do as they please and legally go where they please."

Another article in the *Christian Century* magazine brought forth commendations from all over the country, but few, if any, came from Colorado. The article was written by pastor Stanley Hunter Armstrong, who had grown up in Colorado while his father was the pastor at the First Presbyterian Church in Denver.

"I am trying, within my limitations, to show the people of my state what is required of them as Americans and Christians," the governor wrote in thanking him for the article. Carr was seen nationally as a beacon for those who wanted to help the Japanese in the United States, the one leader willing to stick his neck out or, in his words, "carry on with my crusade."

A former college classmate of Carr's, now teaching Biblical Literature at Mary Baldwin College in Virginia, wrote "I am sure your stand has taken much courage—of a much more difficult variety than armed warfare demands."

The list of war dead and missing was growing.

As the bad news arrived, criticism mounted toward the Japanese from within the state. The Delta Veterans of Foreign Wars #3571 from the western part of the state passed a resolution protesting the importation of any Japanese citizens to their county. "We believe that the Japanese are given too much freedom especially when they are permitted to tour the county and visit our Lakes and Dams and to be permitted to live anywhere in the city limits of Delta and mingle around in our own population," read their unanimously passed document.

Carr's announcement that he would be running for senate brought out the Democratic opposition. Prominent Democrat Phil Hornbein said, "We must find a man to beat Governor Ralph L. Carr." The party openly challenged him on his decision a few years back to shift the money previously allocated for schools to balance the state budget, saying it was simply a way of passing new taxes onto school districts. But the major Democratic criticism of Carr was that although he waved the flag of patriotism and duty when talking about accepting Japanese evacuees, at the same time he was highly critical of President Roosevelt's policies during this time of war.

"Constructive criticism is always helpful," said James Marsh, who would be Senator Millikin's Democratic opponent in November. Marsh used a Biblical analogy of the twin sons of Isaac and

Rebecca who had vastly different demeanors to describe what he called Carr's conflicting views. "But the voice should not be the voice of Jacob, while the hand is the hand of Esau."

Pueblo's Democratic organization attacked Carr, saying he had spent the last few years "in the furtherance of his personal ambitions for election to a political position of greater trust and responsibility." It accused him of "meandering about the country as the curly-headed cupid who sits at the speaker's table at all Republican banquets from Maine to Mexico, campaigning for the office of U.S. Senator."

Although they didn't say it to the press, the Democrats went right to the voters, deriding Carr's association with the Japanese evacuees. The war showed no signs of letting up, and the presence of the Japanese made people afraid that these new neighbors could be wolves in sheep's clothing. The public attitude toward the Japanese remained antagonistic and the governor knew it.

The National Opinion Research Center (NORC) located at the University of Denver had followed up on its poll from March, attempting to gauge how perceptions had changed in the last four months. Harry Field's questioners, the best-trained in the business, would once again ask twenty-six hundred people around the country for their feelings about America's chief enemies in the war.

"Which of the following statements come closest to describing how you feel, on the whole, about the people who live in Germany [Japan]?" was the first question on the survey in both March and July. In the spring, 21 percent of the respondents felt the German people "will always want to go to war to make themselves as powerful as possible." In July, that number climbed slightly to 23 percent of those asked.

When asked this same question about the Japanese, 41 percent of those surveyed in March felt they had desires for ultimate power. Four months later, that number had climbed to 46 percent, or twice as many as those who believed the Germans wanted nothing more than world dominance.

Another statement was: "The German [Japanese] people do not like war. If they could have the same chance as people in other countries, they would become good citizens of the world." The wording had changed slightly from March, but the intent from NORC was similar, as were the results.

Twenty-nine percent of those participating said that the Germans would become good citizens of the world. That was significantly down from the 42 percent who agreed with that statement in the spring, evidence that the struggle in the European theatre was taking its toll on the American psyche. Asked if they agreed the Japanese would become "good citizens of the world," 18 percent had answered in the affirmative in the spring. Just a few months later, that number had dropped to only 11 percent.

It was significant, Harry Field found, that "Twice as many people think the Japanese people [are] incorrigibly belligerent as think the German people will always want to go to war. And over twice as many think the German people do not like war as hold that opinion about the Japanese."

In a sample taken across America, respondents were also asked what form of government each of the Axis powers would want after the war. For both the Germans and Italians, a growing number of Americans believed they would want some form of democratic representation when the conflict ended. But the number of Americans who believed the Japanese would want to continue its present form of government following the war grew from 41 percent in March to 46 percent in July. "There is growing feeling," Field concluded, that Americans believe "the Japanese will wish to retain their present form of government."

Hollywood soon produced a movie that both confirmed those feelings and stirred the pot. Twentieth Century Fox came out with *Little Tokyo, U.S.A.*, a sixty-four-minute black-and-white film that began with a prologue describing the Japanese American community as a "vast army of volunteer spies" who remained "blind worshipers of their Emperor." The movie was set late in the fall of 1941 and starred Preston Foster as Los Angeles police detective Mike Steele investigating a series of crimes inside Los Angeles's Japanese community, known as "Little Tokyo."

Steele discovers that an American-born Japanese man named Takimura is responsible for the bombing of Pearl Harbor. Takimura uses a woman in his community to try and seduce Steele, and when that does not work, he kills the woman and tries to frame the detective for the crime. Steele ends up proving his own innocence, busting the spy ring, and saving America from further death and destruction at the hands of its Japanese residents.

Cameramen actually filmed the evacuation of the Japanese quarter in LA for the final scenes of the movie, but close-ups and nighttime shots were taken in the city's Chinatown since the Little Tokyo neighborhood had been evacuated. A Chinese actor, Richard Loo, played one of the leading Japanese spy roles in the movie. The movie was condemned by the federal government as being an "invitation to the witch hunt," preaching hate for all people of Japanese descent, but nonetheless it was shown to packed audiences during July and for the rest of the summer on Colorado's movie screens.

The governor knew he would be required to address the ongoing hatred at the Colorado Republican Assembly that July, yet he continued to fret about its importance in the eyes of the public. Unsure why they could not simply understand that the country's underlying philosophy did not permit the treatment of American citizens in such a way, he would not back down from his position.

Nearly two thousand people gathered inside Denver's Municipal Auditorium on July 15 for the Republicans' first wartime political convention in twenty-four years. The building had hosted the Democratic National Convention in 1908, where William Jennings Bryan was nominated for a third time to run for president. Operas, circuses, auto shows, theater and concerts had been featured inside the stone structure with the plush interior and stunning acoustics.

Delegates sat on the main floor as well as in the balcony and along the private boxes where Denver's elite would sit to take in the best shows the city could afford. The big unknown was which candidate would emerge to run for governor. All three of the candidates had connections to Carr: Lieutenant Governor John Vivian, Revenue Director Farrington Carpenter, and State Auditor Charles Armstrong. All three announced that they would enter a primary to determine the Republican nominee.

One race that would not have a primary was that for U.S. Senate. Carr was nominated by Colorado Supreme Court justice Haslet Burke, his longtime friend. Burke used to refer to himself as the "last of the Mohicans" because he was the only Republican elected statewide in 1938 when Carr was first elected. Now, he stepped aside to allow Colorado's chief executive to address his party.

The governor's standing ovation lasted for several minutes. The man who liked to claim he always wanted to be a lawyer until he "got sidetracked," smiled, waved, and basked in the moment.

During his keynote address, Carr championed the cause he had traveled from coast to coast discussing, saying the consolidation of power by the federal government was a threat and menace exceeded only by a military attack by foreign powers. "It will avail us nothing to win this war abroad if at the same time we lose the basis of our form of government at home," he told the crowd. "Certain persons in authority forget that the basic idea of the men who penned the Constitution was to permit the people in each section to determine local questions.

"This is the philosophy of the American theory of government. This is the law of human relationships under an ordered government where the individual is free. This is the hope of civilization."

He also spoke about Colorado's financial success under his administration—the state had gone from a budget deficit nearing $2 million to a budget surplus of $2 million. Seventeen pages into his talk, he addressed the issue of the Japanese evacuees. He told the audience that "regardless of the political affiliations of its governor ... every suggestion, every request, every command from our leaders has been obeyed and complied with and met." Referring specifically to the minority group in Colorado that had grown exponentially since the war started, he simply said, "No invitation, no request was made for them to come. We have no choice. We have no voice. A nation at war commands. We can only obey."

Newspaper headlines told the story of atrocities and pain delivered at the hands of Japanese forces. Max Hill, son of Denver East High School's principal, was the Associated Press Tokyo bureau chief when the war broke out. He and fellow AP colleague Morris J. Harris, who ran the Shanghai bureau, both complained of being treated as criminals and mistreated by the Japanese forces in prison camps, leading the *Pueblo Star-Journal* to write an editorial asking, "Should It Be an Eye for an Eye?"

"When we read of the horrible experiences of Americans and British who have been captured and kept in filthy prison camps for weeks and then look at the swank and clean camps in which Jap aliens are placed in this country, it makes every American feel that he would like to personally have a part in cruel punishment of those who are within our borders."

The editors concluded, "Our time will come when the easy flowing grace of the underhanded and back-stabbing Jap will be called upon to answer for what he has done. At that time we will be prepared and ready to deal with that race to teach them a lesson, rather than let them go free with a slap on the wrist."

U.S. attorney general Francis Biddle again warned Americans that simply because there had been no large-scale act of sabotage in America, "no false sense of security should be derived from these facts.

"The threat to our internal security deepens with each day that the war continues," Biddle told the Associated Press in Washington. "It is reassuring to know that the defenses which we have erected against these threats have, so far at least, proved effective."

Still, the war was not going well. The homeland may not

have been attacked again, but abroad, the Japanese Imperial Army inflicted massive casualties. Just across the New Mexico state line from Colorado, the small town of Springer was missing two hundred men out of a town population of only seventeen hundred after fighting in Corregidor and Bataan. A candle was burning in nearly every window in town to signify bereavement. Five hundred New Mexicans in all had been killed in the Pacific fighting.

The governor took a short time out from the war effort to continue his battle with the federal authorities over a number of issues, and he had the help of Lowell Thomas, who brought his national radio program to Denver in late July. As they broadcast from the club car of the Union Pacific's Pony Express, Thomas asked his old friend what the recent mining order from the War Production Board meant. That was the order that said any mine with more than a third of its haul as gold or silver would no longer be entitled to buy the explosives and equipment needed to operate, even though those same mines also produced lead, copper, and zinc needed for the war effort.

"What will that do to Victor, Cripple Creek, and other mining camps where you and I used to live, Governor?" Thomas asked.

"Both of them, Lowell, and many other cities of brick and concrete and steel built up at high altitudes will become ghost towns within a few months. And the red-blooded Americans who know no other work will be driven from their homes and forced to work elsewhere."

The sheer ignorance and arrogance of an administration filled with East Coast residents who knew nothing of the issues of the West truly angered Carr. He used to mock the administration by telling a story of a "young man who was out here a few months ago and told the hard-rock miners to go out and hunt brass mines because we needed brass in the war effort."

In a Colorado audience, where people realized brass comes from copper and zinc, the joke always went over well.

An incident just after the state party convention perfectly illustrated the governor's problem with the administration. He was sent a letter from an underling with the federal Work Projects Administration (WPA) announcing that Colorado had been awarded roughly $1.2 million to help the state's defense councils and other civilian war agencies. The underling suggested to the former newspaper editor turned governor: "You [should] prepare a statement for the press, announcing the big grant and giving some indication of what it is expected to do ... WPA has no press agent, and since I happen to be versed in that line, I have been given a free hand to assist you in promoting the war services program.

"Let's try to get it off to a good start by making an appropriate initial announcement."

Assuming the intent to help was genuine, Carr could not help but look with disdain at the condescension and the impudence of a low-level administration official "suggesting" what he should do rather than asking the chief executive of the largest state in the region what he thought ought to be done in his own state.

There was no better example of this disconnect than the relocation camp being built in Granada, in Colorado's Prowers County. Carr read a letter from his friend and fellow attorney Arthur Gordon: "There are a few sore spots in Prowers County over the placing of the Jap camp [here]." Carr wrote back his familiar refrain, claiming he had nothing to do with it. "It is difficult to understand how they can blame me for the Japanese relocation center at Granada," he wrote Gordon. "That was placed without asking me and with the express statement from Colonel Bendetsen, aide to General DeWitt that they did not need my approval and would not heed any protest. They just phoned me that it was their plan."

Surveying had been completed in the middle of July on the heavily guarded site and actual construction was underway. Numerous one-story, barrack-type structures divided into compartments about twenty by twenty-five feet for a family of five or six would be built first. A dining hall would be constructed later. James Lindley, who had been appointed to run the camp, arrived on scene to supervise the program first-hand.

Secretary of War Henry Stimson would soon designate the area a military zone, meaning "No person of Japanese ancestry who resides within the boundaries of a Center will be permitted to leave without written permission."

The news came on the heels of headlines about American struggles in the Pacific conflict. In early August, the navy announced that the Japanese had reportedly machine-gunned survivors of an American freighter that sank in the North Pacific, killing two. The Japanese attack in the Solomon Islands, north of Guadalcanal, resulted in huge losses for the Americans. Three heavy cruisers and one destroyer were sunk within an hour; another cruiser and two more destroyers were damaged. In all, fifteen hundred sailors were lost in the fight.

Back home, Coloradans found themselves in the midst of conflicting values and feelings. Residents of Lamar, some sixteen miles to the west of the camp, were somewhat soothed by the news that the Japanese would hardly be allowed to move freely. At the same time, help was needed in the fields of many of the state's 51,436 farms and some were willing to put ethnic fear aside for practicality.

The farmers had entered 1942 encouraged by the government to produce the largest number of farm products in U.S. history. To meet that goal, 25 percent more acreage was planted in sugar beets and barley. Double-digit percentage increases were also planted for beans, sorghum, oats, and onions. The heavy winter, which had dumped large amounts of snow, provided fertile opportunity for a terrific season.

But now, at their so-called "zero hour," when crops would be ready for harvesting, many of the farm boys had been called into the service and others had gone to work for more money at one of the many defense industries now operating in Colorado. The farmers of Colorado knew they needed help.

La Vern and Furth McClure had written from tiny Fowler, Colorado, on the Eastern Plains, "The farmer does not expect to shirk his responsibilities—has never done so—but he expects when he plants a crop to be able to harvest it." From the Western Slope and Grand Junction came a plea from the Mesa County Peach Marketing Board of Control. "The Japanese angle," wrote E. W. Austin, the board manager, "still holds the best promise of a solution. ... Sentiment concerning the presence and use of Japanese labor has altered considerably."

But the plea of Jim Colian, who ran the largest produce company in Pueblo, best illustrated the conundrum facing Governor Carr. Colian wrote directly to the governor "It is of utmost importance that everything possible be accomplished to gather every pound of food to feed our nation and our allies. ... Unless something is done, three fourths of Colorado's crops will rot in the fields."

Yet, his antagonism remained. "Japanese labor is unwelcome by the farmers of this area, and we don't propose to use any. ... If it becomes necessary to use Japanese labor, it is recommended that they work in groups supervised by armed guards. ... Japanese aliens running around loose would be considered dangerous to the welfare of the farmers and citizens."

The governor created a labor committee to help come up with solutions to the problem. High school students, retirees, even those with physical handicaps that could be overcome were enlisted in the effort to bring in the crops.

The problem was exacerbated by the authorities on the West Coast. They wanted the governor of the various inland states to sign a document that any Japanese employee coming into their state will be provided "adequate protection." Carr had broached this problem with military authorities earlier. He would not use Colorado's National Guard to watch over American citizens.

He traveled to California in late August, ostensibly to dedicate a warship built for Britain's navy using mostly parts made in Denver.

Privately, however, while in Los Angeles he was focused on how to help Colorado's farmers who wanted Japanese evacuees to work in their fields. He dictated a letter to Julesburg mayor George Thompson about the labor shortage in the agricultural area along the Nebraska border. "It really remains only for local officials to agree that they will enforce the law and protect persons and property, and then arrangements I am certain can be made for the employment of these people during the season when they are needed, and then they will be returned to the reception center," the governor wrote. "This must be the solution."

He met with General DeWitt to voice his concerns. "I know these places. I know the officials and I know the people in those sections," he told DeWitt. "They will enforce the law, protect the lives and property of all persons, and see to it that violence and un-American activities are discountenanced and held in check. If farmers feel the need for such labor and ask for it, I believe it can be accomplished safely."

Before he returned to Colorado, the first group of two hundred and eleven evacuees arrived at the Granada camp. They were laborers, truck drivers, food preparation workers, and others needed to help prepare the camp for the thousands who would follow. Ninety military police officers from Fort Sill, Oklahoma, had arrived a week before to prepare as well. They all arrived at a location that was not even half complete and "probably as bleak a spot as one can find on the western plains," according to the *Denver Post*.

Just a couple days after the first evacuees arrived, the *Pueblo Star-Journal* wrote an editorial encouraging the "continuance of the campaign to bring to light every dangerous enemy alien in the country." More than twelve hundred people had been arrested since Pearl Harbor, mostly foreign nationals who were feared to be engaged in fifth-column activity. The paper wrote, "Much credit is therefore due to … the FBI and the Department of Justice for at least cleaning out over 1,200 human skunks with the hope that all of these agencies will keep the good work up."

As September approached, it was reported that the Granada Center could hold up to eight thousand evacuees. The same day's Pueblo newspaper printed the story of Joseph Grew, the former American ambassador to Japan. He told of how Americans caught in Tokyo at the outset of the war were denied food, fuel for heat, and clothing, while being confined to the embassy, unable to make it back to their homes. "The blot of uncivilized treatment of Americans stranded in Japan when the war broke out," the paper wrote, "it makes every American boil to know what has happened, especially when considered … with the treatment meted out to American citizens in Japan and Jap-occupied territory in light of the excellent accommodations which we have provided many thousands of Japs in this country."

Thousands of evacuees would shortly be on their way to Granada. In case they wondered about the attitude they would receive, the Pueblo paper ended the month with a big feature article by the former International News Service Tokyo bureau chief entitled "Let's Burn Up the Japs!"

Colorado's general election was only two months away.

Chapter Fourteen
September 1942

Within a ten-year period, Colorado had two very different governors with interesting similarities.

"Big Ed" Johnson, governor from 1933 to 1937, physically towered over Ralph Carr, who governed from 1939 to 1943. Both had huge personalities, and people always listened when one of them spoke. Both objected to the New Deal policies of President Roosevelt; both believed in a sound fiscal policy and a balanced budget. Carr was a Republican; Johnson was a Democrat.

On his first day at work, Johnson saw lines around the state capitol full of hungry, desperate people. It would have scared many governors out the back door, but not Johnson. It was January 1933, and the state's newest chief executive told staff to let them in. If he couldn't give them physical sustenance, at least he could listen to their problems and offer emotional solace.

"The Depression had destroyed credit so completely that you couldn't sell anything and you didn't have money to buy anything," he later told the *Denver Post*. "People couldn't pay their bills. ... People had to sell their livestock and their farm implements and their furniture. They couldn't work and they couldn't eat.

"I remember taking part in jackrabbit shoots in Weld County. A hundred or so men would march in a line and shoot jackrabbits until we got a truckload, and then we'd take that truck back to Denver and just hand out the jackrabbits. When people have to eat jackrabbits, things are serious."

He addressed his fellow Coloradans during the country's worst economic conditions in history with candor that would make him an icon. He had no magic solution and wouldn't pretend he did. What the son of Swedish immigrants, who had emerged from a northwest Colorado dirt farm to sit in the back row of the state legislature before becoming governor, would promise was that if the day lasted twenty-four hours, he would give them twenty-four hours of effort. During leap years, he'd give them that extra day.

Political observers marveled at his skills. If he was speaking with those who were struggling, he could tell the story of how he came to Colorado on a stretcher from Nebraska, sick with tuberculosis. If he was speaking to business owners, he could share the personal experience of making the Farmers Milling and Elevator in Craig, Colorado, one of the biggest businesses in the area. If he was addressing teachers, there was the story of his stint at the Sugar Loaf schoolhouse.

"Johnson is distinguished as an accurate prophet of the political weather," *Rocky Mountain News* editor Lee Casey wrote. "His political sniffer has given him exceedingly accurate information through his career. Other politicians talk about his luck, but in reality, his rise has been due rather to [his] ability to gauge situations in advance."

Everyone knew the six-two, two-hundred-plus Johnson as "Big Ed." Big shoulders, big eyebrows, big voice, big personality, he dominated a room simply by entering it. Ed Johnson had big plans for Colorado when he took over in 1932. Despite a political affiliation as a Democrat, he was no fan of the New Deal, instead launching a reorganization and reform program specific to Colorado.

During his tenure, tax reduction, civil service reform, and a balanced budget helped restore economic credit for both the government and businesses. A $20 million highway construction program provided jobs and helped promote trade throughout the state. He would years later be a major proponent of building Interstate 70 through the Rocky Mountains. It was up to Coloradans themselves, who he encouraged to "trust in [their] own integrity, hard work, and common sense instead of visionary promises of politicians."

He overwhelmingly won reelection as governor in 1934 for his second two-year term.

One year later, he made national headlines for a policy created right before the spring planting season. With economic conditions still brutal, half of all the residents on Colorado's eastern plains were on relief rolls and newspapers called "for heroic and drastic action."

Johnson announced plans to deport all "alien Mexicans" then in Colorado to their native country.

Colorado attorney general Paul Prosser told General Neil Kimball, who ran the National Guard, that there was no law in the state authorizing "any wholesale deportation of aliens" and that it "would be practically impossible to deport any great number of aliens without prohibitive expense, and probably not without giving each [alien] an opportunity to be heard in connection with his deportation."

Yet, Johnson plowed ahead, writing a telegram to *Newsdom, Inc.*, a popular Depression-era trade journal: "We are determined to segregate them if we cannot force deportation." He told reporters that he was declaring "martial law on the southern border of the state."

Johnson knew approximately eight hundred Mexican families were on relief in Pueblo County, almost 7 percent of the total number receiving government aid. Another two hundred nineteen families (thirteen hundred people) were on the rolls in Morgan County, and the situation was similar elsewhere in the state. To say his policy of cleaning up the "alien nests in Colorado" was popular would be an understatement.

Fowler police chief Robert Richardson wrote that when he heard of the policy through the press, he "felt like yelling Hurrah."

"There is absolutely no valid or legal reason why aliens should be allowed to remain in this country," wrote Fort Collins resident C. F. Baldwin. "Under normal conditions, as you know, they are the source of the crime problem. Under present conditions crime is greatly increased, to say nothing of the aggravated problems of unemployment and relief."

From the citizens of Colorado, the people Johnson loved,

he got an outpouring of positive support. "There are those, right there in Denver, among Mexicans, who are not citizens, never will be, never intended to be, and are a worthless, shiftless, dirty outfit, who ought to be chucked back into Mexico," wrote R. H. Faxon from Denver.

S. B. Wonder from Durango wanted to congratulate the governor for deporting noncitizens and ridding the relief rolls "of these parasites." J. H. Bailey from the Bailey Garage was happy that Colorado would not "have to feed so many of just such kind of people that impose on our white American race."

The *Pueblo Star-Journal* and a number of other newspapers endorsed Johnson's plan. "While there is no occasion for stirring up racial prejudice, we must face realities and realize that our own family of American citizens must be taken care of first," the *Journal* editorialized. "Therefore, we support the action of Governor Johnson in seeking authority and finding ways and means to rid the state of aliens that are a burden on the tax-paying public."

Spanish-speaking groups across Colorado also rallied to the governor's side. Many Coloradans of Spanish descent who had lived in the state for generations resented those who came from Mexico during the growing season to work and then stayed around on the relief rolls for the rest of the year. For example, J. F. Arguello of Prowers County complained that Mexicans "have all the jobs while some of our citizens have to wait. ... We feel that citizens ought to be protected and something ought to be done to remedy this matter, our Spanish-American citizens being ignored in every point by the relief forces."

On the Western Slope, the Spanish American Citizens Association in Grand Junction said its community had been "besieged" by aliens who had taken work from them because they "have been classed with the Mexican immigrant and have been ignored for that reason."

Signs were posted around the state by a group calling itself the "Colorado State Vigilanties [*sic*]," which read, "WARNING...

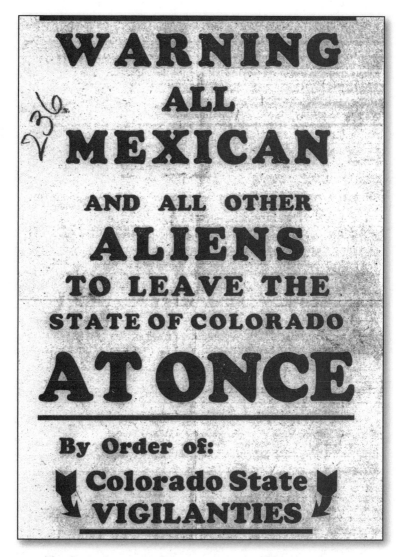

This flyer and numerous others were posted in 1935 after then governor Edwin Johnson ordered out the National Guard to physically drive all "Mexican aliens" across the border of Colorado and into New Mexico. The Depression-era policy drew significant public support, even from numerous Spanish American societies throughout the state, but was terminated after the federal government complained. Johnson and his supporters regularly reminded voters of this action during the 1942 U.S. Senate campaign against Governor Carr.

ALL MEXICAN AND ALL OTHER ALIENS TO LEAVE THE STATE OF COLORADO AT ONCE." The Ku Klux Klan offered, "entire support in this action. You have but to command and we shall move in any assistance we can give you," the letter from "No. Eight" in Denver pledged.

Johnson defended his decision by saying to reporters, "It was not my intention to keep anyone out of Colorado desiring to establish residence or visit here except those who were aliens and indigent without means of support. Aliens are not citizens of America."

However, a month after the calling out of the National Guard, Johnson knew he'd have to pull back. The railroads and sugar beet industry, both significant employers of Mexican laborers, had been putting enormous pressure on him, as were the governors of surrounding states who were not necessarily willing to deputize Colorado Guardsmen "accompanying the aliens" to the Mexican border. He withdrew the guard in late April.

"Martial law will do the job, but unfortunately it cannot be invoked without working a distinct hardship upon the good citizens of other states, and it necessarily puts Colorado in a most unfavorable light, even though our purposes were for the best interest of this state, and do reflect the wishes of Colorado citizens," Johnson said. "No state alone can cope with the alien question. It is a national problem, pure and simple."

His popularity skyrocketing, Johnson took what he saw as an opportunity at a promotion, and was elected easily to the U.S. Senate in 1936.

Ralph Carr's experience with the Spanish-speaking population of Colorado was much different than Johnson's. As a country lawyer working in Antonito, a large number of his clients spoke Spanish. The May 1917 court docket before Twelfth District judge Jesse C. Wiley showed Carr representing Pedro Ortega on charges of larceny, Celedonio Martinez on a charge of assault, and Manuel Maes, accused of larceny of livestock.

He enjoyed telling the story of Juan Jose Lopez, the rug maker of Antonito, who called him a "curly-haired boy." Carr wrote a story about "Don" Juan, his friend, in which he stated, "[Whoever] I meet, no matter how strong their personalities or kindly their hearts, none possessed truer nobility than the little Rug Maker of San Antonito. … From a more advantageous take off in a different place and time, his flight might have shared the eagles."

During his first gubernatorial campaign when he traveled back to the San Luis Valley where he had lived for so many years, he made a point to stop at the home of an eighty-year-old patriarch of a Spanish-speaking family that had lived in the valley for generations. "They talked the whole time about Shakespeare and Cervantes," Carr's son, Robert, remembered. "They also talked about their families. As we left, the old man put his arm around Dad and said, 'Don't worry, Rafaelito, everybody here is for you.' That was the extent of the political conversation.

"They knew him for all the battles he'd fought for them out there. They knew his character and his integrity and his compassion and they didn't have to talk political things, about this problem or that problem. They had had this kind of evening many times before."

Carr marveled at the Spanish tradition where friends would gather around an open fire for a social experience, to experience the classic *Don Quixote*, the "beloved of all storytellers." For someone who loved to spin a yarn himself, the roasting of *piñones* (pine nuts), first mentioned by the prophet Hosea in the Old Testament, could not have been more appealing as the sun set behind Sheep Mountain in the valley of the Conejos River.

Carr became so fluent in Spanish that he delivered entire speeches in the language and wrote numerous letters. On the campaign trail, all the other candidates would have him introduce them to the Spanish-speaking audiences. "Dad would give part of the speech in English and part of it in Spanish," his son said. "Then he'd introduce them in English and Spanish. He'd always do gentle jabs at 'em in Spanish, at the other candidates, with funny remarks. The Spanish-speaking audiences loved it. Whatever he said, they'd laugh."

In the summer of 1942, his quick attention to their needs saved the jobs of thousands of Spanish-speaking workers at the construction site of Camp Hale in the west-central Colorado mountains. Camp Hale was where the army trained soldiers for high-altitude warfare. The Pando Construction Company was supposed to build everything from mess halls to barracks to a hospital, chapel, fire station, stockade, and guardhouse, in addition to physically relocating State Highway 24, the major route through Leadville, the nearest city to the camp.

The major in charge of the project ended up firing 3,456 workers because they were "Mexican." The decision had nothing to do with performance. Carr found out about this in a telegram sent by New Mexico senator Dennis Chavez while Carr was at a conference in North Carolina. Some of the workers were from New Mexico and some lived in Colorado.

"Many of [those fired] are fathers and brothers of men who died in Philippines," stated Senator Chavez in the Western Union message. "This appears outrageous. ... Advisable that you as Governor of Colorado should investigate the matter so that this outrage will not continue."

Another telegram immediately followed from a committee representing the fired workers. "Most of us have sons or brothers in the armed forces," wrote Juan F. Romero. "We [are] unable to understand why if people of our blood are willing to die for our country we are not allowed to do an honest day's work in a government defense project."

Myrtle Graham immediately tracked down Carr at the governors' conference in North Carolina. He instructed her to send the following note to the military commander and the contractors who he knew: "Governor Carr has received telegram from committee of Spanish Americans at Pando stating they have been dismissed from work on project. The Governor has asked that you wire me immediately furnishing explanation."

Later that day, a telegram was sent to the governor's office saying that "all qualified workers that have been dismissed from the project will be reinstated upon application from the employee without regard to racial origin." It also said that any foreman or superintendent found responsible for discrimination on the job due to race or creed would be dismissed. Future vacancies would be filled solely on the basis of merit.

"I think you know my attitude toward these people and their rights," he wrote to Senator Chavez. "I have spent many years fighting for them and trying to see to it that they reached their place in the sun in Colorado."

As the September 1942 political primary loomed, there remained some question over whether the anticipated battle of Colorado's political titans—Carr versus Johnson—would actually take place. Some members of the state Democratic Party, with the support of President Roosevelt, felt Johnson had been too critical of the administration, a cardinal political error, they said, during a time of war. Before Pearl Harbor, Johnson had warned against intervention in the armed conflict with words the president's friends could not forget.

"Political considerations shrink to infinitesimal proportions when one contemplates the blood, the sorrow and the treasure involved in the issue of intervention; for intervention inevitably must result in war," he wrote in a June 25, 1940, letter to the *Rocky Mountain News*. "I do not propose to be a party by my silence or my vote to such a grievous disaster ... when I see it creeping upon us like a thief in the night, inch by inch, I must speak out. The blood of the sons of American mothers is not going to be on my soul.

"In my opinion, President Roosevelt is not only an avowed interventionist, but he is the high priest of that dangerous cult."

He was complimented by the *News* for his determination. "Even those who do not agree with his position cannot help welcoming Johnson's forthrightness." Johnson would not hesitate to take reporters and editors to task for their comments about him, especially if he felt they were "trying to build a skeleton in [his] political closet out of the bones of falsehood."

"From the sidelines it would appear that Senator Johnson may have burned some bridges behind him," wrote the *Pueblo Star-Journal*. "He has shown remarkable political independence … that it is a question whether he can reverse himself sufficiently to satisfy the pro-Roosevelt wing of the party in Colorado."

In the 1942 Colorado senate race, that pro-Roosevelt wing threw its support behind Colorado Supreme Court justice Benjamin Hilliard, whom Johnson had sued for slander for saying that he had called President Roosevelt a "warmonger." He later withdrew the suit, choosing instead to engage in the inevitable battle at the polls. "We can't send one isolationist [Johnson] to beat another isolationist [Carr]," Denver attorney Philip Hornbein said while nominating Hilliard before the Democratic Party convention. "We can't send one Rip Van Winkle to beat another Rip Van Winkle."

"A vote for Hilliard is a vote in support of the president and his policies and a vote for Senator Johnson is a vote against the president."

Hilliard had already served on the court for more than a decade, earning the title from some as the "Oliver Wendell Holmes of the Colorado Bench" for his understanding of the misunderstood, and his judicial caring for the state's unfortunate. Ironically, the one-time Colorado congressman would later be profiled by Carr as one of the state's unsung heroes. He had voted against declaring war in 1917, when the world situation was becoming tense and most Americans were clamoring for it. Hilliard was only in his second term on Capitol Hill; his vote would later be described by Carr as "an act of independent courage which caused his defeat for reelection to Congress and threatened to work his complete obscurity. … In the years ahead after criticism, hatred, and abuse had been his portion, he smiled through the clouds and kept his fellows laughing—friends and enemies."

A quarter-century later, Hilliard sought to allay any concerns about his stand as America once again faced war. "It is my belief that Democrats feel the hope of the nation in this war and the peace that will follow lies in the policies and the leadership of President Roosevelt," he told delegates. "If my party is in power, I will regard the president as the leader."

In this case he was taking on Big Ed Johnson, the man *Rocky Mountain News* editor Lee Casey called "the most formidable and consistent vote-getter the Democratic or any other party in Colorado has yet produced." While maintaining he was a "rubber stamp" for no man, including the president, Big Ed did have the letter FDR had sent him when he was battling Governor Carr on the Arkansas River Authority, the note that read, "You are absolutely right on AVA and Carr is wrong. More power to you." He felt it showed he could be independent and yet still have the support of the head of the Democratic Party.

Johnson would not adhere to any political party edict on how he should act or how he should vote. He spoke regularly about bucking the system, telling the graduating class of Pueblo Junior College at its graduation, "Your classroom instructors tried, with some success, to mold you into so many peas in a pod. At recess you developed a personality—a God-given personality—and learned to fit that personality into the lives of others. You learned to give and take. ... There is nothing quite so important as the ability to get along with other people. It is an art! It is a science! It is a religion! It is the basic foundation of all civilization."

Showing his true populist roots, Johnson had Private Robert Metzger from Denver announce his candidacy at the Democratic Convention. The young man, stationed at Fort Warren in Wyoming, was set to shortly earn his corporal stripes. He focused on Johnson's legislation, which benefited the men in the armed forces, specifically the measure unanimously passed that raised the monthly pay for soldiers and sailors to fifty dollars a month.

"I can't tell you what he means to us," Private Metzger told the crowd. They erupted with a huge ovation. Johnson would win a nearly four-to-one (1,049 to 291) victory over Hilliard among the delegates in the Colorado Springs high school gymnasium. He then announced that he would leave immediately for Washington and would not campaign at all in Colorado through the September 8 primary season.

The latest revenue bill was coming before the senate finance committee, and Johnson said that as the only member of the group from the western states mining region, he felt it his responsibility to represent Colorado's interests in the crafting and drafting of the measure. During the debate over the previous revenue measure, which took eight weeks to resolve, his office received up to fifty letters per day from constituents worried about its contents.

"I do not like to take chances with political situations," Johnson said, "but I will not have time to participate in this primary campaign … I am content to leave my candidacy in the hands of my friends."

Johnson ran a letter-writing campaign and ran newspaper ads proclaiming, "Ed C. Johnson is on the job. Keep him there." He turned his noncampaigning into a campaign theme. "Duty is duty and no one knows this better than Senator Ed Johnson," read one ad, which ran in many Colorado papers. "He didn't lock his Washington desk and come back home to campaign for reelection. He remained in Washington to work. LET'S KEEP HIM THERE!"

When Colorado citizens went to the polls on Tuesday, September 8, less than half of those who had cast ballots in Colorado's 1940 primary showed up the day after Labor Day to participate in 1942, making it the least-attended primary election since the turn of the century. The end result had Johnson dominating Hilliard among the Democratic faithful, receiving more than 60 percent of the vote.

Governor Carr, running unopposed, cast his ballot in

Antonito on primary election day, having spent not even a penny during his primary campaign. He told columnist Alva Swain that he didn't expect "to get off that easy in the November election." Carr versus Johnson would be the race Colorado's political observers had been not-so-secretly hoping for since the governor took control of his party over the previous few years.

"Both men are very adroit in a political battle," Alva Swain wrote in his "Under the Capitol Dome" column a week later. "Let it not be said that there will be no issues. There will be. Each will see to that."

The tameness of the primary season was not expected to carry over to the general election. "It was anticipated that more personal attacks would be leveled by candidates of one party against those of the other party as the campaign progresses," wrote Willard Haselbush, looking ahead to the main election. "Democrats are believed certain to attack individual acts and policies of Gov. Ralph L. Carr."

As if on cue, during the first part of September, headlines blared details of more Japanese attacks in the Pacific, and at the same time, shouted that thousands of evacuees were coming into the Granada camp.

The Japanese were landing forces in the Solomon Islands, continuing to press the fight on Guadalcanal, with casualties on both sides escalating rapidly. U.S. admiral Chester Nimitz, commander in chief of the Pacific fleet, told Americans they should not "for a minute assume that we have the Japanese on the run." The Red Cross announced Japan would not allow any ships or vehicles carrying supplies for American prisoners of war to have access to them.

On September 3, the first major group of Japanese evacuees arrived at Granada, 557 in all. Two days later, more than 1,100 left the Merced Assembly Center in California for Colorado. On September 7, another 553 left, and on September 9, 527 more. One week after that, two more train loads pulled in, with more than a 1,000 former residents of the West Coast. The day after that, the final transfer from Merced had 481 people. Immediately, the headlines came: "Japs Brought to Granada Camp."

Would any of these evacuees be allowed to leave the camp to help with the Colorado harvest? While the crops ripened for harvest in the fields, the question remained unsettled.

Luscious peaches would be ready for picking first on the Western Slope, then came a sugar beet crop estimated to yield five hundred thousand more tons in Colorado. That would be the big test. Joseph Smart, the newly established WRA director in Denver, told reporters, including Alva Swain, that "a plan will be worked out in the near future whereby any Japanese who are needed will be at work in the agricultural fields of the state."

Smart's goal was to have farmers ask for help, say how many men they needed, what type of work was it, how much they'd pay, what housing facilities they have if they were located too far from Granada, and what protection could be provided for the evacuees and the farmers. The long-term goal of the WRA was to use Japanese evacuees, who grew 70 percent of the seeds in California, to help sustain the country's needed food supply during the war.

Swain recognized the immediacy and importance of a decision being worked out. "This much is certain," he wrote in his September 4 column. "If Colorado is to produce the seeds and the other farm products ... that she is supposed to produce, some satisfactory plan will have to be worked out or the total output will never be reached."

The governor was not nearly as confident as Smart that this would all work out because the government was continuing to require he guarantee the protection of evacuees and citizens alike. As he wrote Nebraska governor Dwight Griswold, who was also struggling with how to deal with this issue, "This would mean to change our Constitution and statutes or else for me to declare an emergency which would justify using the defense force."

He continued to wait for General DeWitt's response. When

he received it on September 10, it appeared the governor's fears were finally addressed. "I am sure," DeWitt wrote from his San Francisco headquarters, "that everyone concerned will understand that you can only guarantee the adequate protection of the laws to the extent that the Constitution and statutes of your State permit." So, on September 12, the same day the Granada camp was renamed Camp Amache after a Cheyenne Indian who used to live in the area, he issued a statewide order certifying that employment of "workers of Japanese ancestry ... has my approval and sanction.

"It will be the responsibility of the county and city officials, under Colorado law, to provide adequate protection for these workers, and to see that law and order are maintained. Should the necessity arise the appropriate instrumentalities of the state will also be made available for these purposes."

As he told a statewide meeting of the Republican central committee in Denver, the issue would be in the hands of local communities to determine what's best for their respective areas. "That state authority will not be brought into play unless there might be trouble and the local authorities could not take care of the situation," Swain reported. "Then, the state would treat it just the same as it would treat any other similar situation and restore order."

With all legal obstacles removed, the pleas for help could finally be addressed.

At the urging of sugar beet company workers and farmers, Prowers County, which housed Camp Amache, agreed to allow Japanese evacuees to help harvest the crops. Ironically, the area that initially provided the fiercest resistance to Japanese within its community became among the first to ask for help.

Financial reality overwhelmed wartime hysteria in La Junta, where the *Tribune-Democrat* reported, "Almost every farmer in the La Junta district will use Japanese labor from the Granada relocation camp." City officials determined that only American-born Japanese would be allowed to work in the fields and they would not be able to "roam at will" or go around the La Junta air base. However, in the community that threatened open violence against them six months earlier, Japanese evacuees were now needed to be recruited "to save county crops."

But not all communities were jumping at the opportunity to bring West Coast Japanese into their areas. Pueblo County commissioners held off recommending the option despite the pleas made by area farmers like David Ciruli, who offered to house, protect, and cover the expenses for any evacuee who would help him harvest the crops. "There has been quite a dispute in this County as to your action on the question of using the Japs from the relocation camps on the farms, where their services are badly needed," Pueblo County attorney Riley Cloud wrote the governor.

Carr knew the labor shortage was so acute in certain areas as to allay any fears, and yet there were other parts of the state he knew would not be so genial when it came to using Japanese in the fields. For example, he wrote WRA regional director Smart that residents of places like Costilla County, located on the New Mexico border, had seen their relatives and their neighbors killed by Japanese forces in the Philippines in staggering numbers. Antagonism toward the enemy ran high. "There is a feeling in that County," Carr told Smart, "that the Japanese should not be permitted to enter."

By the middle of the month, Colonel Bendetsen had ordered the transfer inland of an additional three thousand Japanese evacuees from the Santa Anita Assembly Center outside of Los Angeles. All would be headed to Amache. Roughly every other day for a couple weeks, groups of five hundred would arrive at the Southeastern Colorado camp, making it by the end of the month, the tenth largest city in Colorado, with a population of roughly seven thousand people.

When the final group arrived, all of the barracks had been completed, thirty blocks long in all, but plumbing had been installed in only twelve of the blocks. Mess halls were available in only nineteen. Still, the magnanimity of Colorado's governor was an allure for Japanese still waiting to be moved inland. A petition signed by 793 Japanese Americans and resident Japanese at the Manzanar Relocation Camp sought to trumpet the agricultural successes of its signatories in an effort to help Colorado's harvest.

The Japanese who had moved to Colorado before the internment were assimilating as best as possible. The Denver YWCA Nisei Group saw its regular Thursday night social climb from an attendance of sixty to almost two hundred, with new faces seen each week. Japanese American youngsters in the Swink and La Junta area were meeting, the *Rocky Ford Enterprise* reported, "to discuss their duties as citizens of this country and to suggest ways in which they may be of help to this country during the war."

Despite efforts in Congress by some to remove their citizenship for the duration of the war, many American-born Japanese clung to the belief that the values of the United States were worth fighting for. During a tour of Amache, Ross Thompson, a reporter with the *Lamar Daily News*, talked to George Noda, a twenty-seven-year-old American living in the camp. "Now that we're interned, we treasure our freedom more than ever," he said. "For any people who think the freedom of America isn't worth fighting for, I would prescribe such medicine as this."

Patriotic declarations aside, there remained a sentiment throughout southeastern Colorado toward what was referred to as "the Jap Camp." WRA Reports Officer Joseph McClelland believed a majority of residents were opposed to the center and remained that way through the conflict. Robert C. L. George, who would later do a master's thesis on one of the Amache schools, wrote, "With minor exceptions this populace has used every opportunity to discriminate against the Japanese. In many of the stores, for instance, there are two prices, one for the local gentry and the other for the Japanese."

When it came to the Boy Scout troops being set up inside Amache, the Japanese kids would be forbidden from participating in any parades, yet they were sold large numbers of scout uniforms.

Itsako Kuruma said in a taped interview later quoted by Robert Harvey in his book, *Amache*, that when camp residents would go to towns like Lamar, the reaction was the same. "Some stores, they didn't want us to buy anything. They asked, 'Are you Chinese or Japanese?' I would say Japanese and they would say 'No!' … It was sad—everyone would just look at us and say "Are you Chinese or Japanese?' Later on we'd just tell them we were Chinese."

As September neared its end, the governor tried to keep hysteria to a minimum. The FBI, it was reported, had determined that Japanese and Nazi spies had collaborated within the United States before the Pearl Harbor attack. "Remember Pearl Harbor" was showing in theaters around the state with a tag line of "America's Stirring War Cry … Ringing Across Oceans … Striking Fear Into the Heart of a Sneaky Foe Who Dared to Stab Uncle Sam in the Back." Some of the state's newspapers were running a multipart series entitled "Our Enemy in the Pacific."

Carr instituted a program called Colorado's Hero of the Week to promote positive contributions to the war effort. Winners included a man nicknamed "Hamburger Mac," who sold war savings stamps from his seven-stool Denver hamburger establishment; Delta druggist Gray Sheek, who registered every single man and woman in town for volunteer war work, and Merle Reynolds of Boulder, who turned a small machine shop with four employees into a small factory with fifteen workers turning out tools used all over the country.

As for the governor's own contribution, his twenty-year-old son would soon be on his way to war. A headstrong lad, as stubborn as his father, Bob had married Bonnie Sandlin that summer in Nebraska without his dad's permission. The governor had wanted the teenagers to wait until they were older, but when they eloped, he said, "No use to get dramatic about it. They are married. She is a swell girl."

Bonnie's sadness was evident that day in the induction center. She kissed her husband, watched him shake hands with his father, and then, watched as he signed up for the army specialists corps as a private for radio training. She planned to continue her classes at the University of Colorado and her new father-in-law would obviously continue his work at the state capitol, but Bob's plans were more worrisome.

He would spend roughly three months in boot camp, followed by an assignment overseas, likely in a combat zone. Whether his young wife wanted to acknowledge it or not, the governor knew that it would be a matter of months before his only son would surely be fighting the Japanese in the Pacific, battling to ensure that those of similar ancestry to his enemy would continue to have rights in Colorado when he returned home.

Chapter Fifteen
October 1942

Congressman William Hill had been in politics long enough to know that when he heard a rumor enough times, it was either true, or without widespread correction, would become true in the minds of the people hearing it.

Hill, who was Governor Carr's personal secretary during his first term and before that superintendent of the Fort Collins–area school district, was known for possessing a legendary attention to detail and for multitasking. It earned him the nickname "butterfly" from other Carr staffers, for his ability to gracefully flit from one issue or one person to another.

Now, Colorado's Second District Representative, the Republican was up for reelection, and being only in his first-term, he was somewhat concerned about his chances. His opponent, June Hill from Aurora, was a well-known insurance man who had been involved in Democratic politics for the last couple of decades.

Hill had seen George Gallup's poll analyzing the upcoming election of 1942, which indicated many factors working in favor of Republican candidates, including a strong majority of the region's voters (56 percent) thinking the GOP could do a better job than the Democrats. Gallup also thought the Republicans were "at present a more cohesive and unified party than the Democrats and fired with a greater intensity of partisan feeling so far as politics is concerned."

The early fall political primaries had been cruel to Democratic candidates, with four senators and thirteen of Hill's colleagues in the House bounced from office. In the last mid-term election, held in 1938, the Democrats lost four senators and seventeen house members, whereas the Republicans lost none.

The rumors that most concerned Hill were about the Japanese evacuees, which were always associated with Governor Carr, the most visible Republican around and the head of the ticket. It had been a long time since he and his friend had stunned reporters by singing "Happy Days Are Here Again" after a legislative committee finally took action on one of their proposals.

But now, Carr couldn't catch a break, even when newspapers said positive things, like this editorial from the *Pueblo Star-Journal*: "Throughout the Governor's terms of office, he has not pussyfooted on questions which involve the people of the state. He has taken positions on some questions which have been opposed by some, but always has he done it with the idea of the welfare of the state in mind and without trying to injure anyone."

This election would be unique, as stories in all the newspapers pointed out, because Colorado had experienced the greatest shift in population in its history since the last time ballots were cast. Forty thousand new voters were in Denver, 75,000 new voters if you counted the surrounding areas, many of which Hill represented. Both parties figured there would be roughly 150,000 new voters throughout the state, but no one knew if they were Republican or Democrat. Hill realized that though the Gallup poll showed 62 percent of Coloradans knew their Congressional representative, that left nearly four of every ten voters he would have to reintroduce himself to. Plus, with a war raging, and tens of thousands of Coloradans called to duty, there didn't seem to be the interest of two years before when 545,000, or 77 percent of all of the state's eligible voters, participated in the November election.

According to columnist Alva Swain, "Leaders of both parties say that this is going to be a very close election ... there are many elements that will tend to cause it to go either way. Those elements are in the minds of the voters. The voters are not saying very much. They are just thinking and keeping still. No one knows if they approve of this policy or that policy. Not a single leader of either party can guess what the average voter is thinking this year, nor can they guess what he is going to do when he or she gets in the ballot voting booth."

Both parties knew that national political types would be watching. Swain reported, "The Republicans want to hold Colorado as an anti-administration state. The Democrats want to hold it as a state that approves the policies of the national administration. Because of that it is one of the most discussed states in the union so far as this election is concerned."

The governor, who rode at the head of the Republican caravan to rallies, noticed the crowds were significantly smaller than they were two years before when he had won an overwhelming reelection. As Carr stumped, he stressed the impact a centralized bureaucracy was having on the Colorado farmer, the Colorado small businessman, and the Colorado mine worker or owner. Still, the topic of Japanese living in the state, whether freely or in Camp Amache, kept coming up and got more attention than he wanted to give it.

Stories of Japanese cruelty to Americans or its allies were constantly in the news. Pueblo native Victor Keen, who had worked as a journalist in the Far East for twenty years, came home after being imprisoned for months by the Japanese. He had been kept in a twelve-by-twenty-foot cell with three other American men, two British women, two British men, one Russian woman, one Russian man, and twenty Chinese men and women. Their bathroom facilities consisted of a hole cut in the floor of the cell with no privacy for men or women.

Keen told Colorado audiences that a fellow American journalist had lost his toes from a gangrenous infection that "the Japs would not treat." The Chinese prisoners apparently received the worst treatment; Keen described one man's chest that bore a mass of blisters from burns inflicted with matches.

Marine Corps Private Raymond Paul Nunley gave a front-page account of how dozens of Marines were killed for "honoring a Jap flag of truce" in the Solomon Islands. "A Jap officer carrying a white flag came riding into a marine camp one day and told the commanding officer a bunch of Japs across a nearby inlet were

Ralph Carr always wore a white ten-gallon cowboy hat on the campaign trail. It was his political signature. He loved meeting people and was willing to speak with anybody. Friends would always describe men in three-piece suits waiting in the lobby to see the governor while men in overalls enjoyed the governor's full attention in his personal office. Courtesy of the Colorado Historical Society isolated and wanted to surrender," Nunley said. "[We] piled into a tank lighter and crossed about five miles of water to the point where the Japs were located. Only two of those marines are alive today. As the tank lighter approached the beach, a few Japs were observed and sure enough, one of them was waving a white flag.

"As the boat scraped onto the beach, the marines let down the ramp and started to go ashore. Without warning they were met by a terrific burst from several machine guns hidden in the underbrush. They were mowed down like stalks of corn, except for the two who escaped and swam to safety."

Other stories reported that fighting at Guadalcanal in the Solomon Islands was among the fiercest in the Pacific conflict to date.

At home, the FBI announced it had arrested 11,372 alien enemies since the beginning of the war, including fifty-two in October in Texas. Authorities believed the Houston/Galveston war industries and shipbuilding areas were in jeopardy.

In Colorado, a large number of Japanese evacuees from Camp Amache were being released into the fields to help harvest the crops.

By the second week in October, 243 were at work in northern Colorado and another 150 in the Arkansas Valley, alleviating some of the concerns that crops would be plowed under due to the lack of labor to help harvest it. M. V. Haines, the Pueblo County agricultural agent, told his local paper, "Japanese labor … has solved the problem to some extent."

Life sounded normal for the evacuees at Camp Amache, according to news reports. A girls' glee club had been formed, a fully-equipped shoe repair shop with the latest technology was built, and a fire department with two new heavy-duty Ford fire trucks with state-of-the-art equipment was operating. A dental clinic opened, and two hundred sewing machines were delivered for residents to use. The Red Cross reported that the elder Japanese residents who were not citizens "apparently feel that they are being extremely well treated. The only complaints received by the relief organization were from the American-born younger generation in the camp who had lost contact "with outside Caucasians."

Coloradans learned from a Pueblo newspaper story that two more alien relocation camps would be coming to the state. Neighbors could already hear the sounds of construction.

Engineers were hard at work four miles northeast of Trinidad in southern Colorado on a camp set to hold three thousand alien internees, which could include prisoners of war of any nationality. The army planned to expand it in the future. Military orders went out that month for a smaller alien camp to be built near Camp Carson, in Colorado Springs. That construction was set to cost roughly $2 million, and soldiers from Camp Carson would guard the alien internees.

Only months before, some residents in the state had been threatening open violence against the placement of anyone with Japanese ancestry. Now they were facing the importation of thousands more. With warnings about fifth-column activity still prevalent and mistrust high, many Coloradans must have believed the state was asking for trouble.

Congressman Hill knew all the news put together was not good, especially if people thought Carr, the head of his political party, was responsible for making it all happen. It could hurt Republicans up and down the ballot. People in his district were complaining the Japs had it better than they did. Our boys were being tortured and killed, they charged, and we are coddling their relatives in Colorado. Hill had heard the rumors about beautiful housing and easy jobs paying more weekly than soldiers earned monthly. Constituents had written him letters and telegrams complaining about clothing allowances and public subsistence grants being given to those of Japanese ancestry.

The first-term representative decided to try and control the message. He wrote an article for the *Greeley Daily Tribune* in an effort to stop the rumors, the innuendo, all the loose talk, and salvage his former boss's chances in the November election. "Rumors continue to circulate about the fine treatment received by Japanese in relocation centers," Hill wrote. "I have had many letters protesting this sort of care of our Japanese evacuees when reports from press and radio tell of the many atrocities inflicted on our own boys in Japanese prison camps."

Detail by detail, Hill attempted to paint Camp Amache as anything but a Brown Palace Hotel for West Coast Japanese. Homes were twenty by one hundred feet wooden barracks furnished with army cots and stoves. No other furniture was provided by the government, but some residents brought their own and others were buying more. There were community baths and dining halls, shared by roughly 250 evacuees.

Those who wished to work could do so at a salary that was about 40 percent of what the American serviceman would earn each month. Minimal clothing allowances were granted, and welfare was given to families where no one can work. If people were able to work and did not, they were not given any aid.

The article was published three weeks before the November 3 election, more than enough time, he hoped, to make this a non-issue for Carr in his run for the U.S. Senate among the voters in his district. In parts of the state where farmers could get the help of the Japanese evacuees, the labor program was going well. But for those who couldn't, it was another reason to put the issue at the feet of the governor who continued to be labeled in the media as one who said, "The Japanese workers would be welcome and that law and order would be maintained in communities where they lived during the harvest."

W. R. McKinstry was president of the First National Bank in Julesburg, a community on the opposite end of the state, due north of Amache. He said Sedgwick County needed one hundred fifty men to work in the beet and potato fields, and that he had notified the proper authorities, "but we are not getting results." McKinstry wrote, "Since you were favorable to the locating of these camps in

Colorado we thought you might be able to assist us … in releasing some of these Japanese to our farmers." Carr's repeated denials that he didn't invite the Japanese evacuees to Colorado were apparently never heard.

The problems of assimilation and acclimation of both Nisei and Issei into Colorado were likely most acute in the communities neighboring Camp Amache. The Lamar Chamber of Commerce and the city's Retail Merchants Association hosted a "get-acquainted" dinner at the state armory in town in the middle of October for a number of Amache representatives. As reported in the Relocation Camp newspaper, the *Bulletin*, evacuees were issued a "cordial invitation to shop in their city … and merchants promised a hearty welcome to Granadans who visit Lamar."

Henry Shimizu was one of the camp residents in attendance. He told the group, which included a reporter from the United Press, that "75 percent of the evacuees are American and know no other loyalty. … All of the evacuees are 100 percent with you."

At the meeting, one merchant was heard to say, "Why there's thousands of dollars waiting to be dumped into your laps. The people up there [at the center] are just begging to hand over their money to you. Their money is just as good as anyone else's, isn't it?"

This came after some local stores had already displayed "No Japs Allowed" placards. At least one Lamar business, Payne Liquor Store, had little orange business cards printed saying, "Free: One pint whiskey for each pair of Jap ears. Need not be mates. Conditions unimportant. Unlimited offer." Shortly thereafter, the Lamar City Council passed Ordinance 320 that any liquor store selling alcohol to Amache residents would lose its license and those purchasing the booze would be arrested.

The town went out of its way to make things difficult for the evacuees, refusing them access to their community unless it was to spend money. Lamar residents made it clear that their facilities and their parks were for Lamar residents only.

Meanwhile, the "Boulder Boys" were ingratiating themselves

to the University of Colorado community. The *Rocky Mountain Herald*, in an article entitled "When Greek Meets Jap," described the navy's Japanese Language School as "Colorado's most unique war industry. ... Drinking a Coke beside you in 'The Sink' [local hangout] will be some quiet [navy linguist] who speaks English ten times better than you do and can rattle on just as well in Japanese and can probably write Sanskrit.

"Busy with rice paper and brush, they are cramming day and night to bridge that gap between East and West ... America needs these boys and needs them quickly. ... The Pacific war, linguistically, is analogous to the Indian wars. A Denver marine capturing a Jap in the Solomons has about the same problem as his great-great-grandfather capturing a Sioux."

The group of Phi Beta Kappa and elite college students from around the country was quickly acclimating to life at the base of the Rocky Mountains, forgetting anything but the Japanese they were required to learn in little more than a year's time. Student Frank Gibney said that the Japanese language was convoluted and hard to learn, but that understanding it meant understanding the people better.

Naval officers, realizing the importance of the program, planned to expand it significantly. Although the original group sent to Boulder from Berkeley was less than a hundred, Commander Hindmarsh was under orders to enroll an additional five to seven hundred students as soon as possible. Adding this many students meant the arrival of at least eighty new instructors and their families, all of whom would be American-born Japanese.

"It is hoped that we can find some vacant house and bring the teachers in for the time being as single individuals without families and have them run these houses even with a Japanese cook imported from one of the Colorado centers," W. F. Dyde wrote to President Stearns on October 19. Dyde told his boss that Miss Francis Walne, the head instructor, was going to Amache to interview one hundred prospective American-born Japanese to see if they would qualify for the positions. "We are desirous of moving ahead as rapidly as possible," he wrote.

In Stearns's absence, Dyde had appeared before the Boulder City Council in July to discuss the "point of view of Japanese Americans, not students, who were applying to come to Boulder to live." The council required the seventy-five individuals or twenty-five families of Japanese ancestry, who would serve as instructors, to have a letter of reference mailed directly to the Boulder City Manager from the public officials of the community from which they were coming.

Dyde had promised to advise the council if "there were any significant changes made in the university's plan so that they could confirm or withdraw their approval." Bringing in more than a hundred others certainly qualified as a "significant change" and so, on October 20, he once again appeared before city leaders to tell them what the navy proposed to do.

There was simply no room on campus to house everyone. As it was, the men in the navy's radio school had moved to the field house that held CU basketball games. The dormitories were taken over by the students of the Japanese Language School. There was nowhere to house the Japanese American instructors, except within the city limits.

The school turned to the Boulder Chamber of Commerce, which turned to the *Boulder Daily Camera*. The result was a three-quarter page ad in the daily newspaper that began, "The United States Navy asks Boulder to meet the most important quota Boulder has ever been asked to meet ... and immediately. Here is what your navy asks: To rent, within the next ten days, houses and apartments, large and small for — Japanese American Navy Language School instructors and their families. Each one of these instructors has been picked for the Navy with the utmost care, to teach future naval officers the Japanese language. For reasons of vital military secrecy the exact figures cannot be disclosed."

The ad pointed out the influx would mean "a full town and

stable business conditions" but also a "tremendous leap forward in efficient striking power in the Pacific." Boulder had already provided 1,248 men to the armed services, bought more than $1 million in war bonds, and contributed nearly 1,800 tons of scrap metal to the war effort. Now, its residents were being asked to call the Boulder Chamber of Commerce at once to give more help.

"If the Navy asked Boulder to provide emergency housing for the crew of a battleship that crew would be housed! The men the Navy now wants housing for are the crew of what is perhaps the most vital 'land battleship' the United States Navy commands!" The message was endorsed by President Stearns, the Boulder Ministerial Alliance, the Boulder Chamber of Commerce, and Boulder's mayor, city manager, council, and defense council.

Some residents of Boulder called to complain, believing the privilege of buying homes in the city should not be offered to the Japanese Americans. Paul Irish, who produced a master's thesis on the topic at the University of Colorado, reported some *Boulder Daily Camera* customers came in to complain "bitterly about the presence of the Japanese Americans in Boulder," but the newspaper's editor, A. A. Paddock, did not back down, saying the paper "wished to mold the public opinion to accept the Japanese Language School."

Irish reported none of the instructors felt welcome. "At first, the community felt the Japanese Americans had been dumped on them," said one instructor. Gossip was rampant and the distinction between fact and innuendo became difficult to deduce. People heard a Boulder woman had told the ladies at her missionary society "unless the group could demonstrate a Christian spirit in the Language School situation she was going to stop studying about missions." Another story related to Irish included a "very sensitive Japanese-American" who was spit upon in front of a downtown barbershop that did not let any of the instructors park their cars in front of that shop.

"There was some chalking on the doors of Japanese-

American homes," Irish wrote. "One Japanese-American family had 'garbage' dumped on their premises. ... One Japanese-American was shot at with a BB gun. ... Some people in Denver referred to Boulder as a Japanese colony, as a 'Little Tokyo' and this made the Japanese unpopular."

Other stories included a little girl in kindergarten who met "several ten-to-thirteen-year-old girls who on more than one occasion slapped her and called her a 'damn Jap.'" One family received an anonymous letter containing a *Readers Digest* article entitled "Atrocities by Japanese Soldiers." Another said they had rented their house by verbal agreement and had moved in upon arriving in Boulder, only to receive an eviction notice from the owner to vacate in ten days. No reason was given. Yet another reported hearing someone say, "I don't want any Japs in this town," just a few days after moving to the town.

Rufus Baker said that he never felt the attitude of the community was antagonistic, but he realized the tension inherently involved in implementing what the navy and the university wanted. "I was told on pretty good authority that the Real Estate dealers had among themselves a tacit understanding that they would not sell property to the Japanese," the Boulder minister told Irish for his thesis. "The tension grew as time passed and war progress and war stories came in."

Commander Hindmarsh had instructed the university and the chamber to use the utmost discretion with the Japanese Language School. No names of students or instructors could be released to the public, as their work was top secret.

The rest of the state continued its fight against any fifth-column activity, especially since Japanese evacuees were now working in the fields. The head of the state's Farm Protection Committee warned members they "should be conscious of the dangers of sabotage on our farms," wrote Lee Pritchard. "It has already been reported to the chairman that a few stacks of hay have been burned. Whether these were caused by sabotage or from natural causes is not yet known. Nevertheless, this should serve to remind us that we must take all possible precautions for any dangers that might affect the rancher and rural population."

Cities installed large sirens to send air-raid signals in case of attack. A red air-raid message was an action warning, with a signal lasting two full minutes. In many towns, the Colorado Civil Air Patrol conducted practice runs, with screaming sirens that alerted residents to make sure no light came from their houses that could make them a bombing target. The city of Longmont in northern Colorado was tested on October 14 and accomplished a complete blackout in less than ten minutes.

Senator Johnson stayed in Washington for the first half of the month to continue work on the armed services spending bill, choosing to use the successful strategy he had employed during the primary—that of the dedicated public servant willing to forego campaigning and personal success for public service. He knew he'd "have a fight on his hands" in the upcoming general election. He told Alva Swain, "Carr is the strongest man the Republicans could nominate," and, "neither one of [us] has a cinch by any means."

Carr spent some nights and weekends campaigning, but not like in elections past. The war and its subsequent rubber restrictions had put a damper on "beating the bushes for votes," as United Press correspondent Willard Haselbush reported. The governor knew the challenge before him.

Back in the early part of 1939, just after Carr's inauguration, the two had been photographed seated together. Johnson, a good half foot taller, had his arm around Carr; the governor was smiling with his hands resting in his lap, looking every bit the uncomfortable little kid. Although the two were physically so different, they both appealed to voters with their candor, intelligence, and ability to connect with the average Coloradan.

As the campaign opened up, it was evident the tack each candidate would take. The governor would hammer at the failure of the national administration to live up to the constitutional promise of individual enterprise. In Rocky Ford on October 16, Carr railed at those who had "suggested that the Constitution should remain inoperative through the emergency. When the Constitution fails to function at any time, it loses its value."

One week later in Colorado Springs, Carr stressed there "is not a state west of the Mississippi that has done what Colorado has to co-operate with the federal government in carrying out its policies." But the thanks it received, he said, was an order closing down the state's gold mines, which was "a tremendous hardship on banks, stores, schools, colleges, supply houses, transportation lines, and entire communities," as his friend Harry Robbins of the Golden Cycle Corporation put it.

One night after that, three hundred Republicans braved a Jefferson County snowstorm to hear the governor pound the podium against another federal government decision. The secretary of agriculture had fixed a ceiling on prices for potatoes and onions, which Carr believed would hurt the farmers of Colorado who would have a hard time recouping costs for producing the crops. "Clearly," the governor said, the decision would turn Colorado from "a great agricultural state into a non-producing one."

Johnson stressed his experience, saying voters "must all have faith. That's the way you can support the nation's war effort—faith in the righteousness of our cause, faith in our leaders," of which he was obviously one. He was the only member of the Senate Finance Committee from the West. He was the second-ranking member of the Military Affairs Committee. He also served on the Interstate Commerce, Mining, and Public Lands Committees. His main message: "It would take years for a new senator to attain the position of influence now occupied by Senator Johnson."

He was endorsed by the *Boulder Daily Camera* as "no rubber-stamp Senator. Neither is he a partisan obstructionist. He maintains a keen balance of conservatism and liberalism. He is, therefore, of exactly the caliber to be the most valuable senator to Colorado ...

to Democrats and Republicans alike."

Johnson took aim at his opponent, who was espousing views and promoting solely Republican Party candidates. "Beware of bold, brazen, self-appointed political counselors who plead with voters to shut their eyes, to stop examining candidates," he told the League of Women Voters on October 27. "To hell with party labels. This is no time for cheap, outmoded chicanery. Now or never before we must not buy a 'pig in a poke.'"

Where the senator left off, the Colorado Democratic Party and the state's organized labor picked up, attacking Carr. The party ran newspaper ads stating "that loose talking critics themselves prove the absurdity of their claim that we have lost any of our freedom. Where but in a land of liberty would their voices by heard?" The full-page ad added that Democrats believed "a real and dangerous DICTATOR does exist in COLORADO, a DICTATOR who demands that YOU stop THINKING AND VOTE AS YOU ARE TOLD."

Behind the scenes, Democrats were spreading the message that Carr had invited the Japanese into Colorado, and that with two more camps being built, even more enemy aliens were on their way. The safety and security of Coloradans was being threatened as their sons, brothers, and fathers went to war, and more Japanese, thanks to Governor Carr, were coming to the state.

The message was specifically sent to the state's Hispanic population in southern Colorado. That group had seen their neighbors in New Mexico endure a staggering number of casualties. It was estimated that there were 2,800 New Mexicans in Bataan, a large percentage of whom were Spanish Americans, and that only three officers and 104 enlisted men were evacuated when it fell. The balance of roughly 2,700 men either paid the ultimate sacrifice or became prisoners of war.

"I have never seen such a campaign of hatred as was manifested among certain classes of the population over that Jap lie that Johnson cultivated so carefully," Judge Joe Thomas wrote the governor. "Some of them were so wrought up that they were ready to fight about it."

Lamar attorney Arthur Gordon wrote his friend Carr that his community was still somewhat "sore" over the placement of Camp Amache and recommended he pay "a visit to Prowers County between now and November." The governor knew the standard stump speech criticizing the administration for infringing upon individual rights needed to be amended.

The *Colorado Springs Gazette* reported that he specifically stated he had "not invited the Jap camps into Colorado" and that he was simply cooperating with the federal government's wishes to win the war. He added that the first he knew of Amache was when he received a call telling him it was a done deal and that he "had nothing to say about it one way or another."

Reporters covering the senate race continued to point out the differences in the two candidates. The United Press reported that the governor's "acquiescence to federal plans to move Japanese evacuees into Colorado resulted in much criticism." The *Rocky Mountain News* in its editorial endorsing Carr over Johnson pointed out when the evacuation order came, "Colorado was the only Rocky Mountain state, whose governor cooperated with the military program. Senator Ed C. Johnson, now his opponent, tried to make political capital for himself by opposing this policy ... [Carr] considers winning the war more important than his own election."

Headlines screamed of the Japanese attack on American positions in Guadalcanal. After air raids, continuous bombing, and significant troop activity, a huge page one headline in the Pueblo newspaper not long before the election read, "American Pacific Positions in Peril." The headline underneath was "Japs' Superiority in All Combat Services Darkens U.S. Hopes." At theaters across Colorado that weekend, audiences watched *Flying Tigers*, a John Wayne movie advertised by the following tag line: "So long, 'Jappie,' your number's up ... you're signing off the air with a little tune we play just for you—we call it the 'Lullaby in Lead.'"

Carr had to win Denver in order to win the election. The Republican Party headquarters on the second floor of the Brown Palace Hotel had Carr endorsements from the Pueblo newspaper and the Durango newspaper pinned on the wall, but insiders hoped the endorsements of the *Rocky Mountain News* and the *Denver Post* mattered more. The state's largest city could either deliver the election to the governor or take it from him.

There were roughly 713,000 registered voters in Colorado. A record 545,130 had voted in the 1940 presidential election and all estimates from both political parties were that the turnout would be anywhere from 250,000 to 350,000, a significant drop from the last Carr victory. With the labor shortage potentially keeping the solidly Republican agricultural vote in the fields, there was a great emphasis placed on winning the big cities. None was bigger in Colorado than Denver and about a third of all Colorado voters were expected to cast ballots in the capital city.

Three thousand people came to a rally at the city auditorium the week before the election, giving Republicans reason to hope. The crowd exceeded their expectations, leading party chairman William Lloyd to predict "Carr will carry Denver" and that the governor "will pile up a stunning majority." The *Denver Post* reported that "veteran observers characterized the meeting as the largest and most enthusiastic held in Denver in a decade, except when a national figure was the principal attraction."

The governor had told the overflow crowd, it was a "difficult swan song to sing. I should like to continue being the governor of the great people of Colorado the rest of my days, if it were possible, but it just can't be done. We have got to get a tall, slender, thin man to continue this job that no fat man can."

Although he laughed with his lieutenant governor, John Vivian, who had been his college classmate and was running to succeed him, he quickly turned serious, reminding those in attendance: "You must vote principles, principles, principles. And the only party which recognizes principles in this state and in this nation tonight is your Republican Party."

Winning Denver would be no easy chore for a governor whose individualistic political identity was anathema to the Democratic political machine that operated in the city. Both Democrats and Republicans had political organizations that did not look fondly on outsiders like Carr who made political hay by attacking the status quo.

Denver mayor Ben Stapleton was first elected to the city's top job as a Ku Klux Klansman in 1925, and survived a recall election after telling a Klan rally, "I will work with the Klan and for the Klan in the coming election, heart and soul. And if I am reelected, I will give the Klan the kind of administration it wants."

He would later renounce the group, but its nearly 20,000 members was strong at the time. The Denver Klan chapter took out an advertisement in the *Denver Times* in 1921 declaring itself a "law and order organization ... we are not only active now, but were here yesterday, and we are here today and we shall be here forever."

One of Carr's friends from college, Philip Van Cise, a fellow Delta Tau Delta, led the fight then against the Klan and would encourage him during the initial debate over the Japanese evacuees. "Your radio talk ... was a masterpiece of statesmanship," Van Cise wrote Carr. "It won't get you votes immediately, but in the long run, it will pay dividends with the people who for a change like sincerity in office."

Members of the Denver City Council apparently did not accept the "sincerity" of the governor on the Japanese policy. Perhaps moved by the exhortations of the *Denver Post* to prevent a "yellow peril on our hands," the council twice openly condemned the governor and his policy on the issue. The first vote came in a March meeting when members debated Councilman Harry Rosenthal's resolution protesting the importation of West Coast Japanese.

Councilman H. C. Dolph said before voting, "I am opposed to any Japanese being brought into the state for any reason."

Both Denver daily newspapers editorialized in favor of the council decision the next day. The *Rocky Mountain News* said, "The Council undoubtedly expressed the views of a majority of Colorado citizens."

Less than a month later, the council once again sought, as reported in the *News*, "some way of preventing any of the West Coast migrants from moving to Denver." Councilmen Rosenthal, Dolph, and Harry Risley all reported that they "already had trouble with Japanese families moving or attempting to move into their districts." Rosenthal reported that on a recent trip to Salt Lake City, he had counted ninety-seven cars containing Japanese evacuees presumably on their way to Colorado and "criticized Governor Carr for his stand."

Dolph told the council he had prevented the sale of one house and the rental of another to Japanese families after speaking to the real estate men in his district. Risley followed up by saying that one Japanese family had moved into his district over his protestations to authorities who told him he could not do anything about it.

However, it was the political machines of both parties that truly feared Carr's success. Neighborhood papers like the *Park Hill Topics* had reported that Mayor Stapleton "knows if Carr is [elected] … his political power will be broken" and the *Pueblo Chieftain* had also reported the machine's antagonism toward the governor. Carr had taken on Stapleton publicly over the last few years. When he suspected vote fraud, Carr had twelve thousand letters sent out to test the authenticity of names and addresses appearing on election books at Denver precincts. His informal survey resulted in the return of nearly three thousand, when postmen could not find the people whose addresses were on the election material. Carr called it a "plan to perpetrate wholesale election frauds."

Then, in his second term as governor, he vetoed Senate Bill 290, which would have permitted the use of voting machines in Denver elections. His major concern was that the plan "does not provide individual ballots be preserved … it is possible with the machines to vote for all members of one political party by one plunge of the device."

Republicans in Denver were not too fond of Carr either. Van Cise wrote a letter suggesting cleaning out the influence of former Senator Lawrence Phipps from the party. Phipps had opposed Carr's candidacy for governor when he first ran.

Rocky Mountain News editor Lee Casey later wrote that "When a hell-raiser pops up in the Republican Party in Colorado, as a rule he is either smothered in the primary or killed off in the general election by his fellow Republicans." Carr had bucked that system two times in a row as the party's leading candidate, and hoped to make it a third time as he headed into the final weekend before the November 3 election.

The major story in Sunday's papers was about the impending election in Colorado—but it came out of Washington.

Arizona Democratic senator Ernest McFarland announced the Senate Campaign Expenditures Committee would immediately investigate charges of "exorbitant spending" by Governor Carr and Senator Eugene Millikin. Johnson immediately disavowed any knowledge of the investigation or who caused it, and McFarland would only say that a complaint had been lodged by a Colorado Democrat.

Initial campaign filings showed Carr had spent $4,759 to Johnson's $1,925. Millikin had filed a preliminary report with $7,635 in spending, whereas his opponent James Marsh claimed $3,801 in spending. McFarland told reporters in Washington he hoped to have an investigator in Denver before Tuesday's election. Republican leaders called it a "stale political trick" from a senator who in February had been at a fundraiser for Johnson, calling him "a man who is ever sincere and true to his convictions."

Governor Carr was in possession of "some ammunition" of his own to use against Johnson that had been sent to him by a supporter. But, as he wrote after the election to Frederick Lilley, "I looked it over and felt that I didn't want to carry on the kind of a campaign that [Johnson] did and so I left it unused."

The article, though sure to rile up Coloradans during that pre-election weekend, was written by Marjorie Young and printed in the magazine sections of many papers statewide. She had served as a correspondent in Tokyo for many years. It was entitled, "America's Strangest Problem: What to Do With Thousands of New Jap Babies Here." Young advocated separating the Japanese men from the women in the internment camps to prevent more babies from being born.

"Japanese women were quick to catch our war time spirit of mass production and are breeding, at top speed, colonies of pure blooded Japanese babies," Young wrote. "Uppermost in the American mind is 'are the Japanese we have in our camps loyal?' Of course they are. Loyal to their blood and to the souls of their honorable ancestors."

The national pundits were watching Colorado. Carr was featured in *Life* magazine and profiled in *Time* magazine as well. The latter called him "a bright new phenomenon in Rocky Mountain politics. Able, courageous and independent ... [he] proved his statesmanship and urbanity by his handling of the vexatious Japanese evacuation problem." In summary, the national publication said that the election results would either raise Carr to "new national prominence or throw him into temporary eclipse."

In the *Life* magazine article, Carr was shown standing in a sugar beet field with Spanish American women on each side, and it was reported the governor was "likely" to be victorious in the election.

The governor spent the final day before Tuesday's election preparing his remarks for a statewide radio address that night. He began:

People of Colorado, four years ago you bestowed upon me the highest honor which can come to an American citizen—the governorship of Colorado ... by your verdict at the polls tomorrow, will you record your satisfaction or disapproval of the job which I have about completed ...

I am dedicated to the proposition that the Constitution must operate and function in time of war just as it does in time of peace. If permitted to sit as the representative of my state in the Senate of the United States, I shall devote my thoughts, my energy, and my life to the prosecution of this war to the only possible conclusion, while I will demand that we protect and preserve our form of government and the rights of the individual under that government as defined by the Constitution. Without this last, victory would be an empty thing ...

I leave my future plans in your hands. I am yours to command.

The sun rose at 7:32 A.M. on Tuesday, November 3, with highs in Denver expected in the low fifties. The city's four hundred polling stations had already been open for thirty-two minutes, as had the 1,669 precincts throughout Colorado.

As usual, the newspapers were full of war news: A former Denver woman was now interned by the Japanese in a Manila camp. Denver native Elden Elliott, a technical sergeant in the army, had been killed a week earlier in fighting in the southwest Pacific. The women's page of the *Denver Post* had a story titled, "Every Pound of Fat You Save Means Shells to Shoot Japs." Apparently, two pounds of grease drippings created enough glycerin for five anti-tank shells.

The governor had cast his absentee ballot the week before, faithfully sending it to the Conejos County clerk in his hometown of Antonito, where he still claimed residency. He had pushed himself so hard, he was suffering from an advanced case of the flu and his voice was going. Against the wishes of his friends and his Christian Science practitioner, he had kept going over the weekend, but relaxed in bed most of Tuesday, knowing there was nothing else he could do.

Rocky Mountain News editor Lee Casey told others that weekend it was a shame that Colorado "would retire to private life, one of two men, when both should be kept on in some outstanding governmental position. ... [Carr and Johnson] are the best officials this state has had in years. If there ever was a time when Colorado needed the guiding hand of both, that time is today."

Due to the importance of the race nationally, the National Broadcasting Company had set aside time for at least two national radio updates by a KOA announcer stationed within the *Denver Post* newsroom. Voters would be casting ballots for either Carr, Johnson, James Allander with the Communist Party, or Carle Whitehead of the Socialist Party.

Turnout was noticeably light throughout the state early in the day. In Greeley, election officials reported half as many ballots cast as at the same hour in 1940. Republican watchers there predicted strong margins for their candidates continuing through the last hour of voting, when farmers would come to vote, because the weather was perfect for the harvest during the daylight hours. Ward Three, Precinct Six had eighty votes by noon and the strongly Republican area showed Carr up 58–22 over Johnson.

Vote totals from Boulder were significantly down as well. Early returns, according to the *Boulder Daily Camera*, showed "Republican candidates with the exception of Ralph L. Carr were running well ahead in most urban precincts." Low turnout was also seen in places like La Junta and Pueblo.

However, in Denver, turnout was heavier than expected in a number of precincts. Early reports showed strong voter participation in the Republican areas of the city, including the Capitol Hill area and parts of south and northwestern Denver. The headline of the *Post* was "Early Returns Indicate Carr Will Carry Denver." The paper reported that Democratic precinct workers were disappointed and admitted the trend was against their candidates, but their state chairman Barney Whatley said Democrats tend to be "late voters" and cautioned against any premature claims to victory.

The Associated Press called it "one of the strangest campaigns in Colorado's political history," with little sense on anybody's part how it would end. Political analysts of both parties told the AP that whoever won the Carr-Johnson race "might well sweep the majority of his ticket to victory."

Hours after the polls closed, the *Rocky Mountain News* was put to bed with a headline of "Johnson, Carr Neck and Neck in Senate Race." Maurice Leckenby described the candidates as "sweeping on toward a photo finish" as Carr led by a mere 222 votes out of more than 184,000 that had been counted. That represented roughly half the votes cast. The *News* described returns pouring into its office showing "one, then the other surging to the lead with the certain indication that the result will not be definite until each of the state's 1,669 precincts has been tabulated."

The governor could not stay still. Comparatively calm through the day, he had to be where the action was. Around 11:00 P.M., he bundled up and went to the Republican Party headquarters at the Brown Palace Hotel.

From one of its rooms, he would watch the returns come in through the wire service and listen to the radio stations for statewide updates. Alva Swain described it as "about as trying an ordeal as any candidate ever went through. First ahead, then behind, then ahead."

Johnson was restless as well, going over to the *Rocky Mountain News* shortly after midnight to watch returns at the newspaper. He had visited the newspaper each primary and general election night since 1932, never losing a race in that time span. The trip into downtown Denver to the city's oldest paper became a superstitious one.

The Rocky reporters described him on election night 1942 as "calm, considerate, humble." When the numbers turned against him, they wrote, "We thought we were seeing a man fake defeat in a grand and sportsmanship manner with malice toward none."

However, for the morning edition, Johnson said that he expected to "win by an eyelash."

The biggest news seemed to be that Republicans were advancing up and down the ticket.

Lieutenant Governor Vivian was dominating in his attempt to become the state's chief executive. Millikin was coasting to victory, as were Republican candidates for treasurer, secretary of state, attorney general, auditor, supreme court justices (three candidates), and University of Colorado regent (two candidates). All of the state's congressional representatives won reelection, three of them Republican. The only statewide Democratic candidate faring decently was Inez Johnson Lewis, who was running for superintendent of public instruction.

Returns from El Paso County, including Colorado Springs, came in after midnight, pushing Carr's lead to approximately thirteen hundred votes. When the votes from Pueblo came in, Johnson surged ahead. After 1:30 A.M., Johnson led by fourteen votes. The senator was so nervous, he left the newspaper and went to one of the local radio stations to look at the returns, hoping the broadcast outlet would receive results faster. While he was there, he learned the governor was horribly sick with the flu and sent word to him to, as Swain reported, "go home, get a nurse and go to bed."

However, the governor couldn't rest. He studied the results, wondering which precincts were still out. How were they trending? What could he foresee? Carr's friends and closest allies encouraged him to return to 747 Downing Street, where he could sleep in his own bed, and told him they would wake him if new information came out. But the governor insisted, according to Swain, "that he was not going to have anyone say he was a 'quitter.'"

Johnson heard that and reportedly turned to his campaign staff and said that if he heard anyone label Governor Carr a "quitter," then, that person "will answer to me personally."

The sun rose again and the morning wore on before it became clear to the Associated Press that "U.S. Senator Ed Johnson appeared reelected to another six-year term Wednesday, the only Democrat holding firm against a Republican tide which swept all major Colorado state offices in Tuesday's election."

It was one of the closest races in Colorado history.

Johnson won 174,612 votes to Carr's 170,970, or 50.05 percent to 49.95 percent, a difference of only 3,642 votes. He would be the only member of his party aside from Lewis to survive a statewide race. In Denver, where Republican Party Chairman Lloyd had predicted Carr would dominate, the governor lost 58,339 to 50,715, too big a margin to overcome throughout the rest of the state. The race was so close, the *Denver Post* concluded that a shift of only two votes in each of Denver's four hundred precincts, and just one vote in each of the state's 1,297 precincts, "would have changed the results."

The Republican dominance filtered down to the legislature where both chambers turned to the GOP. In the state house, fifty-five of the sixty-five members would be Republicans and at least twenty-two of the thirty-five state senators would also be Republican. In Denver specifically, all four state senators and all fifteen state representatives elected were Republican.

"The fact that Denver—considered a Democratic stronghold—elected a solid Republican legislative ticket shows beyond the shadow of a doubt the PROTEST NATURE of Tuesday's election," commented the *Post*. "Republicans scored the most sweeping victory in Colorado Tuesday in many a year."

Governor Carr waited until Thursday to make sure of the vote before calling Johnson to congratulate him. Johnson told reporters afterward this was the "sweetest victory in my life." He thanked his friends and said he was "glad this nasty, faith-destroying political campaign of disunity is over. Now we must repair the harm that has been done and settle down to the business of winning the war."

The governor released a formal statement saying that he planned to return to his law practice in January. "We have waged

In one of the closest races in Colorado history, Johnson edged out Ralph Carr. A one-vote switch in each of Colorado's precincts would have led to a different outcome. When Republican candidates overwhelmed their Democratic counterparts at all levels of Colorado government in the 1942 elections, Carr and his supporters determined his standing up for the rights of Japanese Americans as the cause of his election defeat.

a campaign for certain fundamental principles which some of us believe must be sustained if we are to continue as a nation of free men. I stated in my speeches that we must forget personalities and insist upon those principles," he wrote.

"This is the most decisive victory for those principles in a generation. To say that I am happy would be to put it mildly.

"Incidentally, the people have said that they do not wish me to continue to serve them. ... Most of all, do I thank all the people for the help and comfort I have enjoyed during four years as Governor. No man could ever suffer regret who has enjoyed the opportunity to serve which has been mine.

"The results of this election mean a brighter tomorrow—a concerted, intelligent drive toward an immediate victory—and a better United States of America." Colorado's preeminent water attorney would get to go back to his first love, practicing law. "They pulled me out of it," he said, "but now I'm going back."

As he sat in the governor's office he'd leave in January, a number of his friends were discussing the reasons why he lost. Was it that Colorado didn't want to challenge the president? Was Colorado worried about changing leaders during a time of war? They already knew the answer and were sensitive enough to avoid discussing it.

Ralph Carr's stand on "the Japanese question" had kept him from Congress. It was his forcefulness and principle that had even kept it close.

In a scratchy voice that would render him inaudible for much of the following three weeks, Ralph Carr said that the reason he lost was even more obvious. "Gentlemen, you forget the principle reason. Senator Johnson got more of those things called votes than I did."

Chapter Sixteen

December 1942 to September 1950

The young woman's family was known simply as #8482. Her address, where she lived in Camp Amache with her aging father, was 6F-5C. She had been offered a job two and a half hours away in Denver—not as a day laborer or as a worker in the fields harvesting crops, but to become a "house girl" for the most visible man in the state. She was uneasy about the whole thing.

Wakako Domoto, who was twenty-seven years old, was on the first train full of evacuees who arrived at Amache in late August of 1942 and immediately went to work as the assistant director for the personnel records department at the center. She earned $19 a month for supervising eight other evacuees, while setting up, maintaining, and auditing employee time sheets at the camp. She did so well, her supervisor used words like "outstanding" three separate times in her first performance review.

"Very mild-mannered, quiet, unassuming person," wrote Henry Halliday, the Amache senior administrative officer in charge of the camp's administrative duties. "Have had no reason to question her loyalty. Appears to have accepted evacuation and relocation without rancor or feeling of persecution. Her wholesome attitude is best evidenced by her desire to prepare herself to earn a living after the war."

The five-three, 126-pound Domoto had lived in California her whole life, and received the highest scholastic honor in her high school graduating class in Oakland. She attended Stanford University for two years, taking courses in social sciences before she had to leave to help run her family's flower and plant nursery business. For a decade, she did the typing, filing, billing, and all the bookkeeping needed to keep the business running smoothly.

When her family was first evacuated from the West Coast, she worked in the personnel department as a senior clerk at the

Merced Assembly Center before those camps in California were emptied and the residents sent further inland. That experience plus recommendations from three Caucasian housewives in California is what led Amache officials to think of her when the request for a house girl came in. The fact that she was a registered Republican in her home state of California did not hurt matters.

"I refused at first because of my father's illness," she later told the *Denver Post*. "Not many [Japanese women] left camp in those days. I was apprehensive."

Colorado's outgoing governor Ralph Carr wanted to make a moral and political statement. He also needed a housekeeper. He decided to ask for someone from the Amache camp, and said he would send that person to Emily Griffith Opportunity School, in addition to giving them room, board, and $35 a month.

"He felt in order to put his money where his mouth was, to verify how he felt about things, he asked [Amache] to send one of their young women to be his housekeeper," said Carr's granddaughter Katherine Lynch. "He wanted to demonstrate to Colorado, he'd trust them in his own home."

Domoto agreed to come live and work at 747 Downing Street. On January 8, 1943, just days before Carr would leave the governor's office and return to the practice of law, he welcomed the Japanese American woman into his house.

Maybe the best explanation was given by his college friend Jim Lockhart, who wrote Carr on January 13, 1943: "You have done your duty well as a servant of the people of your state. You are still a servant of them, but a freelance servant, able to act and do your best in the way you believe best to do it."

"He just didn't believe they'd be a problem," Bob Carr later told the Tokyo Broadcasting System for a television documentary on his father. "He thought it was a whole bunch of hysteria. Even when he saw he couldn't stop [internment], he wanted to make sure they were treated as humanely [as possible], equal rights for all."

As Domoto arrived in Denver, she said: "I was wondering

who would meet me … I was hoping at least his chauffeur would be waiting."

As her bus drove into the depot, she later told Japanese television journalists, "There was Mr. Carr standing right there himself, standing right there. I had never met the man, but I had seen his picture. I said, 'Now I feel safe.' He was standing there to make a statement and he certainly did."

For the next six months, Domoto was employed and sent to school by Ralph Carr. "He told me one day, 'I live alone and so there isn't a whole lot to do. You can go to school and take up shorthand.'" That gave her the chance to pursue her education, which had been put on hold while she helped in the family business. Her character and ability gave Carr the chance to prove the point he had hoped to make.

"She is the finest person I have ever had in that capacity in my home," he wrote to the War Relocation Authority when he asked for an extension of her initial one-month work contract. "She has fitted into the picture admirably, and is meeting every situation in a manner which calls for intelligence, tact and ability. There is no chance for this young lady ever to become a charge of the state or the nation. She will earn her way always. I hope that you may make arrangements so that she may stay with me as long as she wishes."

From January through June, Domoto lived in Denver. While she was there, Carr's first granddaughter, Catharine Joan, known to all around as "Kitty Carr," was born to Bob and his wife, Bonnie. Mother and child moved into the home on Downing Street with the governor and Wakako while Bob was stationed at Wendover, Utah, awaiting orders for officers' candidate school.

"The woman [next door] started talking to Bonnie over the fence," Bob later told the *Post*. "[She] asked, 'Aren't you afraid that you will wake up one night and find your baby murdered by that Japanese. Aren't you concerned she is going to steal?"

Domoto was unaware of the neighborhood conversations,

but told the Japanese journalists she knew Carr was taking a "big personal risk besides his political career … I was forever grateful for him, so I could do something else besides typing. I certainly appreciated him taking me under his wing—they were strong, courageous wings of an eagle and I felt really protected."

Carr's political standing, however, was not protected. His position on the Japanese evacuees was described by the one of the Denver papers as "a fatal blunder," and moreover, Carr's loss to Johnson was described as a "political career [that] has now fallen apart." Alva Swain wrote, "Yet after having crowned his friends with all of the laurels which they desired, he himself fell short of the goal of his lifetime. Just one of the quirks of politics."

Much of the political analysis of the day focused on the public servant Colorado would be losing instead of why that public servant was retired to the private sector. "[Carr] understood that politics is one of the cruelest of games, and that the only rule is the ancient one of woe to the vanquished," Lee Casey of the *Rocky Mountain News* wrote. "I do object however, to the loss to the state that his removal from public affairs entails. We need, and badly need, men of his character and ability. They are extremely rare."

After speaking with many people, the veteran columnist Swain deduced that Carr himself was done in by his own party in part because of his own determination to be governor "in practice" and not just in name. "He did not consult party leaders nor did he allow partisan events to occur in his administration."

When it came to the governor's stand on the Japanese evacuation from the West Coast, Swain concluded, "Had Pearl Harbor never occurred … it is quite likely that Carr would have won."

That was the thinking among many of Carr's friends. His longtime confidante, Judge Joe Thomas in Antonito, wrote to his friend after the election, "The Jap story was what [Johnson] used so effectively. The Mexicans, who had sons in the armed forces, all turned against you on that story and you actually lost Conejos County [Carr's home county]."

The *Pacific Citizen*, the Japanese American newspaper published out of California, reported that one strategy supposedly used by Carr's opposition was to scare Hispanics in the state into believing the Japanese would take their jobs.

Others intimated there was some chicanery behind the November results. Carr's secretary Myrtle Graham said the story going around the campaign office immediately afterward was that FDR "was trying to figure out who'll be worse for him to deal with ... Ed Johnson or Ralph Carr. He decided Ralph Carr would be worse and a lot of money came into Denver at the last minute," she said. "I think a lot of it went straight into voters' hands."

Carr's supporters tried to understand what seemed to be contradictory election results. A Republican sweep throughout Colorado excepting the state's top Republican made no sense. "I still can't believe that you were not elected Senator and certainly cannot understand the people of Colorado," wrote Merrill Shoup, son of former governor Oliver Shoup. "However, the voting public is fickle."

His Council of Defense public affairs director, J. Fred Thomas, wrote, "It is now my turn to say, 'Keep your chin up!' I know how hard it is and how futile it seems at times trying to carry on. I feel your political career is not over. Something will break for you again. A man cannot reach the pinnacle you did and quit for good. You are only started." Fred Ley from the U.S. Department of Agriculture said, "I am sure that the State has lost one of the finest public servants we ever had." Denver resident George Morrison wrote that Carr "will go down in history as the greatest Governor Colorado has ever had or will have."

Carr wrote to his friend Mary Montgomery a month after the election: "It may interest you to know that the position which I took toward the Japanese was made an issue which was greatly misinterpreted and distorted and perhaps contributed to the final result of the last election. I still believe I am right and I think that the future of constitutional government depends upon the attitude which we take toward these people."

He also wrote a letter to Thomas Bodine, who helped get Japanese American students who were in West Coast universities placed at inland schools, including the University of Colorado. "My position toward the Japanese evacuees caused me no end of trouble in the last campaign," Carr wrote, "but I am honored by that very fact because I feel that no fair-minded man could have taken any position other than the one which I did."

Carr, normally tireless, had been ravaged by the flu in the days leading up to the election and lost his voice for roughly three weeks. He left Denver to see friends on the East Coast in an effort to make sense of what had happened. "He was so exhausted and hated so that Ed Johnson beat him, that it just about killed him," Graham said.

Wendell Willkie sent a telegram a week after the election reading, "Dear Ralph, So sorry you did not make it, old man." Carr replied, "There is lots of room for work among the Privates and I shall try to be a good soldier."

Compensation would be a major issue for the former governor, whose combined income in 1940 and 1941 was a little over $12,000. His successor, Governor Vivian, would benefit from the change in state law Carr helped shepherd through the legislature, doubling the governor's annual pay to $10,000. Carr's law practice had been put on hold while he ran the state, his clients had gone elsewhere for their needs, and he had struggled to make ends meet while he was in the governor's office.

For example, Mrs. Aileen Trevorrow in Denver had written asking for financial help shortly after he was elected and he was forced to respond, "I am sorry that my own financial condition, which has been somewhat aggravated by the position which I have accepted with the State, makes it impossible for me to help you financially."

His friends offered him assistance. James Q. Newton, a prominent Denver Democrat who most likely voted for Johnson, offered him a $500 check, payable to cash. "I am sending this to you with the definite understanding you and I had in your office that this is not political, nor have I changed my political views. I do feel that you can use this check for personal expenses of your family," Newton wrote Carr. "I still feel that you are an idealist and I like you for it."

The proud country lawyer that he was, Carr wrote back, "Since it is not a political contribution, I don't feel justified in accepting it for my personal use. Please do not think that I am unappreciative because I am. I do have some financial problems ahead, but I am going to try to meet them and while your way is helpful, it's not the way I want to handle it."

So Ralph Carr hung out his shingle and leased an office in Denver's Symes Building where he had been located before his four-year hiatus running the state. His reputation allowed him to gain significant clients like the Trinchera Ranch in southern Colorado, a 250-square-mile property full of elk, bighorn sheep, and trout-filled streams. It was the largest ranch in the state. The big-paying clients allowed him to represent those who needed help at discount rates. For example, while working for the United Indian Traders Company, he protested to Gene Autry at the Columbia Picture Corporation about the negative images approaching a "vicious libel" toward Indians portrayed in one of its movies.

When it came to politics, he insisted to one friend that his hobbies were "laziness, itchy feet, and the desire to be where things are going on. The Lord has been kind to me in permitting me to do all those things." His name continued to surface in connection with positions in public life; rumors circulated that he might run for governor again in 1944. But, he wrote a friend, "I am not planning to run for anything, but I am going to keep up my interest in things and speak my piece whenever I can. They will listen to me if they don't put cotton in their ears."

All along, he supported candidates who showed more principle than personality, and invariably they were Republican. "My idea is that the Republicans must make a statement of principle which is so clear and so outstanding that we will need only to convince the people that we are going to stand on that platform and then the man who runs on it will be incidental," he wrote to Ruth Simms in the fall of 1943. "In other words, let's start building for principles which are as lasting as God Almighty Himself, and stop dealing with the personality who may or may not try to make those principles effective."

He would accept the appointment of Governor Vivian to become a regent for the University of Colorado, his alma mater in Boulder, which he called "the most beautiful campus in the world." After the war, both of his children, Bob and Cynthia, returned to the school to finish work on their degrees, giving him more than enough incentive to work on helping the institution get to "where it belongs," which he saw as one of the elite higher education facilities in the entire country. He encouraged a widespread sharing of ideas on campus, saying the regents "should not tell the faculty what they should teach. They must teach all sides and let the students decide." He gathered nearly 260,000 votes to retain the generally apolitical regent's seat, almost 85,000 more than when he ran for senate.

The war ended with Carr's belief in Japanese Americans proving accurate. There were no examples of sabotage committed by anyone of Japanese ancestry living in the United States during the war.

This point was stressed by numerous people attending the March 1946 biennial convention of the Japanese American Citizens League in Denver. Their keynote speaker was former Colorado governor Ralph Carr, who received a gold pocket watch from the group with the inscription, "In grateful appreciation for your courageous stand for Democratic American principles."

Inside the Silver Glade Room of Denver's twelve-story Cosmopolitan Hotel, the self-proclaimed "Host of the West," the former chief executive shared a podium with numerous Japanese

American veterans of the conflict. The 442nd Infantry, filled with Japanese American soldiers, emerged from the war as the most decorated combat unit of its size in U.S. Army history, including nearly ninety-five hundred Purple Hearts. Carr told the veterans and the delegates he opposed the discrimination against Japanese residents based primarily on the fact that their human rights were being violated.

"As the only western governor to oppose the violation of the constitutional rights of the Japanese American, I aroused much criticism," he told the crowd of more than four hundred people, including many Colorado civic, religious, and educational leaders. "My stand four years ago on this issue has been justified by the performance of this group in time of war."

Rocky Mountain News editor Lee Casey wrote that it was "eminently fitting" that the first postwar JACL convention was held in Colorado, as the state had "kept its head in a time of stress and refused to indulge in special legislation against any group." Casey went on to say, "It's good to know that this has been understood and appreciated. Now that the test has been made, it's good to welcome these fellow-Americans who have fought so bravely for American ideals in all parts of the world."

At another dinner held in appreciation of his efforts by the Denver JACL a couple months later, Carr invoked the memory of his good friend Theodore Roosevelt Jr.'s father, whose famous speech would serve as the foundation for his address that night. Roosevelt Sr. had said, "There is no room in this country for hyphenated Americanism." Carr believed the theory applied more than ever at this time. "Hyphens don't exist," he said. "Let's cut that out for Japanese Americans."

Carr's passion for his childhood memories from Cripple Creek came out in his later writings. He wanted to publish them at some point, but felt he always needed to do more editing. He sent various writings to friends as Christmas greetings through the years, "You know that old Biblical saying, 'Oh, that mine enemy would write a book.' That is what keeps me from trying to have my things published." It was a community he remembered fondly, a "great, big, overgrown mining country where everybody was big and gracious and pleasure loving."

Inevitably, he wrote about characters who all seemed to have the slightly mischievous traits Carr enjoyed so much. Traits he could never enjoy when he was governor. He highlighted characters like Jay Peterson, who got in trouble with his elementary school teacher one holiday with the following "Christmas poem": "As I was walking by the lake, I met a little rattlesnake, I fed him so much jellycake, it made his belly ache."

Another story was called "One of England's Greatest Peers," and told the story of London's Venture Company as it was negotiating to buy a Cripple Creek mine. The wife of the company's owner worried about the Colorado frontier, to the English a "wild and wooly" country, so she sent a letter preceding his arrival to the manager of the Palace Hotel, saying her husband was of "English Peerage. Her message was clear."

Now, the Palace did not have private bathrooms and the plumbing was rather rudimentary, but the manager, Jorgenson, selected a corner suite to be renovated and thoroughly painted. The wife wrote again, explaining her husband was to "be coddled and protected from cold breezes, from moisture, from contacts with everything worldly."

When the Englishman arrived, he was shown to his room via the town's only elevator to the hotel's sixth floor. He nodded happily at the accommodations, saying, "Why, man, I'll be more comfortable here than I would be at home." However, when he spied a "shining array of chamber pots" located under his bed, he asked why.

"Why, Your Highness," Manager Jorgenson said, "I thought you would need them. Your wife … said that you were one of England's greatest Peers."

Carr's stories elicited all sorts of reactions. "As eminent as you are in other fields, I think it no hazard to predict that you will be remembered as a man of your letters," wrote one of his friends, Thomas Girault. Even the media members of the day, people who wrote for a living, praised Carr's eloquence and humor. Alva Swain wrote, "You have a way of bringing all your stories to an abrupt ending that makes them outstanding." Maurice Leckenby of the *Rocky Mountain News* told Carr he "should have remained in the newspaper business. You wouldn't have accumulated so much dineiro, but you would have had a lot of fun."

Northwestern University professor Herbert Brayer shared a story about how he had passed one of Carr's Christmas tales to his wife, who was ill with bronchial pneumonia. She "laughed so hard that she began to cough, and believe it or not, broke a rib in doing so! So help me, that's the truth."

In 1948, he was once again being inundated with Republican requests to vanquish his foe of six years past. Big Ed Johnson was quoted as saying he expected "Ralph Carr to seek the Republican nomination for Senate, but I would be well satisfied if he doesn't." He went on to say that despite being out of politics and public office for six years, Carr remained the party's strongest candidate and he regarded him as "his most formidable opponent" throughout his political career. Carr's response was typically pithy. "I think Ed just wanted to make the front page, which he did." When pressed by reporters, Carr said, "I tackled Ed Johnson once. I am willing that someone else tackle him this time."

However, the International News Service reported that "Republican leaders from all over Colorado have been beating a path to Carr's law office" to try to convince him otherwise and that the former chief executive had met personally with Senator Millikin on several occasions to discuss the issue. He told Roy Takeno, JACL regional director, that he would "go to Canada to go fishing" if his friends continued to promote him for the position.

In private, he was equally unambitious about taking on Johnson again. He wrote his friend Judge Joe Thomas that though he honestly believed "Big Ed has come to the end of this strength and the right man can take him," he did not desire to be that right man. "No is the only word which has any taste for me these days. Ten years ago, I should have been eager to battle with Ed Johnson if I had felt that I had the same chance I appear to have this fall."

More important, the issue of the Japanese evacuees that played such an important role in their contest six years before had been settled, and, Carr believed, settled in his favor. "I honestly feel Joe that most of the criticism which was aimed at me in my last campaign has answered itself." He told his longtime confidant he would however be interested in a cabinet position, specifically the secretary of the interior, to deal with issues of water rights and land use, if New Yorker Thomas Dewey were elected president. "I am planning to campaign over the state and through the western section [for Dewey] almost as strenuously as if I were a candidate," Carr wrote.

In reality, Carr was a candidate for a second term on the University of Colorado Board of Regents. Two days after he won, after Ed Johnson was reelected in a landslide and after Thomas Dewey barely lost to President Harry Truman, Carr found himself once again on the front page of the local paper in a whole different realm.

Eleanor Fairall was to Carr the "loveliest little lady in Colorado." He had been good friends with her father for years. The former state treasurer and founder of the *Denver Daily Journal*, Herbert Fairall, and Carr were contemporaries. After her father died, Carr fell in love with "Ellie," who was more than two decades his junior.

On Election Day, Carr told his kids he would marry for a second time. At a quiet ceremony held in a friend's home the following afternoon, Ellie wore a brown afternoon suit with a matching feather-trimmed hat. He bought her a bridal corsage of lavender orchids and with his son, Bob, as an attendant, Carr commented he had "acquired a Mrs. Carr to rule my household and to bless my future life." His daughter, Cynthia, was unable to make it to the wedding from her home in Minneapolis. The smiling faces of the newlyweds were captured exclusively for a page one photo in the *Rocky Mountain News*.

After they returned from their honeymoon in Chicago, Ellie made sure Carr watched his diet and monitored his daily insulin shots to treat his diabetes. "I have been alone so long that I am willing to be bossed by anyone," he wrote a friend shortly after the wedding, "provided that I care for her and I am very much in love with this young lady."

Carr returned to a flourishing law practice, writing about Cripple Creek, and speaking out against the federal power grabs he saw from Washington. In 1949, the issue of the water authorities once again surfaced, causing him to take to the stump again to protest what he felt was a blatant effort to infringe upon states' rights. He wrote Wilbur Foshay of the Alamosa Chamber of Commerce, "My idea is that [water] authorities by their very nature are unconstitutional. The Congress, by their act, would be granting to a small group powers which the Congress itself does not possess."

Carr met and befriended Minoru Yasui shortly before the war ended, well before his fellow lawyer became a Colorado legend. Yasui moved to Denver in 1944 after the Supreme Court upheld his arrest for violating a curfew imposed upon Japanese Americans in his native Oregon. Yasui was the first Japanese American to graduate from the University of Oregon Law School. When he couldn't find a job in his hometown of Portland, he went to work for the Japanese Consulate in Chicago. After Pearl Harbor, he resigned immediately and tried to join the army, where he already served as an officer in the reserve corps, but he was turned down.

He returned to Portland, and when a curfew was imposed upon anyone of Japanese ancestry, he filed a legal challenge to its constitutionality, sent word to the U.S. Attorney's office and the

FBI, and went out into the streets to be arrested. He was sentenced to a year in prison and stripped of his citizenship, which meant he lost his license to practice law. It was a sentence the U.S. Supreme Court ruled constitutional due to "military necessity." He served nine months before joining the rest of his family in the Tule Lake internment camp in California.

When he moved to Colorado, he immediately petitioned to get his law license back, took the state bar exam, and registered the highest score in Colorado history. One of those aiding his efforts to fight discrimination and for civil rights in the legal arena was Ralph Carr, who said that Yasui exemplified "greatness as a man and as an American."

After the war, Denver's Japanese population decreased substantially, as many who had moved there during the conflict returned to their homes on the West Coast. Yet, Mrs. Michi Ando, the director of the Midwest JACL office, reported to her colleagues, "Many Japanese and Japanese Americans have operated very successful businesses in Denver with the result that there are a considerable number of what might be called 'wealthy' Japanese in the region. Nisei and Issei are operating hotels, restaurants, tailor shops, Japanese foods manufacturing establishments, beauty parlors, etc.—all with marked success. ... Because of the economic opportunities and the general attitude of tolerance now prevalent in Denver and Colorado, [it is predicted] a healthy future for all Nisei who decide to make their homes in the Mile-High City."

Yasui credited this future, this climate, to Carr, and wrote in the Denver JACL bulletin that the former governor's stand led to him being called a "Jap lover" and yet "never did he waver in this declaration of high American principle of equal justice, for all Americans, regardless of ancestry. Obviously, this stand by Carr at that time was of greatest benefit and comfort to the evacuees, but we must realize the implications significant to all Colorado citizens. In time of war, when hate and hysteria overruled calm, impartial judgment and destroyed tolerance, the official stand of the highest executive of a sovereign State tends to reduce tensions and hatreds, redounding to the continued welfare of established residents."

When Yasui heard in 1950 that Carr was being lobbied to run for public office again, he joined with other Nisei around Colorado to serve as executive secretary for the "Nisei Committee for Ralph L. Carr for Governor." In a letter sent to Carr's home "in the event that a public knowledge of our support would be embarrassing to you," Yasui and his group offered to help in the placement of posters, campaign literature, and mailings to accomplish the widest possible distribution within the Nisei population.

"Ever mindful of the splendid record which you made as Governor for two terms and deeply appreciative of your magnificent stand on behalf of the American rights of the Nisei in 1942," Yasui wrote, "we intend to contact our people ... to push vigorously your election."

After fighting off the overtures for the last eight years, the pressure was getting to Carr. "I am having a very difficult time right now," he wrote to his friend Frank Hill in the state of Washington. "The idea seems to have been promoted by some of our friends to the effect that if I get out and run for Governor with Gene Millikin the two of us will be elected and if I don't make the race he is going to have trouble ... I think personally that Millikin is all right, because I think I know the feelings of the people of this section, but it would be a terrible blow to me to refuse to go and then have Gene come in with second money.

"I am as deeply interested as I ever was and want to do my part, but really, I don't care for public office anymore."

The lobbying continued. Carr got regular visits from party leaders and read all the speculation in the newspapers, especially when Governor Lee Knous, a Democrat and one of Carr's classmates at the University of Colorado, stepped down to take a lifetime position as a U.S. district judge. Walter Johnson would fill the rest of Knous's term and be ripe for the taking, according to the Republican theory, as he was not nearly as well known state-wide as Carr. However, the fear was that Millikin could not hold his Senate seat without help.

"You are the only candidate in the Republican party of Colorado who can help him retain his Senate seat," wrote Henry Kirkpatrick from Alamosa to Carr. "In fact, I think he needs you running for Governor to win. I hope I am wrong, but I sincerely think he will have a tough battle without your running with him."

In a letter that June to R. W. Dill, Carr said he "was coming under a lot of pressure from all sides to run for Governor again, but just can't see my way clear to do it. I am as much interested as a person can be, of course, and am hard at work; taking a job like that as Governor … is just something I don't feel like trying to do."

But the man who once said that "we get all our happiness in life out of serving others," could not continue to say no. While trying a case in Grand Junction at the same time that the state's Democrats were having their convention, he sent word to friends in Denver that he would make the race for governor in 1950. As he jokingly told his old friend George Robinson, who had worked for him in the governor's office, "You know I was always feeble-minded. My judgment ain't worth a damn."

The reaction was overwhelmingly positive.

Senator Millikin wired from Washington, "The news is wonderful." Otero County Republican chairman Orley McGlothlin sent a Western Union message. "Dear Ralph, your announcement is the best news [I] have heard since the atomic bomb fell on Hiroshima." Clarence Stafford wrote, "I know full well you are making a big sacrifice in money and peace of mind but unless Republicans are elected to start getting our ship of state back into the channel of good government many other fine Americans stand to sacrifice all."

His campaign did not get off to a good start. While working a case on the Western Slope, he hurt his left ankle. Within a few days, an infection had spread to his foot, and he arrived at

Denver's city auditorium to deliver his speech for the nomination desperately in pain and hobbling on crutches. The delegates gave him overwhelming support (787 to 354 votes) over Ray Branna-man, the former national commander of the Veterans of Foreign Wars, heading into the primary race. He blamed his injury jokingly on old-fashioned politics: "I've been kicked by a Democratic mule, but I'll kick back."

He went straight from the auditorium to St. Luke's Hospital, where he ran his primary campaign for the next four weeks. Doctors lanced his foot, but his personal physician, Dr. Lorenz W. Frank, continued to describe Carr's infection as "peculiar." The former governor joked to friends like Frank Gimlett that he was "carrying on a very interesting [experiment] right now, which involves the question of whether a man can win an election campaign on the flat of his back in a hospital room."

His campaign didn't avoid the controversy of 1942, but rather embraced it. Eight years, a victory over Japan, and no acts of sabotage had turned a 1942 campaign negative into a 1950 campaign positive.

In brochures for the Republican Party, he wrote about himself in the third person, saying he had "served people without regard to partisanship, race, religion, wealth, or other classification." If voters did not understand his vague reference to the issue of the Japanese evacuees, they could read more that he wrote: "On many occasions, he knew that his life might have been pleasanter had he sidestepped the issue. ... The times did not call for magic because the answers to public's questions required only the exercise of ordinary common sense applied promptly, courageously, and intelligently."

All along, he corresponded with friends and supporters by using his Dictaphone. The sound-recording device that had served him so well through his years as governor now was his primary means of communication despite his feelings it "is such a cold, unresponsive medium for the exchange of ideas."

Carr was persuaded to run for office again in 1950 to help out other Republican candidates on the ticket. He would overwhelmingly win a primary for governor. Here he is on primary night listening to the returns with his second wife, Eleanor Fairall Carr. He was seated because of an infection in his foot that kept him from actively campaigning. It is the last picture of Carr before he died due to complications resulting from diabetes. His 1950 campaign embraced his Japanese American stand of 1942, but he never had the chance to be vindicated by Colorado voters. Courtesy of the Colorado Historical Society

"I can't have visitors," he wrote Butler Disman in August, "but I can carry on a one-sided conversation with this cold-hearted substitute for a stenographer."

He was released a week before the Republican primary, ready to start "running like a scared coyote with two good feet." On primary day, September 12, in his first political campaign since his loss to Senator Johnson nearly eight years before, Carr took phone calls from friends and listened to results on the radio. He was in good spirits, physically and emotionally, after defeating Brannaman by a greater than two-to-one margin. He received roughly 55,000 votes and the former VFW head received around 25,000.

Wednesday, September 13, was a different story, however, and Carr was struggling again with the infection. He went back into St. Luke's for what his doctors called "rest and observation." Min Yasui and other Carr supporters were worried and forced to tell detractors, "It is merely a foot ailment. ... Governor Carr doesn't think with his foot, as seemingly some of our other politicians do, but that Carr acts according to his head and heart."

Still, his closest aides were concerned, as was Carr. On September 22, Carr's son wrote his dad's good friend Eddie Dutcher in Gunnison, Colorado, that his father "is trying to make up his mind whether or not to stay in this campaign." A decision didn't have to be made until October 2, a full thirty-five days before the November election, and the deadline for when a substitute candidate had to be submitted to be on the ballot. However, rumors began to circulate that Carr was simply going to run and if elected, immediately turn the position over to the lieutenant governor, if he made the race at all.

That day, using his Dictaphone, Carr sent a letter to Bill Lloyd, head of the Colorado Republican Party, and the members of the state central committee. "Your candidate for Governor is in a hell of a predicament. He has not been able to call his soul (or rather his body) his own since the convention. Some very able doctors have been working me over and patching me up after the most serious illness I've ever had. I'm again on the mend.

"My conviction that I can run on the ticket successfully and thereby do my best for [Senator] Millikin is unshaken. I'll never quit thinking and working to that end. I don't mean that I won't listen to advice and accept help, but don't look for a substitute for me so long as I'm above the sod."

Later that Saturday, at 8:42 P.M., Ralph Carr died.

Doctors listed cause of death as a heart attack resulting from complications stemming from an infection, and that because of Carr's diabetic condition the infection did not properly heal. His wife, Eleanor, was at his bedside. Governor Walter Johnson ordered flags to be flown at half-mast the next day and said simply, "Colorado has lost a great man."

When Senator Millikin was called and told of Carr's death by the *Rocky Mountain News*, he gasped "Oh, no! Oh, no!" The paper reported that he was silent for fifteen seconds before stating, "For goodness' sake, that is a terrible tragedy for the state … he had so many friends, tens of thousands of them."

Thousands of people passed by his casket inside the state capitol. The media showered him with compliments. "Rotund, volatile Ralph Carr was one of the most forceful Governors in Colorado history," wrote the *Denver Post*. "Normally a friendly, gracious man with an infectious cheerful manner, he possessed an innate stubbornness that baffled opponents and political advisors alike."

The *Lamar News* described the former governor as "a smiling type of scrapper … [who] knew how to give and to take and at the same time hold friendships." The *Intermountain Jewish News* said that Carr "placed principle above political expediency." The *Latin-American News* said of the man called Rafaelito, "a friend has gone." The *Grand Junction Sentinel* offered: "In the record of Colorado history, Ralph L. Carr deserves a permanent and prominent place."

His longtime friend and columnist Alva Swain, simply wrote,

People of all races, ages, and religions came to mourn Governor Carr at the state Capitol. Obituaries from papers all over the state described him as a champion of freedom, a civil rights giant, and one wrote, "He was a friend to man. What more can be said?" Ralph L. Carr was sixty-two years old. Courtesy of the Colorado Historical Society

"He was a friend to man. What more can be said?"

For Colorado's Japanese American community, the loss was acute. At the Masonic Consistory at Fourteenth Avenue and Grant Street, where the funeral was held, the JACL placed a floral tribute in the shape of boxing gloves near the coffin. As journalist Bill Hosokawa would later write, "Few of the mourners needed to be told what it meant. Carr had been a fighter, a champion of the underdog throughout his legal and political career." Min Yasui called the man he had been helping to elect governor in 1950 a "good and great friend of all little people who needed help."

Maybe the sentiment of Colorado was best summarized by the editor of the *Rocky Mountain Herald*, the oldest weekly paper in the state. "Ralph Carr was a one-man crusade for freedom all his life. When he'd lead off with one of his stories always beginning with 'Dontcha know,' as if you should have known, it was surprising how often somebody's freedom was involved, the rights of some bum, some banker, some sheepherder, the rights of a sign-painter's boy who ended up in Oregon gun-fire, some Penitente, some miner claiming a claim or farmer claiming water. Freedom was a lodestone to his thinking. Colorado was fortunate to share in so much of it," Thomas Hornsby Ferril wrote after his death.

"I've heard it said in the past few days that Ralph Carr could have gone down as a great American, known to everybody in every state, if he'd been willing to wangle more of the breaks his way and be less bull-headed about the constitutional rights of the underdogs who sometimes suspected him and of the overdogs who sometimes suspected him. Well, they can have their definition of what a great American is, but it seems to me that if we had more men like Ralph Carr along the line we wouldn't need to keep puffing up so many great men to bail us out."

Ralph L. Carr was sixty-two years old.

Epilogue

As George Robinson tells the story, he broke the color barrier in American politics because of Ralph Carr. After the governor lost his bid for the U.S. Senate in 1942, Carr encouraged Congressman William Hill to help Robinson get a job on Capitol Hill.

"When I first came here, Negroes had only been porters and janitors," Robinson said. "[Carr and Hill] wanted to give minorities more opportunities." Hill used his influence to get him a job inside the documents room in the House of Representatives.

From the documents room, Robinson would go to work on the floor of the House of Representatives, greeting and getting to know each of the 435 members. While visiting his old friend right before Carr's unexpected death, he told Robinson that because he was the last one Carr hired when he was first elected governor, he would be the first one hired if he were elected again.

As Congress acknowledged the two hundredth anniversary of the U.S. Constitution in 1987, members debated whether to grant restitution to those Japanese Americans who had been interned during the war. The decision to give $20,000 to each survivor was accompanied by an apology by the United States government. Just a few years earlier, a blue-ribbon commission had issued a report stating that the decision to intern Japanese Americans during the war was a decision shaped by "race prejudice, war hysteria, and a failure of political leadership."

George Robinson still wasn't satisfied. "He was right. What credit did he get? In the federal government, not a word in the Library of Congress about what he did. That's a shame. All this time, nothing."

So Robinson recommended Carr's name to a Colorado Legislative Committee, studying which state figure should be commemorated with a statue inside the U.S. capitol. To give his former boss's accomplishments another little push, he wrote Gene Amole, a columnist for the *Rocky Mountain News*. The day before what would have been Carr's one hundredth birthday—December 11, 1987—Amole wrote that Ralph Carr was a hero.

"Most of the heroes I have known just happened to be at the right place at the right time. It wasn't so much a matter of valor as it was of chance," he said. "The real hero is one who ignores personal risk and goes ahead and does something because it needs to be done and because it is right. …

"What this brave man did in Colorado at a precarious time in American history honors all free men everywhere. For this reason, I believe his service should be commemorated by placing a statue of Ralph Carr in the U.S. capitol in Washington. He was a genuine hero."

Happy with the column, but not content to sit and wait, Robinson forwarded the column to Colorado congressman Hank Brown, who finally, on March 9, 1988, mentioned Ralph Carr's name on the floor of the United States Congress. "Many government officials turned their backs on these [Japanese] Americans," Brown said before placing Amole's column in the official congressional record. "However, former Colorado governor Ralph Carr was one man who spoke out against the unjust treatment of these fellow citizens."

Robinson was grateful. "It was my way to thank him for giving me the best job I ever had. I like that job better than the two I've had in Congress. That was great he helped me. It was great to get up and treat people nice and take 'em in to see the governor. I like that job better than any one I ever had."

Colorado would eventually select former Apollo 13 astronaut John "Jack" Swigert for its statue inside the capitol instead of Carr.

Meanwhile, Carr was memorialized with a small bust that sits in Denver's Sakura Square, an area nicknamed "Little Tokyo" after the war. At its dedication, one speaker said that Carr "rolled up his sleeves on the side of the angels and helped the Japanese

Americans regain respectability."

His old acquaintance Minoru Yasui told the crowd of roughly one hundred fifty in attendance that Carr's principled stand was "one voice, a small voice but a strong voice, like the voice of a sandpiper over the roar of the surf."

A plaque in his honor also sits outside the Colorado governor's office, a regular stop on tours throughout the building.

Maybe in the ultimate of ironies, the *Denver Post*, which had pilloried his stand daily during 1942, chose Ralph Carr as Colorado's Person of the Century in December 1999, saying that the choice was one of "style over substance":

> He didn't tunnel through 6 miles of mountain rock, build an airport, or deliver the gush of fresh water that sprouted a foothills metropolis.
>
> He had little to do with the Rocky Mountain skiing boom, even less to do with the brewing of a home-grown brand of beer. He didn't even win us a Super Bowl.
>
> What he did was take a stand.
>
> In one of America's darkest hours, he defended humanity and decency, a move that cost him a career and sent ripples of goodwill rolling through Colorado for years.

Index